MW01202038

Finding Our Fire

Enhancing Men's Connection to
Heart, Passion and Strength

by Martin Brossman
with contributions from
many other men

A portion of the proceeds from the sale of this book will go to support The Men's Inquiry, The Women's Inquiry, and the Triangle Men's Center.

THE PINECONE PRESS
4847 Sedgwick St. N.W.
Washington D.C. 20016

Dayle,
Thanks for your
support.

Publisher: THE PINECONE PRESS
ISBN: 978-0-6151-6385-7

This book may be purchased from www.TheMensInquiry.com

© 2007 Martin Brossman & The Men's Inquiry

All rights reserved. No part of this book may be reproduced or transmitted in any form or by any means, electronic or mechanical, including photocopying, recording, or by any information storage and retrieval system, without permission in writing by the author.

Release 2 8/11/2007

Dedication

To all the men who are modeling emotional courage and supporting other men in being better fathers, sons, leaders and partners, in their lives and to the wise women who support them.

Contents

Preface 1
by Martin W. Brossman III
(the author)

This book is about men and our lives. *Finding Our Fire* opens a window into a world that most people do not know exists. Through non-ordinary questions and often extraordinary responses taken from a decade of The Men's Inquiry meetings, the reader is gifted with an intimate view into a small world that we trust will become widespread, one in which men express their personal concerns and their issues with other men in a healthy, uninhibited, safe environment.

The intention is that through reading these questions and replies, men will increase their insight into their own lives. For example, *Finding Our Fire* may inspire fathers to have richer discussions with their sons. Or it may be a tool for sons to use in initiating deeper-level discussions with their fathers. For those who wish to create a men's team or group, it may be used as a resource handbook. But remember: this book is not written just for male readers; it equally offers women new insights about men and their own lives as well.

Men across the country have emailed to say they're going to use the book to start their own Men's Inquiry group, an indicator of the hunger for real communication that's out there. More and more men are ready for the depth of the issues addressed in this book, ready to step up and do the work. This is soul work that we can no longer ignore and the cost of not doing it in our society gets greater each year. It involves both collective insight and clear action. That is why I end each Men's Inquiry meeting with these questions: What insights did you personally gain from this inquiry? What do you want to commit to or re-commit to out of these insights? Because insights without committed actions are just entertainment!

A preface by my father is on the next page.

Preface 2
by Martin W. Brossman II
(the author's father)

Serving as a reviewer on this book was an instructive and rewarding experience. It has given me a remarkable insight into my own life and the lives of many other men. Reading the responses of men to deep issues in the book made me realize how much I would have benefited from such a dialogue years ago, as I am benefiting now. Had the Men's Inquiry existed in my earlier years, my understanding would have been so much greater and I would have benefited from the insights and experience of many men.

At this stage of my life it helps me better understand my journey and make the rest of my journey more rewarding. Reconsidering the questions / issues explored and the men's responses continues to enrich my life and understanding. However, as a father, reading the section about a critical period in my son Martin's life—a simultaneous struggle with his job and marriage described in Chapter One—was extremely painful to me.

But my son soon persuaded me that it was part of his journey. The whole premise of his subsequent years of "men's work" and The Men's Inquiry was based on being true and open. He also pointed out that the pain of that time led to the subsequent development of The Men's Inquiry which has brought untold insight, and improved his life and countless others.

Had the Men's Inquiry existed in earlier years, the painful period Martin III experienced probably would not have occurred. He would have found deep strength in the associations of what he later created. If I'd had such an association at that time I probably would have had the sense of a problem and opened a dialogue on it. In any event, my life has been enriched by reading the thoughts of men in *Finding Our Fire*—and sharing the collective journey—as I am sure will be the experience of all who read this book.

Acknowledgments

I would like to thank John Sharpe, a widely-published scholar who generously donated a great deal of time and effort to organize the men's contributions and edit my own first draft. John skillfully improved everyone's grammar while retaining the original voices. Other edits followed, thanks to the help of friends: author Conrad Joseph, Coach Chris Custer, and Lisa Dumas who drew on her gift as a dance instructor and course developer to help me sculpt out some metaphors in the book.

Many thanks to: Denis Bunbury from New Zealand, who has offered great wisdom and support to the on-line Men's Inquiry over the years; Mike Hopley, for his work in integrating on-line resources; and Sid Harrell for his work as advisor to The Men's Inquiry. Special thanks to final review editors Dana Gower, Sonia Katchian, Oie Osterkamp and Mike Saleeby.

I want to honor and express appreciation for my father, Martin W. Brossman II, who also assisted in editing, and to my mother, Judy McLean Brossman, for her continuing support. Thanks to my grandparents, the late Dr. & Mrs. Martin Brossman, for lasting inspiration. And deep appreciation to my beautiful partner and wife, Barbara Carr Brossman (www.NaturesFace.com), who lovingly honors me and inspires me to cherish her and be a better man. Barbara serves as advisor to The Women's Inquiry.

Thanks to all the women who have supported this project, including Amy Sky (www.amylsky.com) and Janet Bauer (www.whatsgreataboutyou.com), who have co-facilitated the Women's Inquiry.

Deep appreciation to all the people who contributed directly, or indirectly through their support, and to those who gave inspiration and made suggestions during the creation of this book, and to the men involved in the ManKind Project (www.MKP.org), New Warrior Training, and I-Group. In my worldwide search for contributors, those men who have done this men's personal development training were often the first to step up to the plate and contribute.

Thanks also to more than 100 other courageous men who contributed their responses within the book whose names are not listed here to further protect their confidentiality. You men know who you are and I deeply appreciate this gift of your words. Special thanks to Fred Boyles, Robert Bly, Michael Meade, and Warren Farrell and who inspired me in this work.

And special thanks to my good friend, Dyck Dewid, for his generous assistance with the first book release.

Note: All the names used in the body of this document are pseudonyms. Some contributions have been further edited to protect confidentiality, enhance clarity and make the information accessible to a greater audience.

Introduction
The Inquiry

The first in-person Men's Inquiry occurred in 1997 in my Raleigh, North Carolina, home. We have been meeting once a month ever since. In November 2000, I created an online Men's Inquiry utilizing Yahoo Groups, where I posted the questions that were explored at in-person meetings and threw them open for discussion. This online group now has between 145 and 200 members. However, the Internet version was NOT designed to replace the in-person group. It was created to allow men to have access to a discussion when they have no in-person Men's Inquiry group (or group like it) to participate in. It is also designed to encourage men to create or join an in-person men's group like The Men's Inquiry.

The book

This book is intended to support men who want to create, maintain, and deepen healthy relationships with other men—men who in their lives give and receive support by being the men they are called to be.

In working with men from diverse cultures and beliefs from all over the world, I have attempted to get to what is core to all men. We do not support one set of beliefs over another. In the on-line version of The Men's Inquiry, men from Japan, New Zealand, India, Europe, Alaska, Australia, and Great Britain have shared thoughts and ideas about their lives. In this volume you will meet these men. They model the unique contribution they make to one another in giving their time to this project. Thanks, men, for sharing!

I feel real gratitude for those who have challenged The Men's Inquiry over the years. They have caused me to rethink certain positions I have held or to change my opinions. Their honesty actually increased my commitment to the value of this work. I owe the most to the director of a family shelter who challenged some of the work. He led me to understand that some people sadly are afraid that as strong men we will take something away from women, a concept that is about as far from my commitment and vision as you can get. a mature man does not have to dominate or manipulate women; real strength in a man gives a woman space to be equally but uniquely self-expressed. Only the cowardly and fearful man must dominate and manipulate his environment to gain a false sense of validation.

I am not alone on my journey into mature manhood. Along the way I have connected with men who shared their experiences and opened their hearts and souls as they responded to the questions that are posed in this book. I can't claim that I have arrived somewhere. But I can affirm that more than ever before I am on my own path, having learned from the sum total of all our experiences. I have also learned what it means to listen to my own voice, which occurs through both the interaction with others and working on your own.

This book is intended to:
Touch something new in you, perhaps opening you to more compassion for men.
Give you courage to relate to someone in a new way.
Provide another element to enrich your life.
Move you to take action that makes you more of the person you want to be.
Make you see the value in men intentionally getting together to support one another, and maybe inspire you to join or create your own "team of brothers."
Get you to see a special someone in a different perspective, enhancing your relationship with him or her.
Help you to be a better partner, friend, father, member of a group, or leader.
Deepen your understanding of the difference between "having to be driven" and 'being called to something."

And, I envision that *Finding Our Fire* will illuminate the value of honoring your word, implied or stated, to others and especially to yourself.

Why the title **Finding Our Fire**? Why separate out the masculine and explore it? Why do I think I have any thing new to say that has not been said before? Let me start by addressing the last question first.

Why do I think I have anything new to say that has not been said before?

Over fifteen years ago, somewhere lost in despair and resignation, I realized that I could never collect enough evidence by reflecting on my life experiences that I was "worthy enough." I felt then that I could never be certain that my life would make any difference at all. I gave up looking for evidence of my worthiness. I decided that I would live the rest of my life as though just who I am makes a difference. Undertaking the work of The Men's Inquiry eliminated doubt that I have made a difference in many peoples' lives, just as they have made a difference in mine. Conducting the monthly sessions, structuring meaningful men's issues, recording the sessions and making them available for the benefit of others all made it apparent that we had had something to say that has not been said before in this way.

Why separate out the masculine?

I am interested in distinguishing both the masculine and feminine only to the degree that it gives us all more freedom, aliveness and self-expression. From my experience many of us have both emotional wounds and intrinsic gifts, which are only uncovered by distinguishing the masculine and feminine. For me this exploration has enriched my own life tremendously. When one must define one as better than the other, this separation loses its utility, versus valuing the gift of both the masculine and feminine. I also believe that there is masculine and feminine energy in all of us and distinguishing it is one way to get access to both.

And finally, why the title "Finding Our Fire?"

This is the core of men's work—it connects to our real, flaming, distinctive passion that defines our hearts' deepest desires and expresses them fully. That "fire" will show up in bold, surprising ways—in loud ways, in actively compassionate ways, in joyfully alive ways, and, yes, even in *fierce* ways, connected deeply to our hearts and strength! I want to explore something beyond the "sensitive man," beyond the "aggressive tough man" and, instead, to discover and honor the man with fierce inner compassion and strength!

At the end of each chapter, I invite you to notice the insights you have gained about yourself. Listen to your own inner voice or thoughts. Make note of them. Let insights emerge and make them part of you, with committed or re-committed actions that create more meaning and fulfillment in your life.

Chapter 1
My Journey Begins

Discovering a greater need

My journey began when the book *Iron John* by Robert Bly was recommended to me. It addresses issues men face in the process of maturing. Essentially, *Iron John* reveals what has been missing for men in our culture and focuses on men's rites of passage. Bly outlines ideas about men gathering together to support one another. Some time in 1993 I bought the book on tape since my job required that I drive a lot. While driving and listening to the audio, I was suddenly aware of tears streaming down my face. Though I was not oblivious to my feelings at that time, I truly could not understand *these* emotions and where they were coming from! The pursuit of the resolution of these undistinguishable feelings is what led me to men's work. Through it, I have discovered that some wounds just do not heal except in the company of men who have the courage to explore them. I have also learned that unhealed wounds play out in our lives as repeating undesirable behaviors, requiring more and more work to hide from until we learn the value of facing them.

It seems Robert Bly thought that a particular fairy tale spoke to issues men face in today's culture. Using it as a compelling metaphor, he tells the story of a man named Iron John to illustrate what he had discovered was missing for men today—the several components required for the healthy development of a man. To review these basic components briefly is for a young man to have substantial connection with a father figure in addition to a mother figure. Then the second stage develops, where a father alone does not provide enough of the broader influence crucial to a boy's maturation; a community of men is required to fully bring him along into manhood, a phenomenon historically referred to as rites of passage. And still a further stage requires the young man to have a male mentor who guides him to the mastery and richness of life.

So the goal for the boy entering manhood is to find his mission, his purpose, his great adventure in life, and his contribution in the community. Not that this excludes the wonderful contributions of his mother or life partner. But the fact is that most adult men are not modeling these experiences, creating by default a nation of sons who are not learning them, and daughters who are lacking sufficient models of healthy and mature men to pursue as partners.

Bly explains that men have lost the traditional rites of passage, particularly during that crucial time between boyhood and manhood. Consequently, we have a society filled with shells of men who are spiritually and emotionally immature. Left to their own devices, these men too often seek bizarre and destructive ways to attempt to reclaim their masculinity. Unfortunately, and all too frequently, young men join gangs because they miss the interaction with healthy mature males, leaving them to seek initiation from each other or from negative role models, which obviously doesn't work.

Indeed this is a controversial concept, one I would have argued against before I read *Iron John* and before my own experience. Even if a young man's relationship with his father is a good one, it is not enough for complete maturing. I have always had a great relationship with my father, yet according to Bly, father and son are too close emotionally for the father to be the sole person responsible for bringing his son to manhood. He says this necessary support, guidance, and initiation must come from a community of men, as well as from the mentorship of an older man other than the father. Such customs once prevailed in primitive societies, yet in our "advanced" culture all three components are often missing: the strong relationship with the father, the community of men, and the older mentor.

Memories, marriage and a mentor

While many aspects of Bly's work were speaking to me in a personal way, I was also recollecting and relating to earlier experiences in my life that at first did not seem to have a connection. One of these memories that came forward had happened several years prior while I was taking personal development courses.

I was sitting in a hotel conference room working on my assignment, a writing exercise recalling some past experience. While I was writing, memories of my father sprang into mind. Several months earlier my father had undergone a major operation. I had taken time off from work for a week to be with him and to help out my mother—overall an intense experience that had me feeling confused about what to say or do. As I recalled this overwhelming period of time, a rush of emotions flooded in. Again, I did not understand what was happening to my feelings. The emotion felt close to sadness, but at once very different. I later discovered that this was a form of grieving for the loss of a part of myself. The writing assignment made me realize that I had not developed a useful model of being a mature healthy man to draw upon for handling the demands of my life. I had focused so much on understanding the evils of men—a focus that came out of my younger view that supported militant feminism (an extreme division of feminism, not a description of all feminism.) In the militant feminist's worldview, men are the source of all problems, and there are no good mature males. This way of thinking left me without models of healthy men to draw on in my psyche. I recalled Bly had said that this part, this healthy model, had to be found in the community of men and could not come from the father. It definitely felt like that was true for me.

Growing up in Washington, D.C., I was not very impressed with most models of adult men that I encountered there. They projected the image of men as aggressive, dominating, distant, and "macho." When it became clear to me the extent to which these men had taken advantage of women throughout history I became angry. In the process of working on my course assignment these conflicting thoughts—my father (a kind and good man), the Washington men-cult, and the treatment of women in general— had become very clear to me. Consequently, I began looking for answers to satisfy my dissatisfaction with what I had perceived.

Like a blow to the back of the head, I realized that what Bly was saying regarding the need for a male mentor applied directly to me, even though I saw no available or appropriate male role model for me in corporate America and had few local male friends. The realization annoyed me: I had identified the problem but had no answer. The need for a new support system became even more apparent with severe job and marriage problems looming on the horizon.

There were two key problems in my face: First, my wife had decided that she wanted to have children. That thought filled me with fear about whether I had the inner strength to be a father. At the same time I was facing a personal crisis in my career. My

17

company, IBM, was changing its internal service function to outside contract support. I had focused my career plans on IBM, having majored in computer science with an additional degree in computer applications and an IBM internship; I excelled at my work, receiving the IBM Means Service Award after my first year, a record achievement for a new employee. Then there I was, six years later, dealing with the unwelcome news that my career company was going to be closing out its service business.

And on top of all of this—or perhaps mixed up in both these problems—was my conviction that I was not "good enough" for my job nor did I have any idea what I would be good at. Lack of confidence and low self-esteem were nothing new to me (due in part to my problems with ADD, dyslexia). But I did believe that one of the few things I was good at in life was being a good husband, because I was kind and warm and in touch with my feelings and those of my wife.

Before we were married we had a very honest conversation about our thoughts on parenthood during which I looked her straight in the eyes and said, "If you feel you need to have children then you shouldn't marry me." Because with my ADD/dyslexia I strongly believed that I did not have whatever it would take to be a parent, and, therefore did not want to attempt what I felt would be for me an impossible undertaking and not good for a child. Life seemed so hard and I felt so isolated at that time. Why would I want to take on the responsibility of a child? I was thankful that she said she definitely didn't want to have children.

Because of my deep concerns, I thought it would be unfair for her to marry me if she wanted children. Filled with shame at what I clearly saw as a personality or character flaw, I did not want anyone to know this about me. When she later changed her mind and decided that she really did want children, I attempted to make our relationship work. But my feelings of inadequacy continued and got far worse, even though I tried to hide them, not very skillfully, beneath the surface. I was convinced I was inadequate for the task, which just compounded my belief that I was inadequate in my career. It was as though I had a lead sack on my head; it required great effort just to hold my head upright. The more I anticipated the responsibility, the more inadequate I felt. I had no clue about what I would be good at, and the responsibility of being a father became a burden that only grew heavier. Worse

18

even than the anxiety at the prospect of being a father was the intense shame I felt anticipating what it would be like if anyone were to know this about me.

It should come as no surprise that other issues eventually surfaced in the marriage—issues that neither of us could avoid. When she said that she was not satisfied with the relationship, it was absolutely a great shock to me. Yet continuing to think that being a husband was the one thing I was doing well, I naturally took on the task of "fixing" the marriage. I listed all of her complaints about me. I did a truly gallant job of tackling them. And within six months I had actually changed so much that she became angry. And as her anger increased I worked even harder to change further. Finally, she admitted that she really didn't want me to succeed at conquering the list of shortcomings. I was to learn later that she had given up long before she admitted her feelings to me. That was not because she meant to, but because at that time neither of us had any better tools for dealing with this elephant in the room.

Therapy seemed the appropriate next step. It gave me the opportunity to dig deeper to identify my feelings, thinking all the while that the process would help me repair my sense of inadequacy. The reality was just the opposite. The therapist's encouraging me to get more in touch with my feelings opened a floodgate of shame, grief, and sadness that I had a hard time containing. It has become clear to me now that this was not because of the therapy but because of the therapist's incompetence in understanding men's issues. Obviously he had not done the work on himself around his own masculine issues. A competent therapist, especially someone sensitive to men's issues, would have been more effective during this very crucial time for me. It is clear that when a man has suppressed thirty-some years of feelings, he does not suppress the happy and joyful ones. He suppresses shame, grief, sadness, and into the mix he adds anger in great quantities. Sharing all these aspects with my wife, in a state of having what I know now to be an underdeveloped mature masculine core, certainly did not help the relationship. Instead it made me into someone stuck in his feelings, as opposed to being unaware of them. It was later men's work that eventually gave me access to the feelings along with access to my inner strength, enabling me to experience those feelings without being ruled by them.

During this phase of therapy there were times at work when I would find myself filling up with tears to such an extent that I would retreat to lock myself in a room and weep uncontrollably. I did not understand what was happening to my emotional internal self. When the therapist, feeling so confident in his therapy, assured me, "This is good," I replied, "I could lose my job if this crap gets out."

One time when my wife was in the therapist's office, I just came apart and wept out of despair at the burden of trying to handle a job for which I felt inadequate, and fear at the prospect of the responsibility of being a father. The therapist praised me for how wonderful I had been in expressing my feelings and how endearing it all was. Meanwhile my wife sat there stoically with a look of indifference. I was totally confused. Something very significant was missing and I did not know what.

Despite my gallant effort at changing myself in an attempt to please her, I failed. She still wanted out and ultimately my marriage ended in divorce. With the advantage of 20/20 hindsight, I know now that the effort to change myself just to make the marriage work was a hopeless task. I was only doing it to save the marriage and lost track of my own life in the process. Often men refer to this time as "throwing themselves out the window," only later realizing their partner no longer loved them, for they were no longer "in the room."

Though I was not fully aware at that time how much the trauma in my life was driving me to make changes and find new solutions, I was very aware of needing some healthy structured support. Immediately after the divorce my personal and internal life did not appear to improve. I was very unhappy in my job; I detested the competitive corporate game of deception that I perceived was going on around me.

I resigned from my job to launch out on my own. Soon afterward I joined a diverse and interesting support business group called the Samurai Business Team. It occurred to me that some aspects of the group—organization, direction, agendas, etc., could be improved. Wanting to see the group succeed, I called Fred Boyles, the founder of the group. In our conversation the topic of *Iron John* came up. I told him that I was angry with Bly because of how he seemed to pose the problem so clearly but didn't offer a solution that was accessible to me. Incidentally, many years later when I got to spend time with Robert Bly, I shared with him both my appreciation for his work and the fact that I had been angry with him. He smiled. He *smiled!*

Fred Boyles asked me what I wanted. I said, "I want someone to play the role of a male friend." I mentioned Robert Bly's ideas and thought Bly was right about what was missing in my life. Fred assured me that he himself was that man, declaring: "I'll call you every Sunday night and we'll talk." The idea that he would call at his own expense every Sunday from L.A. seemed crazy, but I accepted his promise.

Well, he did call, every Sunday. Then one Sunday he didn't call, and although it wasn't such a big deal, I was still a bit pissed. I called him in the middle of the week and asked what happened. He said he broke his word and that he was sorry. Then he asked me what he could do to make it up to me. I jokingly said, " How about 25 pushups." I then heard, "Ok, my men's group is here to witness it," and heard him say, "He said 25 pushups." I could hear a group of men talking in the background, and the sound of the phone being put down. Then I heard the guys counting, "1, 2, 3..." in unison. Finally, Fred got back on the line and asked if that was sufficient. I said, "Of course," with mixed emotions. Part of me felt like this was silly, and another, deeper, part really sat up and noticed. I couldn't remember any other time in my life when a man broke his word and then honestly asked what it would take to clean it up. Fred took responsibility. And that meant something to me that has stayed with me ever since.

The flight to community

After many conversations with Fred, I began to identify those issues that were of such great concern to me. I began to put names to them and to point out the places they held in who I was. I told him how I had rejected the John Wayne macho character, and that I'd worked for years to break down my shell, to get in touch with my feelings, to be more sensitive to women's feelings. Then, however, I was left with a feeling that seemed like a tortoise being exposed to the world without a shell, or rolled over on his back in the middle of the road on a hot summer's day. Previously my

21

tough exterior had kept me numb from the neck down and protected me from feelings that made me vulnerable. I had expected to find something great underneath, but instead I felt like I had exposed the inside of a volcano filled with fear, shame, anger, and grief. I told Fred, "In a lot of situations, I feel like a 9 year-old boy in a 36 year-old body, and I am in BIG trouble." He then suggested that I take part in a men's retreat that was taking place in a few months. I agreed, thinking I could talk my way out of it with a good excuse if I had to. Fred was a significant mentor in my development. As a result I am convinced that mentoring is one of the most important relationships in the male maturation process. Mentoring is the non-verbal energy that is shared between the mentor and the mentored—both individuals give and receive with clear and communicated boundaries. The relationship strikes a spark in the mentor, bringing to life something that may not have otherwise appeared, and at the same time it ignites within the mentored something that would have remained otherwise unlit.

As the date for the retreat arrived, I was rather anxious but couldn't come up with any good excuse not to go. I got on the plane. I had a fear that I could not explain, later learning that it was a good fear, the type of fear that lets you know you are about to do something engaging, and that it is important to stay alert. Trying to deal with the fear, I asked Fred if there would be any "high altitude stuff" because I had a fear of heights. He assured me that my feet would be on the ground at all times but the anxiety still persisted. Most of the weekend agenda centered on exploring what it meant to be a man, and there were also more interactive activities. The real gold was not the specifics of the weekend but simply the value of a group of men getting together to address this topic of mature manhood with challenges and support.

Periodically during the retreat I noticed that it was difficult for me to get fully involved. There was my fear of confronting aggression—mine as well as other men's—and the disturbing and unidentifiable risk of being exposed. I discovered I had a background fear and mistrust of other men, though my experience was not unique by far. Other insights included realizing just how much of my life I had spent seeking the approval of women and how much other men did the same at the expense of getting our own lives in order. It seems so ironic since most of these efforts didn't work. Other insights included how even men who had been

22

battlefield veterans were challenged dealing with emotional pain. These of course were not the only issues, just a few of the least-expected ones.

Another discovery of that weekend: It's not so much that men do not share their feelings, it's that many of us have little access to them in a verbal way, to ourselves. Since we have only a little idea of what they are, we are limited in what we are able to express verbally. The loss of our emotional and spiritual self, as well as our fear of connecting with other men, became apparent to me then. And it was present in other men as well.

When it was time to go home, I was exhausted but also exhilarated. We said our goodbyes and I headed to the airport, soon to be surprised on the flight home by an unusual event that was both amusing and self-affirming. I noticed I was seeing life a little bit differently. When I got up to the check-in counter, the counter attendant asked me if I had any special requests. I thought for a moment, deciding what I would REALLY like if I were not worried about how it looked to others. So, with determination and a sense of fun, and my new natural grounded confidence, I said: "I would like a center seat just behind the wing, with two attractive and intelligent women on either side of me who enjoy my company enough to buy me a drink on the way home." I was shocked that I said that, and looked at her for a shocked response. Part of me thought, 'How could I make such a sexist request?' and another part thought, 'After a weekend with men this would be very enjoyable!' She paused, obviously having heard something other than she expected,. She smiled warmly and said, "I will see what I can do for you, Mr. Brossman." I felt like it was more *how* I said it than *what* I said, or maybe it was the fact that I look crazed from the rush of the weekend, not having slept much the night before.

While boarding the plane and walking to my requested seat, I wondered why I hadn't chosen a window seat, which would have been more realistic. As I sat in my middle seat, flanked by empty seats on both sides, I could see from the line of passengers that all seats would be filled shortly, and I was wondering who I would be 'stuck' with for the long trip from L.A. to Raleigh. While sorting out my stuff, I heard a female voice saying to another woman, "We're almost next to each other, isn't that great!" I looked up and saw two beautiful women checking their tickets and recognizing their seats were next to me—one to my right and one

23

to my left. Amazingly we seemed to hit if off right away. One of the women was a professional athlete on a national women's team. The other said she was the lead singer in some classic rock band that I had 'probably never heard of.' I asked the name. "Fleetwood Mac," she said, explaining that Stevie Nicks was doing solo work and she had taken Stevie's place for the album *Time*. Well, time flew by, and they seemed to be very interested in my men's weekend experience. When the flight attendant came for drinks, before I could speak, one of the women said, "What do you want. It's on me!" So I had the first mixed drink I'd had in a long time. We had great conversation, and in no time we were landing in Raleigh. Before I left, I asked the singer for her autograph.

What I gained from the weekend was not crystal clear but I knew it was profound. When I got back home, I noticed that the feelings I had before the weekend had changed. No longer did I feel like a 9-year-old boy in a 36-year-old body. I felt like a 36-year-old man on a path of personal growth and maturity with significant work to do. Sudden—and strange to me—strength had been drawn from the community of men that I carried home with me.

Unfortunately, where I lived there were no men's groups available to keep that weekend alive for me. Then I received a letter from a man in Greensboro, NC who wanted to start a group to introduce men to the experience of the retreat. I also found the Raleigh Men's Center and went to one of their annual gatherings, realizing that I wanted something that would keep me in the conversation of men's issues. Though I was beginning to discover the benefit of men's work in my life, I was also aware that it was going to take long-term work for lasting change to happen, along with the right environment to nurture it.

The man from Greensboro got a group of us together, but distances caused the group to collapse after several months. Yet it was a real start of seeing the value of an ongoing men's group. My girlfriend at the time was always excited when I was going to get together with the 'team' (that's how we referred to it) because she said she liked the type of man I became after the meeting. Out of this group I met my next housemate. He was in the process of getting a separation from his wife. I suggested that we create our own different type of men's gathering, and he agreed to help me with it. The idea was to have a unique meeting of men. I thought about what type of group I would like to be involved in.

My passion for questions and the value they had given me drew me to the idea of a men's discussion group, a group where the questions themselves had a life-shifting effect. I intended that by exploring the questions, we would be inspired to change, commit, appreciate, forgive, accept, or enhance some aspect of our lives. I had a vision that in a healthy society, men would get together on a regular basis to have meaningful deep conversations about their lives, addressing issues and supporting each other around the unique issues that may come up in living your life powerfully. I told a friend I wished this type of group existed and he said, "Maybe the lantern that you want to be lit is yours to light." Out of that statement I took on creating the first Men's Inquiry.

Chapter 2
The First Men's Inquiry Meeting:
Pursuing a Calling

On October 18, 1996, almost a year after the first men's weekend that I attended, my housemate and I had an unusual party at my house, a party to which we invited only men. The party's theme was "An informal inquiry into what it means to be an adult man and what creates and maintains a long term passionate relationship." We invited many of our friends. Some said it sounded interesting, but they couldn't make it. Others just said; "I won't be coming." A few said, "Why would you have a party and not invite women?"

We decided to set up two flip charts in my living room—one stating the theme of the party and a definition of an informal inquiry, and on the other I put three questions to seed the discussion. I looked up the word "inquiry" in the dictionary to complete the flip chart and better design this effort. Dissatisfied with the definition, I wrote my own: An "informal inquiry" is a casual discussion examining something, looking at it as though it had never been examined before with the intention of discovering something new.

When our guests started to arrive, we introduced ourselves and my housemate offered refreshments. We ranged in age from 23 to 65. I started describing how this idea for a party came to be. I began: "We attended a weekend course called the Sterling Men's Weekend and each of us received unique value from it, but I wanted more. I wanted to discuss men's issues that I thought were important with other men. My intention here is to discover something in a group that might not be discovered on one's own. At the men's weekend I discovered that men together could begin to look at and discuss openly things that they may be apprehensive about discussing in the presence of women."

The men in the group were listening attentively to me, so I asked the first question: Who were the role models that supported you in distinguishing yourself as a man? The answers were varied: "My first role model was my father, then later a man at church who represented wisdom..." Another man said, "I took bits and pieces from different people... Davy Crockett and John Wayne were role models for me growing up. The *Rifleman*... It was about a

27

father/son relationship involving power, strength, as well as gentleness also, and my father of course."

To further encourage the discussion, I talked about my role models and, in the process, revealed some things about myself. Another man spoke up: "I grew up without a role model at home because my father was gone, and I resented that. My role models were fathers in the neighborhood. I remember an older man who taught us about cars. He showed us how to fix cars and let us do some of the work. That left an impression on me."

Another said, "Andy Griffith. This was a story about men's relationships. I got strength from my father; he gave me a sense of fair play, not taking advantage of a person when they were vulnerable—also how to deal with physical pain. But he did not offer a model for dealing with emotional pain; he would just run from it."

Some men volunteered to speak, and sometimes I called on others. One man said, "My role models at 16 or 17 were Bob Dylan and Timothy O'Leary, basically because I was rebelling against my parents. Dylan was bright-witted, and cynical, and I liked that." Sadly, one man said, "Most of my role models growing up were negative ...a lot of drinking and anger. Now they are Tony Robbins, Stephen Covey, and John Gray...I guess the most important role models are the ones in front of me today. I listen to tapes of them in the car and worked hard for the last year to change; however, my wife doesn't feel I have changed enough and is still divorcing me. I listen to the tapes of them over and over, but progress seems slow."

Another replied, "We were not taught how to let go, which is necessary for real change. It's a challenge to remember where we want to be." Another man spoke up, "There are earthly and heavenly role models: Jesus Christ offered both to me... I was always a good Christian, husband, and father... then I came home one day and found my wife in bed with another man. I had a complete breakdown...if it wasn't for Jesus, I would have not made it."

"Who else?" I asked, and one man replied, "I tried to draw role models from TV... I could never measure up. ... I really went through an identity crisis during my separation. In fact, I think in my 40's I am just beginning to get together my own identity from role models around me."

28

One of the younger men said, "My father, he was my best friend. I wanted to follow in his footsteps. He was in oil and I am in computers… Oil and computers don't mix."

Another said, "I wonder if I chose my father as a role model. He had a strong nurturing side… I remember what he gave to me in times when I was in big trouble, then he was really supportive… but at other times he was just absent."

There were more comments and the conversations continued. It is hard to put into words how rich the experience was becoming. We discovered that what we were taught or told growing up was not nearly as important as what the people around us were doing. We seemed to learn from who our parents were, not what they said. So, for example, if you give to others and never take care of yourself, you will teach your kids to do the same. We were looking for models of being and behaving from men around us.

Yet my own internal dialogue was not giving me clear feedback as to how well the evening was going. The inner critic was talking about how I should be doing something better, that I was missing something.

I continued to the next question: *In contrast to traditional role models of men, what does it mean to be a man who is in touch with his heart but at the same time strong, managing his responsibilities and loving and enjoying his life?* After reading this question out loud, I realized that it was a bit much, so I stated it in a simpler and slightly different way: *What does it mean to be an adult man, and when did you decide you were an adult man?*

One man jokingly blurted out, "What do you mean 'decided'? You're assuming that I am one." Another said, "What do you mean by *adult?*" I answered that I had picked 'adult' as another word instead of "real man" and he questioned, "Why not just *man?*" I replied that we could use the word 'man' and so the discussion continued. The youngest man spoke up: "I have met a lot of older men who act like small children…I mean, just because you are older does not mean you are an adult."

The man who had found his wife in bed with someone else spoke, "To tell the truth, I am not the right man to call on, I don't know any more. The center of my life was my wife, family, children…I gave up time for myself…that was a mistake. Now I am trying to discover what my purpose in life is." You could see he really did not realize how much he was offering to the rest of us with his courage to speak.

One of the men said, "I guess I have moved from being who I think I should be; now I am looking at becoming who I want to be. Another said, "I guess I had an identity crisis at 30, 40, 50, and now at 60, I am becoming more comfortable with who I am." Someone added, "I remember the moment I realized I was a man, I was doing construction work at the time and the foreman asked me to go up on a high roof and do something. I remember looking up at the high roof, I was tired and I said, "Look man, I'm scared. I don't want to do it."

After some more comments, obviously it was time to go to the next question: *What does it take to create and maintain a long-term, passionate relationship?* One spoke up, "I think it is important in our relationships to work on our relationships with ourselves." Another shared, "Yeah, I have forgotten and remembered that many times."

Someone else said, "You know how much we buy into the romantic fantasy? The problem is that no one has offered me a way to break the pattern. It's like they have offered women a way out (in movies and on TV) but not us." Another reply was, "Yeah, what does the prince do when his princess does not want to be rescued?" One man responded, "To keep the relationship working you give up your men friends and hobbies because you're told that you're away too much." Another said, "What we do is give up ourselves for our relationships." To this another commented, "Then we have nothing left for them to love."

It was 10:30 p.m. and I thought it was a good time to conclude. I thanked everyone for coming and shared that my intention was to further refine leading such group discussions and perhaps write an article. I was still not exactly sure how the evening went, or if this was even a pure inquiry. At the same time, I was moved by what had happened. I felt as if I had played a role in creating a sacred place and it was clear something important had happened.

As we started to adjourn, several men spoke up, "When are we going to meet again?"…"Yeah, we just scratched the surface." I replied that I had already scheduled the next meeting to occur after Christmas, maybe in February. "That's too far away…" "Yeah, we don't want to lose the continuity!" So I said I would look at my calendar and have the next meeting within a month, unaware that our Inquiry meeting was about to take on an ongoing monthly life of its own!

After a year of having The Men's Inquiry every month, I reflected on the experience. Every month on the allotted evening I would wonder why I was doing this since few or no men would RSVP. In my head I was convinced no one would show up at all. It seemed like too much work and criticism for trying such a thing from men who had not experienced it and even from women. I would think maybe men were just jerks, determined not to let anyone contribute to them or to explore fellowship in this way. Then by 7:30 p.m. the men would show up, sometimes the same and sometimes different, but they would be here to see what would happen. So I faithfully kept the Inquiry on my schedule, inviting more men, developing our guidelines and gladly noting the increase in attendance as months went by.

Over that first year I perfected a workable format that is still in place today, ten years later, except for the fact that we now send out the questions via email several days before the meeting. For the original meetings I posted three related questions on a dry erase board at the meeting

The Inquiry format

7:00 to 7:30 p.m. – Arrival
We begin at exactly 7:30 p.m. I tell the men that we start at 7:30 sharp and if they have a challenge being on time I recommend planning to arrive as early as 7:00 p.m.

7:30 to 7:55 p.m. – Getting Present
We use this time to say whatever is required to bring our attention fully into the room and be prepared for the inquiry. I say, "Welcome to the Men's Inquiry, we start on time and end on time. Please respect the confidentiality of the other men. What is said here stays here. I ask you all to speak from your own experience, which means making 'I' statements vs. 'we' or 'they' statements. One reason for this is you begin to realize that your own experience may be a greater contribution than your advice or ideas. You are welcome to give advice if it is asked for. We will go around the room and ask you to say whatever you need to say to

31

be fully present here in this group tonight. That may involve some accomplishment, some challenge or anything else."

8:00 p.m. – Inquiry Discussion

I begin by reading the first question. A few examples of questions explored over the first year are: How do we learn to accept ourselves? How do we develop the way to be assertive without being aggressive? What is a man's role now in a household, family, or relationship? As I intended at the Inquiry's inception, our job is to examine the questions as though we have never seen them before, discovering together something that we may not have discovered alone or in the company of women. I see my job leading the Inquiry as encouraging us to dig deep into the questions, staying with each question until it has been fully explored.

9:20 p.m. – Insights & Commitments

The time may vary slightly according to the number of men involved. Here we take time to review the new insights we have discovered and what actions we are willing to commit to doing in the coming weeks. We always have more to discuss than the time allows. I say, "I want to give us time to state any insights you gained from this evening's Inquiry, and if there is anything that you would like to commit or re-commit to do through your insights." I regularly remind everyone that "Insight without committed action is just entertainment."

9:30 p.m. – Closing

I thank the men for coming, invite them to suggest new questions, hang around to chat, and if they meet someone they would like to continue a conversation with, I recommend they meet for follow-up.

Thinking back to the very first meetings, I knew that I was the right person at the right place. I felt profound satisfaction to be a part of the birth of this new work, realizing we were really making a difference in each other's lives by being there. As that first year and the next decade progressed, with each Inquiry we discovered something new about ourselves. It enhanced our lives and nurtured the development of the courage to trust other men.

The premise of this work is that often the behavior, beliefs, and values that have the most influence on our lives are just outside our individual conscious awareness. It is hard to change something that we are not aware of. Through this type of inquiry we can discover the things of which we had been unaware, allowing us to choose or change them.

The intention of the Men's Inquiry Group is to create an environment where men can profoundly nurture, trust and emotionally support each other. The group is a place where together we can explore ourselves in such a way to be able to embrace our full humanity and enhance trust between each other.

Out of these meetings my personal vision for men evolved: when men can re-learn how to nurture and authentically support one another and to stand together to be the men we are proud to be, then we will truly be mature men.

A widening community of men

As a complement to The Men's Inquiry, I chose to take a men's training program in 2002 called the New Warrior Adventure. This weekend program includes exercises designed to deepen your clarity of your own mission in life and get you to move beyond what may be stopping you. It is also about embracing your strengths and having more access to them. The weekend can be, for some men, a Rites of Passage or Initiatory weekend that honors each individual man's own path. Other men may view it as a tool for transition to the next level in their life. It gives men tools to deal with tough emotional issues so that instead of having to leave a situation that is uncomfortable, we can stay present and even use it to make ourselves stronger. It helps us at work because it enhances our abilities to take more initiative, to be more aggressive. The weekend is designed to challenge, but in a respectful and safe way.

Some of what I have taken away from weekends like this is a greater sense of what I am capable of doing and consistently being in action on it. Before these experiences I did not realize how little I trusted other men and how much it hurt me that this issue was present in my life. From this workshop I experienced trusting other men and at the same time developed better discrimination skills in knowing when I am in a safe trusting environment. I also gained access to more of my own personal energy and resolved a number of issues I had with my mother. This has directly enhanced my personal relationships and my effectiveness in taking initiative in business.

Following the New Warrior weekend, my girlfriend and other friends noticed my deeper level of confidence. The experience also gave me a sense of how to be more appropriately assertive in my life. From the New Warrior weekend I learned what true, strong and masculine compassion can be. It deepened my friendship with my best friend from college, and now I have 11 men in my life, brothers who have experienced the New Warrior training, who I meet with every two weeks. They are committed to supporting me as the man I want to be, as I am for them. For more information you can visit www.mkp.org or see the resources in the back of this book.

Chapter 3
What is "Men's Work"?

Before I got involved in "men's work," I was always very suspicious of men's groups. Proudly, I thought I had evolved beyond that sort of socializing. This suspicion was deep, probably due in part from growing up in Washington, D.C. and the views I developed there—if men were doing it, it was probably bad news and soon in the nightly news. My suspicion did not die easily and continued for a long time, even after I participated in my first men's weekend. What were we doing? What was this stuff called men's work?

My current definition of men's work is men working together to inspire each other to be the best we can be through healthy relationships with each other. It is not men helping other men justify behaviors and lies, since that is the act of cowards. It is about men giving their attention to other men, expecting them to be and do what they say they will do. It is not about men letting each other off the hook for good excuses. Men's work is about learning to trust men in a way where fears, passions, grief, and joys can be expressed. It is something that takes real intentional work for most of us and does not seem to happen automatically in our society. Men's work may or may not be faith based.

The Men's Inquiry is an aspect of men's work where men get together to explore questions, to share experiences, to address issues that are deeply important to men and then take action out of the insights gained. Issues addressed may include ongoing relationships, developing healthy male friendships, being a father, dealing with anger and/or emotional pain, courage, joy or having a mature spiritual life. The vision for The Men's Inquiry is that it will exist as a natural part of men's lives, where men will take time out with other men they have learned to trust and have these deeper explorations of life's questions to enhance their lives and their community.

My own nervousness and suspicion were partially resolved when I interviewed men who had been involved with men's work and their partners. I asked them what their partners thought when they first became involved in a men's group. Some of the women had been suspicious of the group at first and said they initially saw no real benefit. However, the greatest resistance came from other

35

men. They made jokes about men "coming out of the closet," or said they had "gone to something like that once" and did not need it now. All the responses reminded me of my own beginning on this path when I was denigrating socializing in men's groups.

This led me to seek out and interview men who had been involved with men's work for over a year or more. I wanted to find out what their partners thought of their involvement after a period of time. I was amazed at how positive the responses were! Comments included: "I liked the man that he became." "He seems to be more confident and involved with the family" and "I really see the value he gains and it helps our relationship." After being involved in a men's group myself for awhile, I saw the benefits first-hand and was puzzled why so few men were involved in such groups.

Here are a few of my observations about what may be stopping men from participating in—and reaping the benefits of—men's groups.

Fears, Concerns and False Beliefs About Men's Work

Myth #1: It is the man's role to be the sole protector and provider.

We are still highly influenced by the antiquated social role of men as protectors and providers who are self-sufficient creatures having all the answers. Our society has implied that self-sufficiency means handling everything in isolation. A healthier attitude would be that self-sufficiency is the wisdom to seek out and utilize support and resources in one's own environment.

As Warren Farrell noted in his book, *Women Can't Hear What Men Don't Say*, men in our culture are often viewed as "success objects." This viewpoint is as dehumanizing as viewing women as sex objects. Many times the success object bias does not even change when both partners bring in equal salaries, especially in a family with children. There is nothing wrong with the protector and provider role as long as it is not used as an excuse to avoid male friends or to avoid taking care of yourself.

Myth #2: Men's Groups Equate to Oppression of Women

Both men and women may be suspicious of men's groups. Some believe that men's work is misogynist by its very nature. They believe it exists to support men who hate women. Nothing could be further from the truth. Men's work supports men and women living in harmony. It takes a certain level of personal courage for a man to work on himself and get clear on what is truly important to him, as is done in men's work. It tends to create more balanced and grounded men who honor women as equals. The truly strong and confident do not need to attack or dominate anyone.

Myth #3: Silence Means Strength

Many men have developed the habit of isolating themselves emotionally, especially from other men. They have learned the unwritten rule that a man should develop only superficial or competitive relationships with other men that solely revolve around business or sports.

In contrast, men's work helps break through this two-dimensional socializing. Conversations involving more personal topics become easier with practice and support, as does distinguishing emotions vs. ignoring or reacting to them. Silence alone allows no one to contribute to you, and what courage does that take? When men learn to develop trusted friendships with other men, they learn that they connect to their challenges in life and become better equipped to engage these challenges. They also gain greater skills in developing ability to appropriately use support and let others contribute to them.

Myth #4: If you are in a relationship there's no benefit in being in a men's group.

Some men don't notice that they are missing the male relationship because they have become overly dependent on the women in their lives. As a consequence they are not able to take the risk of being emotionally available to their partner. This is where the man has no real friendships with other men. For these men, this over-dependency is often unconscious. Too often, however, it rears its ugly head as jealously, domination, control, or even in resentment of her friends. Men's work provides a support structure for these men safely to discover and change this dependency. By developing healthy relationships with other men, they have less at stake in their relationships so they can become more emotionally available to their partners and to themselves. Without men's work, a man may get all his emotional needs met through his partner. But the fear of losing this singular connection is what causes him to have more at stake and, consequently, he actually shares less and takes less emotional risk. With men's work and having emotionally healthy men in his life, he has the connection of fellowship for support and can be more available in his relationship with his partner. The paradox is this: A man can be more emotionally intimate with his partner if he has healthy relationships with other men from which he can gain greater understanding of his life and purpose. He can mirror himself, and from that greater confidence develops.

Myth #5: Men's groups are made up of gay men

Homophobia may keep heterosexual men away from men's groups, while a gay man may stay away out of fear of being ostracized. The core of men's work is about creating a safe place where active sexual energy does not exist as it often does in situations with men and women or in places where there are only gay men. Men's groups provide a place to learn within a safe environment—a community of confidence and trust—to distinguish between sexuality and intimacy for both heterosexual and gay men. Hashing out sexuality issues is central to living as a healthy adult male. In fact in a men's group a man's "sexual" preference seldom arises because there are so many other issues that rise to the top of the agenda. There are issues like anger, personal goals, parent issues, purpose, as well as specific issues with family members or a difficult boss or employee. In other words, the business of just living in a diverse community is a fruitful source of issues.

Myth #6: Only the weak need support

Some men think men's groups are only for men with problems or for unsuccessful men. What a misunderstanding! A man who can move smoothly through his feelings instead of suppressing them or being driven by them, who is clear about what he is up to in life, is a strong and powerful man. Actually the wise seek the support that helps keep them at peak performance. An Olympic athlete would not attempt to achieve a gold medal without a supporting team. While he must do the work himself, he is successful because of the supportive community that not only encourages but also cajoles and instructs.

Myth #7: Men's groups would take more time away from my family

If you are a father working 40 hours a week or more, you may not have a lot of free time. What harried fathers do not realize is that their lives within their family may be enriched through extra-family structure that supports them as *men*. They not only become more emotionally available for their partners and children but they also have a different perspective on themselves. So why on earth should something as important as fatherhood be handled without support?

What Insights did you personally gain from this chapter?

What do you want to commit to or re-commit to out of these insights?

Remember!
"Insight without committed action is only entertainment!"

Chapter 4
The Benefit of Men's Work

Why is it important that men's work expand its scope? What is the social and personal value of men taking time to address issues about our lives, learning to talk straight with each other, supporting each other in living our missions, visions, and values? Why even make the effort?

First, men who are more conscious and able to experience their emotions fully and determine their needs tend to live a more fulfilled life. Second, men who have healthy relationships and feel connected to others tend to be life-supporting, compassionate, and less violent yet still capable of being appropriately assertive. Men's work also helps develop essential role models that are stable and mature. The flip side of this is that men who over-isolate themselves cause many social problems and often suffer more from depression. Young boys need healthy mature role models in order to learn to become worthy men. And furthermore, they need specific rites of passage that delineate their transition from being boys to becoming men, something more evolved than gang allegiances that some teenagers use to initiate themselves into manhood. Without a doubt, well-directed men's work can reduce violence in our society. I attended both public and private schools in Washington, D.C. in the sixties and seventies and from my experiences there I observed that violence frequently comes from emotional isolation. This isolation creates resentment and anger that often leads to violence toward oneself and others. Men need a form of sustenance from other men that we only get when we learn to trust each other—a special type of emotional connection. Perhaps men's work offers this needed food, a balanced diet of emotional support that allows us to be whole and complete in our lives.

In each of the following chapters we will explore different questions that I have crafted during the past 10 years of leading the Men's Inquiry meeting. Each chapter has the same format: a list of related questions around a theme, a short perspective of my personal experience on the subject, and a collection of responses to the questions from men of differing ages, backgrounds and nationalities. The men's contributions were requested and received via phone and e-mail. Responses were submitted by over 100 men who agreed to have their answers published anonymously under a pseudonym. Many of these men have been a part of the in-person Inquiry meetings or the on-line Inquiry. All understood that they were expressing themselves in the same context of genuine listening and speaking that a Men's Inquiry provides.

To take interpersonal communication to the next level we must commit ourselves to action based on expanded understanding and insight. It is my vision that this technique of inquiry and discussion within the confidentiality and trust of a group will be further developed. You, the reader, may wish to follow this simple yet powerful model in your own place. The chapters to come will give you an experience of the unique environment the Inquiry creates for gaining life-enhancing insights. I invite you to explore these questions with yourself and others.

What Insights did you personally gain from this chapter?

What do you want to commit to or re-commit to out of these insights?

Remember!
"Insight without committed action is only entertainment!"

Chapter 5
Building Fellowship & Friendship:
The Value of Having Male Friends

How do you create close male friends you can confide in about your joys, passions, fears, anger, and desires?

How could meaningful relationships with other men support you emotionally so that you are more available to your partner, children, and yourself?

What does it take to rekindle and maintain a male "best friendship"?

What type of friend are you to other men?

Do your friends justify your bad habits, or do they inspire you to be a better man?

Do you realize how having close men friends helps you to be more effective & balanced in business, in fatherhood, and with family issues?

If you are not modeling healthy relationships with other men, how will your son learn about modeling healthy relationships?

Who are men who you admire in your life? Have you told them what they mean to you?

Do you allow other men to contribute to you? Do you know how selfish it is not to let other men contribute to you?

Do you invalidate another man's contributions by acting like you are humble, or do you respond with a simple "thank you," personally receiving the acknowledgment?

Do you "see" other men or just "look through them?"

♦ **Martin's comments on this topic**

♦Don't men have enough male friends they play golf with? What about male friends on softball teams, in church groups, hunting pals, or old high school "drinking" buddies? Can a bunch of guys doing 'guy stuff' equal the incredible support and insight a network of male friends getting together to explore questions (as in this book) or other healthy men's work can?

◆ How can you say that a support network of male friends isn't as meaningful and significant as meeting with a bunch of guys doing "guy stuff?" I 'm not discounting sports activities as unimportant or less meaningful because they truly have their value. Besides, many men don't even have that level of traditional buddy friends, as they are only connected to their jobs and daily family responsibilities.

◆The questions that I would ask most men are these:

If you were on your deathbed, would you look back and say, "These are the kinds of friendships I always dreamed of?"

If you have a best friend, do you have the courage to tell him how much he means or is important to you?

Do you have men friends (not family members) who you could call in the middle of the night if you were in trouble that would help you?

Do you have men in your life that you would want in a foxhole with you? That is, if there were real danger present and you had to rely on someone to survive, do you know who you would want with you (family members excluded for this question.)

◆You can't imagine the richness that is possible in life when you have friends at this deeper level. Learning to see, hear and trust selected men in your life can enhance all aspects of life including traditional male activities.

◆It is easier for men in committed relationships with women to have more solid male friends than female friends. I don't mean that it does not work for men to have women friends; just that it is worth the time to examine the effort you have made to develop strong male friends as well.

◆Good male friends support you and challenge you to be your best and stay aligned to your mission and core principles. They acknowledge you for being your best and call you on your justifications. Poor male friends support you in your own personal justification and help you live a reasonable life of mediocrity and white lies. Just the other day one of the men from my men's team took me out to lunch to see how I was doing and challenge me on my progress with taking care of my health and completing this book. It was not comfortable to face the truth that I was not living up to my own capability. I recommitted to the entire team (who will not let me off the hook), to a new workout program and new goals for completing this book. It is hard to express in words how valuable and blessed I feel to have men in my life who care that deeply. I want everyone to have people like that in their lives. Even as an only child I can still say I have a team of brothers who will not let me hide out in my life or fall without being there to catch me! These types of friends generally do not develop without making some effort as adults. A good start is to seek out men you admire and make the effort to get to know them and what is important to them. Realize that despite how much you may admire them, they are also a person like you, a man with concerns and goals. Friendships develop when dealing with challenge as well as celebrating successes. This lets me bring more strength and support back to my family.

The Men Address Selected Questions

How do you create close male friends you can confide in about your joys, passions, fears, anger, and desires?

Fredrick
For me, with my male friends, the trust has always developed more slowly than with my women friends. I think with a woman I can bond, wisely or stupidly, very quickly. But with men, there's got to be some track record. We have to prove ourselves to each other. Often that happens "under fire" somehow – in a work situation, or in some kind of conflict. It feels very primal – you and me against the mastodons, or something. I think it works this way because there is more at stake. The risk seems bigger but at the same time the benefit of close male friends is greater, too.

Bob
My greater problem was sustaining healthy male friendships. I had that problem until I gained more self-esteem and self-confidence. At that moment, other men were not any longer semi-gods I would worship, but peers I would recognize as men and who would recognize me as a man. In my opinion, this is the most important thing in male-to-male friendships: learning to trust each other for a real sustainable friendship to develop and trust each other as men.

Barry

I've always had male friends, and for the most part they were superficial when I was younger. My ability to really "see" other men deepened significantly when I did the New Warrior training in December of 2000. For the first time, I felt in touch truly with the good parts of my masculinity. I grew up with a father who was the classic silent type until he blew up. As a result I grew up scared, particularly of men. I no longer feel that way, and even when I talk with a man who is angry, I can see past that and connect with him and validate him and his anger.

Since my New Warrior weekend, I truly see men differently. I used to have trouble holding the gaze of a powerful man, and I don't any more. No matter who the man is, I now see the little boy in him when I look at him, which helps me stay compassionate and strong.

I am a good friend to other men, mainly because I am willing to listen. I'm also willing to share my feelings, judgments and wants with them in a clean way. Men trust me as a result. Having close male friends is a stabilizing factor in my life. They keep me in touch with the powerful parts of masculinity, which serve me in business and in my relationships.

There are so many men I admire in my life. One of these men was my dad, with whom I've now built a stronger relationship. He taught me so many good things about how to live life: a strong work ethic, responsibility, sacrifices. Another man I admired was one of my first bosses who was also a mentor. We've now been friends for the past 20 years. Many other men have filled the role of big brother or mentor or simply friend.

Of my 50 years on this earth, it has only been in the last 10 years that I have experienced the power of truly close male friendship. I really did not make any effort to create close male friends before that and now see the effects of that. My own feeling of isolation got me to change. In allowing myself to open up to male friendships, I have discovered a new way, a better way to live. Instead of viewing other males as independent competitors, I now see them as interdependent allies. That simple change in my perspective has reduced my stress level immensely.

Ken

Until fairly recently, I didn't create male friends and didn't have any close ones. After being involved with men's groups over the last 8 years, I now create close male friends by taking risks. I share myself and my successes and struggles. I honor the other man in his successes and struggles. I listen with all my heart. I ask him for his advice. I offer to go the extra mile for him.

Dave

I create close male friends through Doing, Sharing. Knowing, and then Trusting. I would say these are the 4 keys to creating close male friendships. I believe that in doing things and sharing times with a man, I really get to know that man...what they're made of and what they're about. After really knowing a man I can decide if I can really trust this man...if I can confide in him about what's really happening with me and not just BS with someone about football or whatever. So far, I have one great man who knows me through and through. I see how rare this is and I see how few men have this.

Ross

I am involved in what we at call an I-Group (The ongoing support groups following the basic New Warrior training.) This circle of men meets weekly on Tuesday night. One of the first things we do is 'check in' with how we are feeling – from the heart. We follow that with a process that offers us the opportunity to reconnect with another man, e.g., if there is something keeping me at a distance from that man, some strong feeling or judgment I have about that man. The process offers me the opportunity to learn what that "charge" is and to transcend it so that I can bridge that gap and be in closer connection with that man.

Jeff

For me the men who are most trustworthy with my confidence I have found to be in spiritual groups. But the group needs to have a leader who is courageous enough to look at his own issues or the whole group will remain superficial. I am a member of AA and also a churchgoer, and there I have found confidants who have augmented and replaced the shortcomings of my familiar relationships.

Charles

The men in my life bless me with the gift of our journeys shared. They are good friends to me when:

-They do not pretend to stand in my shoes because they know that only my feet fit there; they do, however, stoop to do up my laces when my back is too sore to bend.

- They do not pretend to walk my journey for me because they know that only I can tread those steps; but they walk with me, at least for some of the way.

- They do not speak crap to me (well, almost never) but speak of their own unfinished adventures, even those which are full of pain and sadness.

- They don't take crap from me (well, almost never) but seek the truth of my own exploration of the highways, the byways and, especially, of the dark lanes and alleys.

- They are not afraid of my silences, nor I of theirs; but we are both enchanted by the magic of that wordless electricity which sparks between men who are in a trusting and companionable silence with each other. It strengthens!

I am such a fortunate man to have found close male friends who hang in there with me, especially in my later life! I am so fortunate that there are men to whom I can say, "I love you" without threatening their sexuality or mine. Or to whom such a declaration is an affirmation that it is OK to be who they are. Or to admit to a secret knowledge about myself. But it wasn't always so. My saddest regret is that it took me most of my life to discover that the secret to achieving close friendships with other men was first to discover an intimate friendship with myself. I found that there was absolutely no point at all in seeking friendship with anyone unless I was first and foremost my own best friend. That was the major discovery that led me to greater intimacy with other men.

So how did I learn to be my own best friend? That is an easy question to answer: Other men taught me that it was OK to be me. And to fall in love with who I am, and with whom I was becoming. I had always been under the impression - no, I always *knew* - that I was a dud, a failure and a fraud, despite the career, the degrees, the mortgage, and the family life with beautiful children and an attractive wife! I had to learn to unlearn that script for my life, and did so, thanks to other men! Sheeeeshh!! It was a hard thing to unlearn!

They walked with me in my Men's Group, and were available for hours on end to hear my grief. Over and over and over, for months, they heard my sadness at the loss of a marriage and a dearly-loved spouse, of my children growing up and leaving home, of the death of both parents, of a brother and a sister, of a career loss, and broken health, of a fire that destroyed my first new home,, of financial desperation in mid-life.... The misery of it all must have bored them rigid. And the repetition. And the length of time to tell and retell the story. And retell, and retell, and retell...

I even managed to bore myself to sobs, eventually, eventually, eventually...Such forbearance from those men! Such sticking-with-it until I was through the darkness!

Never did they prescribe solutions, nor diagnose my condition. Not once did any of those men in the group tell me to pull my socks up, get over it, and put it all behind me. Not once did they tell me to 'get a life.' They just acknowledged that I already had a life and that it was immensely sad and broken, because that was what they heard from me. And they confronted me when they could clearly see that I was talking crap. And quite regularly they hugged me and made me coffee.

They listened. They acknowledged. They were present. And they stayed with me, always respectfully hearing and acknowledging me and what was going on in my life as I reported it.

These men were trustworthy! They gave me the space and the courage to deal with my history, to get some tentative handles on it, and to begin discernment of a new way ahead. They gave me space! Space! Safe space!

Men! How magical your persistence is! Your ability to put up with crap, because you see the gold in it, is seemingly endless! Your courageous fortitude and comradeship is your glory!

The men also shared their own lives open-heartedly, softly, loudly, fervently, timidly, soberly, drunkenly, profoundly, profanely, religiously, raucously, demurely, casually, stupidly and insightfully. We brewed pots of tea together and solved the world's problems. We boozed on cheap wine and boasted of conquests. We engaged each other in the reconstruction of each other's lives and loves. The Great Australian Novel never got written, but the fabulous exchange of stories in drunken (and sober) stupors was the stuff of Nobel Prizes for Literature! The first new date, the doubts and fears of ever engaging with a woman again. The encouragement to learn from each other about opera, car maintenance, art, plumbing, woodwork and metalcraft. A deep re-engagement with religious faith happened for some because they finally had time to nurture and develop the inner life. The excitement, shared by phone at 3 a.m. one morning, of sex with a woman for the first time in years! Tips on shopping, swapping recipes and cooking hints! A demonstration of how to sew a button on a shirt.

A profound understanding grew that we men could be whole and complete and functional and valid all by ourselves. We did not need women to validate, approve, or define us. We did not need a relationship with a woman to give us permission to exist or to approve us or to demand that we behave ourselves and get a job. This lets us be a 'real partner' to a woman.

The wonder of it all was that when we formerly-partnered single men understood and integrated the knowledge that we were complete, whole and valid all by ourselves and on our own recognizance, we could at last entertain the idea of a relationship with a woman once more, but on new terms, on our terms as independent and affirmed men. As equals not as servants, providers, endless suppliers of funds with no money to spend on ourselves after grinding at boring jobs, or as protectors and reliable lap dogs. As equals! Some of us actually found women who were prepared to treat us as equals, to pull their weight in a new relationship.

Whew! What a relief!

Some of us found that it was equally OK to be single and to deal with those ladies who saw matchmaking opportunities for desperate-and-40 women-in-need-of-husbands-with-money.

Hey! It's too late! We have escaped!

The truth is that the more I loved myself, the more I developed as the French say, *'amour propre'* (self love), then the more I attracted other men who wanted to know me and to be my friend. And a wonderful woman became my second wife!

That is, roughly speaking, the value of male friendships to me.

Go for it, fellas!

Fred

To other men, I am friendly, reliable, sociable and always ready to give of myself and ready to show respect for others—a man who humbles himself and apologizes when he has either hurt someone or does something wrong.

Yes, I do allow men to contribute to me. I have only recently started doing so. I never knew that it was selfish not to do so until recently. I have felt better since I have started. I have also returned the favor. I usually thank them and if I forget, I apologize and I try to remember to say "thank you" the next time.

Ralph

How do you create close male friends in whom you can confide your joys, passions, fears, anger, and desires? That's just it! The way I have created close male friends is to confide in them about joys, passions, etc. What a great way to take the friendship deeper... by sharing a bit of who you really are. If they are a friend to keep, then they'll really listen. Maybe they won't have the courage to share with you just yet, but I'm sure that after a while they will. If they end up stabbing you in the back by making fun of you or by talking to other people about what you said, then probably they aren't a friend you wanted for the long term anyway. Might as well learn that now.

Arthur

I think part of having close male friends is expressing my feelings one-on-one. I have to say, despite the amount of work I have done, it is still difficult for me to express my true feelings, especially, one on one. Just this week I had the best of intentions around both my wife and my best friend in telling them both how important they are to me. I eventually got there but for me I notice how a part of me does want to shrink away from this, which affects how graciously I share myself. In a group situation I am more comfortable, so currently I am dealing with how much of this is 'theatre' and how much is real. I notice the theatre in others first, then reverse the perspective ...yes there are times where I seem to perform rather than practice.

I believe that I am as honest as I can be at any given instance with my brothers, and my journey will continue with this.

One thing I am happy with is how I model masculine relations to my four sons. This is not to say it's perfect, rather that it is a quantum leap from my own upbringing and therefore a vital shift in the evolution of the psyche in my lineage.

I am in a group and also run groups. I get so much from this both personally and professionally. I have a deep knowing that I will be doing this for a long time – it sustains me, gives me strength and humility, and it never ceases to amaze me how powerful it is for so many men. This is where I belong!

Stan

I think that being gay in a married relationship has added to my challenge around having close male friends. I knew that I was "different" from an early age, and as a gay man I have struggled all my adult life with how I might create and maintain close male friends with whom I could feel confident and comfortable. It was very difficult, since my sexual orientation seemed somehow to always preclude the possibility of a genuine friendship. With straight men I was afraid of losing what camaraderie I had, however shallow, and with gay men there seemed to be always looming the question of "what does one do, now that the secret is shared?" Have sex? Enter the guilt! End of relationship!

With marriage to a woman and the onset of family duties and career responsibilities, the absence of male friendship beyond the superficial continued. Maintaining the fear of disclosure to straight men and, with no further attempts to relate to gay men for shame of sexual intimacy, life became an endless series of shallow pleasantries highlighted only by the occasional joys of family and work. Meanwhile any possibility of authentic relationship with men was put on a high and distant shelf. I still struggle with this today.

Wilson

First, I am open and honest about my feelings, fears, and desires. I have learned the biggest boon to developing my male friendships is listening and speaking ONLY from the context of my own experience. The biggest detriment to creating a close male relationship is substituting advice, judgments, and opinions for true intimacy. Unfortunately, most men do this and for me it keeps the relationship on a superficial level. I work hard not to fall into this trap. I also learn a lot about whether a man is worth knowing by how he handles problems.

Benjamin

I create close male friends through intentional friendships. These are friendships that begin casually. I draw a man out by seeking to find out his interests, his joys, and, if it's not too prying, his pain. Once I decide that I want to have a particular man as a close friend, I place him in my "intentional friendship" group, seeking to find opportunities to meet in whatever way interests him. I find it very important to listen carefully, to remember what is said, and to avoid taking over the conversation.

As the friendship progresses, I seek to discuss what it means to have a good friend, how I have found that I need close male friends, what not having close friends can do to a marriage and to society as a whole.

Further, I begin to discuss the importance of touch. I will have already begun various non-threatening touch such as a side-hug around the shoulders, a touch on the arm while chatting, and I will attempt to covenant with him to replace the handshake with a hug. I have found it useful to keep this light. I may say that a 12-second hug is the bare minimum; that a 6-second-er is acceptable in a rush; but that a 3-second hug or briefer isn't even civilized. Sometimes we end up counting off the seconds in each other's ear as a joke, but it can break down the fear of male/male contact.

Ultimately, I attempt to bring individual friends together for group activities. I have found that the men I truly enjoy and who enjoy being with me nearly always enjoy each other. It's fun to watch the dynamics of meeting, and how quickly friendships form.

Anthony

The quicker way I have found to create close male friends is to join a men's group – preferably a structured men's group. I find that connecting with some men outside of the men's group can be a slower and more gradual process. I am open-minded and pretty non-judgmental (on a good day!) and find that I am often more open and trusting than other men are. Therefore, through consistency and open-heartedness, I gradually allow another man to feel his way while challenging him to think outside his own paradigm. As I have come to know, this helps!

Relationships with other men have taught me that I do not have to be perfect as a partner, husband, brother, son, and future father. I know from my training and my own experiences that I respond much better to observing and listening than being told how to lead my life, to be in relationships, to be at work, etc.

Peter

About male friends, this is an area where I have failed. In the past, I have had male friends that I would consider 'close,' yet I cannot point to a single one at this stage of my life. I think it has to do with some of the choices I have made for my own life and especially because I have a terrible habit—although come by honestly—of offering my opinion and advice, unsolicited, to friends about their lives, work, spouses, financial decisions, etc. As I have become more conscious of this defect, I have realized how difficult it must be and must have been for some people even to tolerate me in the same room. Many don't anymore. Not that the nearly unconscious habit of doing this has not been a choice of sorts; I believe after a certain period of time in adult life one owns his own life, his own choices, and his own behaviors and consequences. The 'find somebody to blame for your problems' act gets old very fast.

However, I also believe that the male role models that are in your life from grade school age through early high school have the most influence developing a male's view of what it means to be a man. In my case these men were, of course, my father and his father, as well as his two brothers (my uncles). They started a business together when I was an infant. I grew up around this business, which was eventually broken into numerous devalued pieces when I was in my early 20's because the group simply imploded under the non-fusion of its owners' mutually exclusive self-interest agendas. This happened shortly after my grandfather retired to a part-time participant and a coincident divorce of one of the brothers. The story is long and sordid, but suffice it to say, there are wives and relatives who no longer speak to one another over the dissolution of the entity. The original entity still exists. But it is just one uncle, and my own father continuously looked over his shoulder, although my father himself was operating his own form of the business in a different market. The 3rd brother does something completely different nowadays. My grandfather died essentially alone nearly ten years ago. Whatever business each of the three brothers do, it must generate revenue sufficient to satisfy personal legal guarantees they made, as extracted by my grandfather in return for claims settlements, to pay a pension to their stepmother, my grandfather's surviving wife, for the remainder of her life. They reap only what they sowed.

My father, as the oldest of the three, sees it as his role in life to be everybody's father. He is right always as far as he is concerned. I don't believe I have ever heard him express himself without being somewhat or extremely insulting and condescending toward whomever he was speaking to. He denies this completely. I stopped seeing him or speaking to him a little over 6 years ago when I began to understand this influence and listened for it more actively during a few encounters. I had no idea how bad it was. There also was a climactic incident, which is too long a story for this context, but it was enough for me. The worst of it was learning how readily, seemingly naturally, as in second nature, and unconsciously I did and do the very same thing. I cannot describe the extent of my resentment about the fact that I was taught that being a man meant to belittle, demean, criticize and speak in derogatory terms about anybody I knew to anybody who would listen. It sucked to figure that out and realize this behavior was precisely why I had such difficulty maintaining adult male friendships.

The bright side, I guess, is that I am conscious of it now. Whether that results ultimately in successfully changing the behavior for good is an open question. I do believe that male camaraderie and relationships are important. Its practice, however, from my observation and experience, is usually hierarchically based and having become a cynic as well, I believe often related to a personal gain motive. People who have taken the time to be my 'friend' usually want something from me: Favors, a promotion, a raise, or a consideration of some kind. I've never cared much for that reality. It's one thing when there is mutuality to the development and maintenance of a relationship; it's quite another when it's one-way and manipulative. One of the side effects of my 'defect' apparently is that I appear to be one who can easily be taken advantage of. Many have tried. Some have had a measure of success. I've noticed a lot of relationships I thought were above that level vanished when I was no longer in a position to provide the advantage sought. I haven't decided exactly how the two factors are related, cause or effect or cause and effect. Am I bringing this on or is this just the truth? I am not sure.

So while I understand the value of these relationships and I wish to make a measured effort to pursue some of them, I will do so cautiously as the grafts on my wounds have not yet entirely healed.

Wilson

Before I answer this, I feel I need to give you some background about me so that you can put my answers in perspective. I am 59-years old. I have been married twice, the last one ending at age 35 - I have lived alone since that time. I have a son from my first marriage at age 19 and a daughter from a non-marital relationship between the two marriages. Both children remain estranged despite my reconciliation offers. My decision to live alone was actually based on the realization that my failure in relationship might not be my choice of mates! Unfortunately, the living alone became isolation and depression and a vow to never put myself in a position to be hurt.

I am a recovered alcoholic and drug addict since 6/10/1987. As part of my recovery, I participated in men's groups for over 7 years and a mixed group for 2 years. I went through years of intensive psychotherapy and spiritual growth. My return to the church and faith in Jesus Christ is the most important part of my life.

In the late 80's and early to mid 90's, I was very active and interested in the Men's Movement (as it was dubbed). I read Bly, Keen, and Farrell and looked for other men who were interested in the plight and path of men in the modern era. I also participated in *Promise Keepers*. I found it very difficult to find men who were really interested in pursuing true growth and contact with other men. I think the press jaundiced the movement in the early '90's by presenting it as anti-women. Also, unfortunately, the largest groups of men who are active and outspoken are gay men - the perception that men speaking their true feelings and fears was tied too closely to the gay community chased away many men that I knew. This is a shame, for there were almost no gay men in the men's group I was involved in.

56

I am still having difficulty today finding men in the church who really want to honestly work on true personal and spiritual growth. I feel called to continue this search. There is some renewed interest as a result of John Eldredge's books and I certainly hope it continues.

I am (was) an executive\upper manager. In January of this year, I made the decision that I no longer wanted to remain in the corporate world. I quit my position with only the promise to myself that I would not work 'corporate' again. I am giving myself a year sabbatical to listen to God's call for my life and dedicate myself wherever He leads me. It feels shaky but it feels right!

It has been a challenge to get men together but the payoff is great enough that I still pursue it.

Theodore
It has taken me time to make friends. Only a few do I trust absolutely. Only a few (one or two) can I share everything with. Because that does not surprise me, I do not feel lonely. However, I am open to meaningful friendships when that possibility presents itself.

Jerry
I now welcome men into my life, by being vulnerable and authentic, allowing men to see my pain, sharing with them about my father, my mother, and telling them how I imagine my parents saw me as a child, and how they would describe me today if they walked into the room. I found out that this kind of vulnerability has made my life richer and the men that love me know who I really am, no pretending and no bulls--t.

Kyle
I don't create close friendships. Friendship has always been a mystery to me. People seem to go back and forth in their response or acceptance of me and I haven't usually been able to figure it out. Now that I'm thinking about my relationships with people, something else is coming up. In my younger pre-50s time in my life, it was always important for me not to seem needy. Of course the opposite of that is to be independent. To cultivate that image was very cool to me. I though about that word "cool" and that it was the thing to be back in high school So, the behavior this

produced in me was to appear confident and self-sufficient and aloof. As I developed this on into my 20s, it became my trademark, and it had the effect of making people afraid of me. It allowed me to be in control, or so I thought. But, this attracted the wrong kind of people to me. I didn't like people who didn't have a mind of their own even though they tended to worship or idolize me.

And in this persona I had problems finding ways of showing my true passions (while acting cool) so, this is the backdrop of my current persona. I relish friendship when it comes. Yet, at times I catch myself doubting, holding back, trying, disengaging, and walking away. At one level I'm afraid of getting into it and just letting it happen- afraid they will make me appear needy for their attention by brushing me aside or embarrassing me by just using me for their purposes. On another level being in a Friend-Relationship makes me part of something brand new, something good for itself, another way to know humanity and myself, where communication is not only in words. From another angle, I might like someone, and see they're having problems, and want to help them. But, this is actually selfish, and a way to approach that gives me the advantage. I think," Who am I to help? Isn't that arrogant and presumptuous?" Wouldn't it be better to come to a relationship tentatively, humbly, reacting to what is there at that moment instead of what it could do for me? Why would a healthy person want a friendship that wasn't equally based?

There are fledgling friendships I would like to develop because of my admiration for the potential friend. However, often they don't have time or inclination or courage to help cultivate the friendship. They don't have a way to tell me they do not want this friendship. It's often a sad matter of just giving up after many attempts to get together. So I still struggle with male friendships and see the real value at the same time.

Dave

Friendships with other men are essential to my well-being, and I feel blessed to have quite a few of them. In the early stages of an acquaintanceship, during which I'm exploring the potential for a real friendship, my technique is to put forth "a little something" and observe how it is received one bit at a time. If my openness startles the other man or causes him to withdraw, then I respect his need for distance and either settle for an association that is superficial or nonexistent. In this way, I minimize the chances for either of us being hurt. If, on the other hand, he responds with encouragement or, better yet, by proffering something a bit intimate about himself, I put forth a little more. Depending upon the circumstances, this process for developing a warm association can take place in the space of a single conversation or over the course of a much longer period of time.

My experience with men is that we thrive on appreciation, and I find that the more I extend to others, the more I receive in return. There are some men for whom my feelings of appreciation include actual admiration, and I have told them so. When, after years of maintaining an intermittent, friendly acquaintanceship with one of them—Warren Farrell (who is one of my life mentors)—an appropriate moment arose during a recent face-to-face encounter when I could embrace him and tell him I loved him. Recounting this to another man I admire—John Guarnaschelli of the New York men's group *On The Common Ground*—my eyes welled up with tears of happiness, awe and gratitude over having been able to express myself in this manner, and to be warmly received too! Fellow members of NCFM who I admire include Stanley Green and Marc Angelucci, each an inspiration in his own way. And then there's my beloved co-sponsor, Michael F., in Al-Anon Family Groups.

Andrew
For much of my adult life I've had few or no male friends to confide in at all! I simply didn't trust most men enough to be vulnerable and genuine with them.

It seems that the phenomenon of men not having male friends occurs frequently in this culture. I reach a certain age and find that my college friends are long gone, replaced by professional colleagues and/or competitors. I think also, given my terrible relationship with my father, that this situation is exacerbated for me in that I am afraid of most men.

In December 2004, I did the *New Warrior Training Adventure* weekend largely because I was interested in forming deep, meaningful friendships with other men. The biggest takeaway from the weekend for me was that my having the guts to be vulnerable was the key for my continuing personal development, as well as for my building real relationships with men.

In the six months since that initiation, I've become acquainted with literally dozens of terrific men with whom I'm pretty comfortable and trusting. I think much of the reason for this is that I know of their commitment to authenticity and connection to feelings, and it therefore feels safe for me to be vulnerable and genuine with them. Surprisingly, though my affiliation with New Warriors usually feels pretty safe, I'm still often afraid of men in the world at large. I'm slowly growing out of that fear, however.

Mark

I belong to a team of men whom I can trust from our "point" experience and this has been proven over time. These men are my mirrors and I am theirs. We practice agreed disciplines such as getting to the truth quickly, tough fathering, not buying any bullshit and overall, telling it as we see it. Most of all we always know and say how much we care about each other and remind ourselves that it is this type of caring that allows us to be receptive to how we are behaving.

Larry

I start with someone who has common interests in areas important to me: openness, spiritual awareness, helping make the world better. Then I build trust, which is easy for me. I usually share myself and if the person responds in a trusting manner, relationships are easy to grow.

Ike

I inherently make acquaintances because I am very extroverted. It is my desire to be who I really am, wherever I am. One way I make that concrete is to choose to make short, honest/self-revealing statements without concern with the response. I find that people who want to be real are respectful of others so people can respond as they see fit.

Damon

I identify with some men who seem to be coming from a similar background or experience as myself. I tell others when they are being the man I wish I could be, that they are, in fact, someone I wish I could be like.

Benny

How? I seem to think more in terms of why? Granted, I do have male friends, but I only confide in one, my best buddy. Unfortunately, he is in another state now. He's going through problems similar to mine. So, by phone and e-mail, we find that we are growing our relationship into another stage. He tells me his pain, and I do likewise. Putting the stubborn male ego aside I find we are helping each other through difficult times.

Darryl

In my experience I have engaged three principles, either consciously or unintentionally, each time I have ended up with guys I deeply trusted. The first is that I have shared some deep ordeal or emotional stretch with the other guys, such as intensive experiential trainings or graduate school study or living in communal housing situations. The second is that I have made and received an explicit commitment to personal development, specifically including the attainment of emotional literacy and full responsibility for our emotional lives/emotional reactions. The third is that I have entrusted my care to these guys, and they have to me. That is, I have specifically asked for help and allowed the advice, care and protection to reach me, and the guys have done the same with me. I'm talking about taking care of each other on life's critical challenges, such as doctoral work, financial security, death, divorce, marriage, child-raising, severe illness, etc. The most enduring expression of these three principles, and the most enduring gift as a result, has been in my relationships in the ManKind Project community, specifically in my every other week group that has been meeting for the past ten years.

Phillip

I don't create close male friends, and I have never had the kind of male relationships I want. The only person I have to share my joys, passions, fears, anger, and desires is my wife, and I often don't share these things even with her. I have come to understand that this is a fundamental problem I face.

Don

Mine have evolved from long friendships or common struggles over several years, supporting one another.

Randy

For the most part, I don't. However, the few male friendships I have created were created only because I thought them to be sensitive enough to trust.

Alexander

First of all there is no easy answer. In some instances personally, it has been intentional through associations I have had with other men in groups such as church, sporting events etc. However, some of these relationships have been accidental. Regardless of how they are first formed, I believe those friends that I am closest to have taken a great deal of time to develop. Also, I have found that my closest friend wanted to invest time into me. So, I guess for me, it starts with some passion that we both enjoy, and then there is regular fellowship, then over time spent with this person privately, and time investment, then a level of trust is built where we are more vulnerable.

Tom

After a friendship has been established (by either me or the other guy) I let it be for a while... I give it some time. Then, if I have come to believe that this is a person with whom I would: 1) want to and 2) be able to create a closer friendship with, I test the waters by revealing something of a more personal nature about myself. Then, I see how he responds. If he reacts with empathy and reciprocation, I gradually proceed... step by step.

Blake

Spend time with them, be truly interested in them. You cannot play one-up. You must be open to them as well as open for them. Most men really want to help, to teach, to be there. I believe most of us need little pats on the back from time to time but no sucking up. If you are open and true with them, they will be with you. Take little steps moving deeper as time allows. Try to remember the friendships of your youth and how they were developed, nothing has changed. You must spend the time doing things you both like.

Andrew

For me, there's a requisite first step before any such sharing can occur with anyone, but especially with men. That first step is that I see in the man that he is open to a friendship and that he's a safe person with whom to engage on that basis. I judge that by the openness I detect in him, in regard to how he talks about life and about his relationships and in how he describes his thoughts and feelings. In most cases, I will assume that a man is open to such a relationship if he is initiated into emotional work, as in MKP, or if he is a therapist or openly mentions having had therapy.

Once I establish that a man is a suitable candidate for such a relationship, it unfolds as with anyone, a little at a time, usually with smaller confidences shared before larger ones, building trust over time. When I detect a man's acceptance of me and his willingness and ability to match my openness and trustworthiness, I have a relationship I will nurture and maintain, by making "face time" and offering support, as well as asking for it as needed. That type of man is usually one who can be told directly that I value him and his presence in my life. I let him know through my works and actions that he is a trusted and valued friend.

Brent

I create close male friends by being with them, experimenting with new ways of being together, ways that change the ways I have learned to be with them, spending time with, sitting with them, breaking bread with them, hanging out with them, eventually I begin to speak, I begin to share with them . . . time gives way to these friendships. I create close male friends by sharing my secrets, as deep and as dark and as vile as I may judge them to be. I seek witnesses to my accomplishments and the sharing of my joys. And I get closer by hearing from men secrets that are more secret than my own. That is how I learn what goes on in the hearts of men.

Al

I don't know how to create close male friendships. When I start getting close to another man, I seem to find ways to keep me away. For instance, I find excuses to not return a call. Not sure why.

Clark

The way I create close male friends is to tell the truth. A simple example will explain. Tonight I was talking to my tennis partner. He has a rough time handling when he blows a shot and gives an excuse or just plain misrepresents what just happened. For example: I put in 80% of my first serves, when he put in more like 15%. I tell him the truth, that his success rate on serves was close to 15%, and that his protests to the contrary reveal that he was trying to protect his ego with bullshit. When I ask him what is the truth, he usually fesses up, and recognizes he was trying to protect his ego. We have a great time not only playing tennis, but helping each other to stay in the game on the court. Here's an example of us under fire helping each at the moment of truth. We were losing a doubles match at 2 to 4 and I was serving. I put in 4 good aggressive serves and my partner blew 4 shots at the net and then I was so depressed I doubled fault the last point of my serve. He turned to me and said, "I know I screwed up, what we do from here is more important then the past mistakes" I agreed and committed to giving my best. His ownership of having missed 4 relatively easy shots made me feel better and he told me the truth, the next point was more important then the last mistake. Telling the truth and being there for each other when you are down and in some ways celebrating your victories is more important then the actual game. Somehow when I tell him I was proud of his shot and acknowledge his choice and execution of that shot it goes to his heart and I feel the pride.

Werner

I make male friends very different from how I did when I was younger. When I was younger I looked for men who would let me 'hide out', let me be comfortable, let me be small. I of course did not understand this then. Now I have male friends at many different levels—some for business, some for inspiring me. But the important ones are the ones who I feel a little resistance being with, for they will inspire me to be more than I currently see myself as—men that support and appreciate my mission, not my complaints. If fact I don't value men who let me 'hide out' now.

Darryl

I honestly don't know how to answer this question. You see, I don't have what I would call close friends, either male or female. I've never learned or figured out how to nurture a relationship well enough to maintain a long-term friendship. Usually the relationship is initially based on proximity and mutual interest, and when that initial reason for connection is gone or over the relationship eventually fades. My role models didn't have, or at least didn't show me; strong male-male connection, and I haven't taken the time or energy to figure it out for myself.

Roy

I have learned in today's busy day that it takes real intentional work to keep male friendships alive and worth the effort.

Chad

I create them easier than I maintain them. Creating them—and maintaining them—means making them a priority—making time for them. I've never been much into the traditional male bonding stuff like team sports, cars, fishing, whatever. But I have found that the best way to build a friendship with another man is to make time for fun, whatever we define that as, and the more physical it is, and the more outdoors, the better. Examples are things like paintball contests or mountain biking or even just helping each other with yard work. I think I'm hard-wired to connect better with another man if there's "shoulder-to-shoulder" intimacy— shared physical experience—that builds some sort of trust. The hours I spend doing that kind of thing with one or two men makes me more available to the other relationships in my life. It's like it anchors me or puts me on more solid ground or gives me a better sense of myself.

How could meaningful relationships with other men support you emotionally to be more available to your partner, children, and yourself?

Andrew

Rather than seek validation, I ask for an honest commentary in case I am off balance or inappropriate. The men I trust have views of me that often help temper my behavior, my responses. This I get from the company of men.

Ross

Quite often in the men's group, we share our feelings and concerns, etc., about our relationships with other people including family, partners and friends. When I do this, I am given the opportunity to share what I feel, think, and judge to be true for me. I am then able to ask for feedback and/or advice from the other men in the circle. Often when I share with other men and they share with me, I/we learn that what we feel is common amongst us. This helps me to feel included as part of the group. Also, from time to time the men will share some advice/techniques/philosophy that I hadn't thought of before, and this helps me to overcome a negative belief I had about myself or another, to move into closer relationship with them.

Mark

Only strong relationships within the spirit of a team seem possible for me to have any support in my life. I have many friends and, from experience, these friends care enough to be involved and interested in my life; however, for me, it is only the most relentless of men who can break down my bullshit and allow me to reveal myself to myself for the first time. Uncovering these layers and recognizing whether I want to use them or dispose of them has given me the ability to pay much more attention to my spouse, my children, my friends and family, my career, and—most of all—myself.

Wilson

There are some things (thoughts, desires, and needs) that only another honest man can understand and reply to. I have found that any opening of my heart in this way does carry over to my other relationships. I can't process it all on my own, and I need answers and support of 'men who have been there' or are experiencing the same things in their lives.

Jeff

Meaningful relationships with other men allow me to model spiritual principles in my own life and enable me to serve my family in a similar way. In addition, I am then able to burden them less with some of the trials they should not be party to.

Ken

As I learn to become closer to men and accept their support, I stop expecting my partner to provide everything for me. She doesn't have to carry things any longer that should be shared among men. Also, being supported by other men helps me in my daily interactions with men in the world. I used to simply fear men. Now, I also have a place in my heart where I can accept them.

Roy

With real fellowship of men I bring myself home as an adult man to my partner instead of part-man and part-boy looking for 'mommy's' approval, which I did in my first marriage. Women understand this I think faster than men. Like Robert Bly said, most men, when you ask them how they are doing, will say, "Fine," while they are dragging their guts behind them.

Carl

The way I see it, only a man can know what a man feels and thinks. We are designed so very differently than are our female counterparts. I have an experience of being 'known' when I let men into my life, just as women have similar experiences with other women. How well do you think a man could truly understand what it is like to go through childbirth? There are some places where women can connect more to the pains of women and the same is true for men. Of course, most of us have not developed deep enough male friends to experience this.

Phillip

I believe meaningful relationships with other men will balance me as a man and give me the strength to be a better partner, parent, and person. I need validation and support from other men to feel part of something bigger than myself. Without it I am isolated—physically and emotionally.

Larry

To me, being available includes all the sides/facets of who I am. Other men can support me in being a man—strong, supporting, and protecting. They can encourage me and hold that space by being it in themselves. By holding this space myself I'll be more available for all those around me.

Don

We relate very well and can challenge each other in non-threatening ways.

Alexander

When it comes to my wife, I am an exception rather than the rule when it comes to our relationship. Quite honestly, she would rather I worked more and be less attentive. Truth is I wish she would spend more time with me. My children—because they are older or have moved away—are not really interested in having me interact with them. I know that I have always been healthiest emotionally, mentally, and spiritually when I have had men who I can have open dialogues with.

Danyl

I would think that having a resource of men—people of similar thinking styles, would allow me the opportunity to have simple conversations—to be understood as one who "is a part of." I would not be one continually needing to explain or defend my thoughts or words as if I was speaking a different language.

Joseph

Sometimes I need to be able to discuss feelings, issues and challenges with other men that my wife would not understand. These are areas that my wife would not understand or relate to. It lets me bring a husband home with these issues resolved.

Brent

I think about it like this . . . I am a buoy. The fluctuations on the face of a body of water, say the ocean, is my life's timeline. Sometimes the waves are strong, sometimes the water is still, sometimes there are storms, etc. The buoy, me, is tethered to the ocean floor, linked by chain, rope, what have you. The tension in that chain, rope, may increase or decrease with the rise and the fall of the tides, the conditions at the ocean surface, etc. Meaningful relationships over a period of time help tether or ground me to a center, to myself, and to meaning. When I encounter the world, or the surface of the ocean as in this metaphor, right behind whatever I am dealing with in life is the awareness that somewhere, with some group of men, I am good enough, I will be validated, I can have my needs and wants fulfilled. It is that sense of belonging that helps fill my wholeness and makes me available to other folks in my life whether it be a child, a partner, etc. That sense of belonging allows me a sense of self, identity, boundaries, which then aids in taking folks at face value. It helps keep me clear on what is my stuff, what is their stuff, and how to dance the tango.

Al

A meaningful relationship with other men could give me a sounding board for discussion of the various strains and stresses that all families have to deal with. I really did not think of this until I read the question. Maybe I should do something about it.

Merlin

The support I get from meaningful male relationships solidifies my self-concept as a man. Ask yourself this: If you associate with caring and solid people, wouldn't you take on some of those attributes? It just starts to rub off and makes me a better person. I feel better about myself, can let go of my hang-ups, and be more available to others in my life. Another hidden value I found from meaningful relationships with other men comes from a kind of hidden support mechanism just knowing they're around. For example, I recently took a trip and a family crisis developed. I held up fairly well during the event because I saw in my minds eye the guys from my *New Warrior* Integration Group standing behind me. I knew they were there for me in spirit and knowing that, I received the strength to soldier through the crises. I didn't call them for support, didn't need to. Just knowing they were there got me through.

What does it take to rekindle and maintain a "best male friendship"?

Werner
It usually takes giving up being 'right' about something that I am still holding on to. Making contact, picking up the phone—very difficult things like this that I tend to resist.

Darryl
About rekindling male friends, I don't know.

Randy
I believe to maintain a best male friendship I must be willing to listen (even when I don't want to), for those times have proved to be the most valuable and nurturing for me, and for them. Also, when I can ask for help—when the barriers of looking good are broken—that is when, I find myself having compassion for myself.

Blake
Once again, be there. If there ever was a best male friendship it still is, it just needs a little time to test the glue that binds.

Jeff
What does it take to rekindle friendships? Just a phone call away!

Fredrick
A shared sense of humor is a huge part of it. I could say more obvious things, such as shared values and a history of coming through for each other. Those are true too. But there's a kind of shared understanding that men have, based on my experience, that comes very directly through humor. It is important that men have time to just be with other men and their humor, a way to connect! A woman can kill this off with a simple comment like, "The boys want to be with the boys," or "Another boys' club," and if they knew the harm they do with this, I know they would stop.

Ronald

I had a best male friend only once in my life. We were close in age and shared many of the same interests. For years we hung out together, sometimes sharing specific activities such as golfing or fishing, but mostly just sharing time together in a relaxed and friendly kind of way. About the only thing we didn't do together was socializing in groups. He had his circle of friends and I had mine. The time we spent in each other's company was mostly just the two of us.

In the years we spent together, I don't think we ever once actually talked about our relationship. We just accepted it for what it was. We didn't need a reason to call each other up to see what was going on, and I doubt we ever had a phone conversation that lasted more than a minute. Sometimes those were emergency calls because if I was ever stuck, his was the first number I'd dial. It was the same for him.

I don't think I ever got angry with him although I can think of one or two occasions I irked him, but considering the number of times we were in competition together, everything from foot races to spitting contests, those few would hardly count. I think that maybe it was that acceptance that kept the friendship going. There was no need on the part of either of us to test the relationship. It was comfortable to be with someone who accepted my young man's masculinity and never required me to prove it. It was a comfortable, safe place to be alone and together at the same time.

Andrew

To rekindle and maintain a "best male friendship," a mutual understanding that trust can be rebuilt is needed.

Chad

I have to remember that my natural tendency is to "retreat into the cave" when I'm having a hard time and that other guys often do the same thing. Which means I can't take it personally when my phone call doesn't get returned, or I don't hear from the guy for a couple of months. Neither can the other man. If I want to contact, I've got to call again. And again. And if I don't want contact? If I don't return a call, or take the initiative myself? I need to ask myself what's going on—what is it I'm avoiding? The answer is almost always the same—if I get with a man I'm close to, I'm going to open up, and opening up hurts. Sometimes I just don't want the pain, as much as I may need the support. I don't know sometimes if I'm breaking through my shell or his, but I can't make up something in my head, or say "Screw it," or write him off. Leave me and another guy like me to our natural tendency to isolate when we need male contact most, and years can go by before we reconnect.

Jeff

The best way to rekindle and maintain a friendship with a best male friend is to first create a time that you regularly make contact. If you are unable to do that, make a thoughtful gesture or overture when you have time, i.e. a gift to his children or a personal letter. Transparency is important as well. Taking the first step to share some of your own struggles is a positive step in rekindling that friendship.

Jerry

It takes dedication, time, compassion, meeting the other men half way. Healthy friendships don't just happen, we make them happen. Call a man, make time to see him, listen to him, challenge and support him. The way I see it, it is like a sparring partner, friendship has a life of its own, so I take time to see my friends because if not, they will find other ways to get their needs met.

Ross

Honesty, integrity, accountability, compassion, forgiveness and a sense of humor. Maintenance of the relationship requires me to be real with my friend about who I am. My friends are very good bullshit detectors. I care enough for them to let them know (in a good way) when I see their bullshit, e.g., when I see them lying or pretending to be something/one they are not and they do the same for me.

Ralph

When you find this out, let me know! Haha... I've always had lots of good or close friends, but as an adult, I can't recall the last time I had just one best friend who was a guy. Perhaps I've traded quality for quantity? I hope not... but a part of me thinks maybe I have.

Jeff

For me, building a close intimate relationship with another man is not easy because you cannot trust all with personal information. Building trust takes time and confiding in another man also takes time.

Mark

Caring enough to listen and show another man that you are just like him but not just waiting for something to change by itself but by owning your own life and being accountable for your actions.

Roy

Sometimes it can just be giving real attention. I mean in the moment when a man lets a glimpse of pain out. If you listen, you will hear it. Realize each man can handle different levels of attention. Honor the man where he is. When you connect to your own soul you can hear other men's souls. Until a man is really mature enough in his masculine core to know who are safe men to talk to and who are not, the man may just talk in generalizations. Just really listen to whatever he gives you and you will be surprised how much even that may mean to him. You don't need to challenge him to go deeper, just listen deeply and you will have a profound effect on his life (this works for children and partners as well). I have had lunch with a man who may have said something like, "its really rough bring up teen age girls as a divorced dad". I heard an ocean of pain behind it; I did not over probe I just listened. I gave him my attention, man to man. I did not say something stupid like, "I truly hear great pain behind that;" this does not work by using some 'listening' trick, just listen! After lunch he thanked me for having such a deep conversation with him. To me it was not that deep, but that's all he felt safe to let out. There is something we can give other men with out attention that is beyond words. Most of us are to busy thinking of the next thing to say, or concerned about something related to ourselves to hear this stuff. This is what can build deeper relationships with almost any man. But I don't do it with any man; if I don't see value in him I may choose to not give this attention. I also discriminate. It's like if you can say "NO," you surely cannot say "Yes" powerfully.

Wyatt

I developed several. Some of my first close male friends I developed as an adult in college. I feel fortunate that in college I was a member of a fraternity that gave me a group of friends that I continue to have contact with, even though it has been more than 30 years. I came out of college not planning to have anything to do with the military, and three weeks later I had a letter from the draft board. I would have never chosen the Air Force but I made some friends with whom even today I exchange cards, notes, and visits. Small groups of men in my church and the programs developed by men's centers have provided groups that I could depend on at various times of my life. This has meant a great deal. There are opportunities for men but it does require persons to reach out. Too often men do not reach out.

Ken

I need to reach out, take the risk of being rejected, avoid judgment, and allow myself to be vulnerable in the man's presence. I also offer my male energy in support for his needs. I have to continually reach out when I find myself going complacent. I find that offering something at times like a hike, a walk around the neighborhood, a dinner, a movie, or some type of sports activity helps.

Wilson

This is a tough one for me. Living alone has kindled an independence that is really selfishness at work. I need an invitation to re-kindle and maintain a 'best male friendship. At times, I don't consider myself worthy to barge in and ask for friendship.

Anthony

I have found that it takes effort, love, yes that scary word related to men—love, open-heartedness, and a listening ear. It makes me really be a man—being empathetic, but also fierceness in my feedback and honest in my relating to what I see as healthy sometimes and a good sense of where my own wounds are, as well as healthy boundaries. I also think that it is important to do work in the men's area together and sometimes apart. I feel that I have a good sense of respect for other men. Empathy for where each man is comfortable and an awareness of where a man may need to head to learn more about himself, having been where another man is, sometimes. I am very aware of protocol and not abusing another person, for my own needs to feel important etc (ego-centric). A level of acceptance and boundaries also are helpful. I do have an understanding of how this knowledge and experience helps me to discern what is going on in negotiations, inter-relating at the office, at home and when out with friends. I'm really excited to have the knowledge – I feel a couple steps ahead. I feel more conscious, rather than wandering aimlessly, attempting to get my needs met in an unconscious way. Working with and undergoing ongoing men's work stands me in great stead for the future. A wise older man said, "This men's work is not a fix all, it is preventative medicine. He checks-in to his men's group for a tune-up and shake-up!"

Benny
Seeing that my best pal was having problems in his long-time marriage, I drove to visit him. He and I used to be quite close, but life's demands and moving out-of-state had made our closeness dwindle. For the past year, he and I have rekindled our wonderful friendship.
Now, I find I'm going through a traumatic time in life, my own divorce. I'm visiting him now. We planned on having a beer to forget about our problems, but found ourselves really discussing them. It sure has helped.

Phillip
Risk. I have to deem myself vulnerable and reach out in a way I have never practiced. I have been afraid to give what it takes to build that kind of friendship.

Ike
I consciously choose to take time and to be open because you can't just tell a man that you like him—that would almost feel like a date or something.

Don
Effort and an appreciation of the value of it.

Alexander
Intentional, purposeful, consistent time.

75

Tom

I think that, whenever possible, both friends need to be supportive of each other (even if they are not always interested in what the other friend is doing). They need to find and create opportunities to laugh together, be non-judgmental (but when judgment is called for, do it with compassion), make a commitment to simply be a friend.

Joseph

Trust. Being able to count on help when needed.

What type of friend are you to other men?

John

In years past I don't think I would have been able to answer this question. But today, I feel differently about how I view having a man as a friend. The type of friend I could be to another man is one is who is supportive of his goal and/or aspirations and who appreciates him for who he is as a person. For me this was a difficult task. I found that I needed to look inside myself and find out why I felt this way about other men in general. Thankfully, I realized that the majority of men might also feel the same way I felt, and I just accepted it and decided to work toward being a better person towards other men. This slowly led toward more male friends, but it had to start with me.

Wilson

Sadly, I am in and out. As long as the friendship is not too demanding and doesn't interfere with how I want to spend my time, I am there. If pressured, I will stay with the friendship, but if the other man shuts down, I will find an excuse to leave–leaving that potential friendship in my wake.

Fredrick

What type of friend am I? An honest one, I'd say. I often find myself in a counselor's role with them, maybe too much.

Ken
What type of friend are you to other men? I am the kind of friend who can listen and share deeply. I am not the kind who sells himself out for companionship by drinking or doing things I really don't like. I am also, at times, a mentor and teacher to other men.

Andrew
Honest and trustworthy. At least that is what I hope they view me as.

Ross
I find it difficult to let men in, to be very emotionally close to men. I am working on this. I make myself available if they need help and try not to offer advice if not called for, but to listen and understand. The fact that men do call me to talk about some of their problems tells me that I am reasonably effective in this.

Jeff
What type of friend am I to other men? I am nurturing but give up easily if I don't receive that back. I have high expectations for transparency.

Ralph
When I'm in a relationship, I'm the friend that lurks by himself most of the time only occasionally popping up to go out with the boys...or to get together when I need their help. Kind of sad, actually. Before I was in a recently-ended three-and-a-half-year relationship, I would always hang out with my friends. Once our relationship got serious, I practically cut them out of my life, which was a REAL mistake. Now that the relationship is over I still don't hang out with them very much, despite my invites over to my house. It makes me sad... but can you blame them? It'll take a bit of work to get my friendships back to the level they were before my relationship, and I'm sure some won't ever be. I'm OK with that. Well, back to the question, I'm the friend that completely disappears when he gets in a relationship, and even when I'm not in a relationship I don't hang out with them much. Ultimately I am the reliable friend that would help them in a jam...like picking them up or driving them two states away if they had a problem and needed a ride. But do they know that? I don't know.

Mark

I am a strong inspirational friend who cares enough to speak little at times and speak up when my heart tells me to. I am a man of my word and live out loud by my personality and success. I can be counted on and men see me as the leader I am. Many men would consider me their friend but it is only the friends I keep who know me for the man I really am, which is a good man and a bit of a jerk.

Benny

I am typically not a truly good friend to my male associates. I protect my thoughts, my fears, from male friends. Usually, I enjoy an activity with them like scuba, tennis, music, etc., but when the session ends, we part and go our own ways, not knowing the inner thoughts of each other.

Phillip

I am a friend to other men in deed, but rarely a friend in spirit. I am not truly bonded to my friends. They don't even know me.

Larry

Hopefully, the same I am to women.

Don

Sincere, trusting, supportive.

Alexander

You probably need to ask them. On many different levels you would get different responses. I think the one thing they would say is, that I am loyal, and a defender of them. I think they would also say that in general I am kind, and care about what's going on in their lives. I think the negative would be that I have a tendency not to call very frequently. I can be self absorbed, and when stressed, pull away.

Blake

I would hope to be one that is there for them when needed. My biggest regret in life is that I allowed so many good friends to drift off as we advanced in our own lives at different rates and directions. It just seemed that there wasn't the time to keep things together. Shame.

Jeff
I am a terrible friend. I seem to like being the lone wolf....

Randy
A good, intelligent, and honest friend I am.

Darryl
Loyal and trusting, once I know you. As available as I can be. (With my schedule, that can sometimes be a problem.)

Curtis
As I see my role as a professional career and entrepreneurial coach, I would view my friendship to be more on that level. On that level, set rules apply, codes of behavior and expectations remain set. This makes more sense to me. If I play a sport then my team and a proper commitment to winning comes with that type of game On the level of professional conduct and loyalty to a cause you could say that and I would consider myself a friend to many. Guys don't come over to my house much. I don't go to the Y or work out with a group of guys. I might go to a hockey game, play hockey or go see a movie like Blackhawk Down or Gladiator with some of my business friends but that's about the extent of it. In fact that movie came out years ago and that's the last one I went to with men who are friends. I would consider hunting for game or playing organized hockey at any time of the week though. That way I could make friends and enemies in the same two-hour game time frame.

Roy
For me I hope I am an honorable man but I know I break my word in little ways far more than I want to admit. I feel I have wonderful male friends that forgive me and always try to do better at keeping my word.

Werner

This just means something to me that it did not when I was younger. I am committed to being a good friend of men who I choose to be in my inner circle.

Do you realize how having close men friends helps you be more effective & balanced in business, family issues, and fatherhood?

Mark

Yes. OK, just a joke about the one liner. Of course I do! Men need to compete and even on a friendly basis; we need to know how we stack up in the scheme of life and that inevitable word called success. Emerson quotes success at its best, and I share this with any man from my heart. Do yourself a favor and look it up and memorize the sentences and then ask yourself if not that, what then? Balance is a process achieved by trial and error with the result being effective after time. Whatever I am paying attention to in my life is better because I am doing my best by doing something better and not just accepting things for what they are. I am consciously choosing to live my life in the present tense and have built a set of core values which I can live by. My life is better than I ever thought and I love the prospect of limitless days of wonderful experiences ahead.

Ken

Yes, absolutely, but that does not mean I have done enough about it yet.

Wilson

Yes, as a sounding board and an accountability station.

Jeff

Yes, the importance of transparency with other males shouldn't be underestimated. Just as in sports, no star can carry a team by himself. It takes others: a good coach, a good defender, and the like to make the star or, corporately, the team, a success. It is just not good judgment to do it alone! Also, if you are a competitive man, having a team to support you gives you a competitive edge.

Fredrick

Absolutely. Male friends give me perspective in terms of my relationship with my wife. They help me keep from taking on too passive a view of things. Of course in business, friends look out for each other and delight in creating opportunities for each other. That is of enormous practical value as well as being emotionally satisfying.

Andrew

I find it emotionally rewarding to have men friends who acknowledge, trust and bless me in my day-to-day life. In my ongoing men's group I have a place to be myself, wrinkles and all, and receive the support, encouragement and love of men with whom I have a trusting, ongoing relationship. On a simpler note, I enjoy having a circle of men I can meet for breakfast and with whom I can joke, converse, share and know that I'm welcome and appreciated.

In the past, whatever woman I was dating was usually my sole source of closeness and support. Thus, I had all my emotional eggs in one basket, so to speak. I often found myself unwilling to assert myself, to set healthy boundaries or to get angry with my girlfriend; because I felt I had too much to lose. I suspect I'll be more authentic and powerful in my future relationships with women because I know that my support system of men won't evaporate if my relationship with a woman ends.

Allen

Helps me to not be as scared of men who have intimidated me in the past, be a better listener, and to actually not be so wigged out about authority figures. Close male friends help me deal with my children better—how to support my son from getting stuck in life. And helping me be proud of him. I also know it helps sharing stories of how I have close men friends—which he never saw when I was younger. Sharing the work I have done and the struggle I have gone through as an adult is also helping him.

Ike

My close friends give me the space and support to practice being my true self, so I feel safe doing it wherever I am.

Darryl

Over time, because of what I have experienced and learned in relationship with my closest men friends, I have come to change my relationship to other men at a fundamental level. It is almost hard to remember now how much I competed with, judged and mistrusted men, just because they were men. Now I see us all in a global community with responsibilities to care for the planet, our local communities, and our families, and we are all doing a better or worse job of it. I think my job is to be supportive of all the other men I meet so that they can be better at these sacred responsibilities.

And I clearly see that we are all in this together. I have a relationship with these men (in business or as neighbors or as other fathers) based on my experience of being in their boots in our daily struggles. I shudder now to think how much I judged and competed with other men, as if I were somehow better than they were.

Phillip

It has taken a career failure, a hard marriage, broken family ties, and parenthood to understand what I am missing in my life. I have always felt it, but didn't understand it—I need real friends to make it in this world.

Don

Absolutely.

Alexander

I think that is true. The problem: the development of those friendships doesn't happen overnight and takes many years to form. And when you work on commission it is difficult to be consistent.

Joseph

As an adult, most of my close male relationships have revolved around sports and business. They have been formed when working together to build or accomplish something.

Curtis

If I focused on or defined friends as those who fight to emulate Christ, then I would like to aspire to be more like them. Some of my greatest influences have been from books that I have read and not friendships or close friendships. My deficiencies lie in coming short of the image of Christ that I would like to aspire to, and that I would like my kids to see in me. So to have more brothers who aspire to live closer to Christ, to me, would and should have the kind of impact and lead to more effective and balanced business, family issues, and fatherhood. But I still would like to work on accomplishing something or building something with them vs. just chatting with them regarding things that happen to me or to them. So I am sure that I don't realize the positives that result in these relationships or close men friend relationships.

Danyl

I don't know the impact, because I haven't had that experience yet of having close male friends.

Damon

I don't really remember getting into conversations with men about what I feel or think about relationships and feelings.

Randy

No, I don't yet realize the full benefit of having close male friends; otherwise, I would be investing more of my time there. These questions are getting me to look at things I have not looked at before and it is a good thing to do.

Jeff

The realization seems to evade me. I tend to self-destruct friendships over time. This is a question I need to look at again.

If you are not modeling healthy relationships with other men, how will our sons learn about doing the same?

Andrew

I have daughters but my honest relationships with good men have led them to want to connect with men who are honest and loving.

Ross

There are men who I have admired at different times in my life in different ways. I have not told most of them how or why I admire them. Since my involvement in MKP I have met more men I admire. I have been humbled and honored when men have said they admired me, and have passed on that gift to others by letting them know how that what they did or the type of person they are has helped me in some way, e.g. by modeling a type of behavior I want to be like. This is evidence to me that I am modeling healthy relationships with other men.

Mark

If we are not modeling healthy relationships with other men, they just won't learn from the man in their life who matters the most. A father is given a passport to a son's future and if he doesn't lose it, abuse it, or confuse it, then he will always be the first thought a son can reference. A sad thing happens when a father steps off this pedestal…a son is lost and may never be found. And what about our daughters? They will make poorer choices in men for we are the first real models of an adult man to them.

Samuel

I come from an addicted, dysfunctional home so the relationships that I had were not the type that I wanted for my son. I wanted something different for him but knew that I didn't know what that looked like, so I have surrounded myself with mature, healthy "elders" who give me the view of what that might look like. This both feeds my soul and gives my son a model to do the same. I even talk to him about my friendships with other men and its value to me.

Ken

If we are not modeling healthy relationships with other men, they will get models of men from TV, dysfunctional mothers, peers, and video games. Ha! Ha!

Wilson

They will not. Most of the young men who I am in contact with learned their relationship skills from women. Those skills are fine, but only part of the picture. When we don't play out all parts, they may get a good part but they only get half of the picture.

Jeff

Our sons will have a difficult time if they don't see the father modeling healthy relationships with other men. It is hard enough when men compete so heavily for success.

Anthony

This question about modeling is right-on! Since I'm a younger male in this work I see it a lot. I see where I have been under-fathered and under-modeled and still have a lot of anger, sadness and grief about my own experience. When I work with these feelings I also tap into a greater well of the above, which is the collective, and that hurts a lot. Being an empathic in this work is a blessing and a challenge at times! I do admire my Dad, appreciate my brother, am grateful for my brothers in men's work, and the elders I respect. However, I have only just recently, in the last 5 days, learned that I unconsciously place my elders on pedestals, without checking in with myself on this as an overall concept. I think it has to do with our conditioning of "respecting your elders," no matter what they say/do etc. I'm in the process of selecting and acknowledging–though I think I will be doing this all of my life.

Larry

It will be hard. Bonding, like in important undertakings or the army or sports, will help bond men. The healthy part may or may not happen, depending on the leaders and others involved. Our children learn from who we are, not what we say. If we don't show them healthy relationship with other men, they will not learn it. But they surely would learn it from TV or the movies! And what about our daughters, how will they choose good men?

Damon

I think many of the problems with my son are because I did not model healthy relationships with other men but just stuffed it inside. I am in counseling with my son now who is coming of age and trying to define his space and place, which put him in conflict with me. Instead of calling it counseling, we found a word that was acceptable to him: we are going to see the *mediator* who listens to both of us and helps us find ways to let the other feel, get, see, do whatever he needs to progress.

Phillip

I can tell my son what I know about relationships but he will see the hypocrisy in my words. He will either flourish in spite of my shortcomings and pity me for my misery or he will suffer the same fate. I don't want to pray for pity, lest he follow in my footsteps I want to give him what he needs but I have to fill myself up first.

Don

My father had, and continues to have, close male friends. It was one of the greatest gifts he could give me by letting me know about how he valued them and seeing how they admired him.

Alexander

That is definitely true. I think though my son knew how close I was to my best friend before he died. My son also saw me lose a couple close friends recently, and now sees me having to start over. The problem is I am very particular, so finding the right people is very important. I am sure that has left him a bit empty since the one best friend who died was a good friend to him, too. We both took a huge loss that has not been replaced, and quite honestly would take years to develop. That's not easy. Chances are my son will not see that relationship develop while he is still living at home.

Blake
I'm not sure this is a problem. As long as you are the man and fulfill that role in the home, you are a father, leader, friend, mentor and confidant to your son. It follows then that he will develop the skills needed to establish a network of friends among his peers as he moves from centering on you to centering upon his own life and needs. Time will tell.

Danyl
I don't know, and I do fear whatever influences my son may fall prey to. I pray constantly for his safety when we are apart and that God will bring strong, positive male role models into his life.

Werner
Children learn from what we do and not what we tell them. So I am clear this is a big problem. My own sons problems with having too many female friends and not enough male friends. If I want to know where he learned it, I can look in the mirror.

Jeff
I have always been close with my son. But I see how my relationship with my son could be improved.

Who are men that you admire in your life? Have you told them what they mean to you?

Laurence
I think my father was the man I most admired in my life, particularly as I grew older and recognized more clearly the sacrifices he had to make in order to support his wife and three sons. I think those sacrifices included emotional ones as well. As I got older, I realized that he had probably experienced many of the same emotional states that I was experiencing but was in less of a position to indulge them than I. As a result, I more keenly felt his sacrifices and admired him all the more. The unfortunate part is that I was never really able to express this to him well. In his last six years of life, in particular from age 70-76, he was infirm, debilitated by the effects of a mild stroke at age 58 and the inevitable TIAs (transient ischemic attacks) that followed over the

years. The last time I saw him, when he was in a nursing home, I still couldn't adequately express my love for him. I've regretted that ever since, though I do believe, on some level, that he did know how I felt about him.

Mark

My father passed away in 1988, and I never had the experience of being able to share the real me with him. This is because it is only recently that the real me has decided to emerge at the age of 50—despite that I recognize the model of fatherhood that he was, and have accepted the lessons he gave me without words. My Uncle David, who passed in 2003, was the disciplinarian in my life who could have "ordered" me to do anything and I would have followed, because I knew how much he cared for me. For a man like me who prefers to lead, this was and remains a strong lesson in heroism. My business partner of 30 years is a strong, stubborn, narrow minded and abusive man who lives with integrity and values despite their archaic origins. Although we don't see eye to eye, I trust this man the most, and if there were a man on earth that I would trust with my life, it would be him and only him.

Wilson

I have a 79-year old poker mentor that I admire. Yes, I have no problem telling men how much they mean to me. I admire any man that is taken with the Spirit of God and not afraid to speak.

Jeff

The man that I model most in my life is Brian Boender. He has been a disciple to me to become more like Christ the last two years, and despite all my flaws, has shown me support, confidence, and everything a young man could want. He has modeled integrity, unconditional love, wisdom, generosity (with time and energy), and humility, and most importantly love for others and Christ. Without him, I would be unmarried, have a child out of wedlock, aimless, ungodly, more prideful, and generally disconnected from God and my fellows. I have intimated to him how important he is to me but have never written him a letter conveying how deeply he has shaped my life and how much I care about him. I need to do that.

Ken

I admire many men for different reasons. Yes, I have told them what I admire about them. I give what I want to receive... recognition. I did not always do that; I think that is also part of being an adult man.

Jerry

Yes, I do admire some good friends of mine, yet what I found difficult is that some of these men I sexualized, it was very hard to have a clean relationship, because for whatever reason, even though I enjoy their company, I keep sexualizing them, I started wondering about my sexual orientation, so one day I talked to one of them, Steve. I said: you know I really like you, He said: I really like too. I said: no, you don't get it, I really like you, to the point that I keep thinking of you and it is turning scary, then I let him know how I somewhat fantasize about him.

To my surprise, Steve didn't run away, he listened to me, and said: I like you very much, I admire you and I am here for you, but if what you are looking for is sex, NO I cannot go there, it does not work for me, that is not my thing. But I want you to know that I like you, I am your friend. We embraced each other and after that day my sexual charge around him has changed. Being vulnerable, taking the risk of letting him see me, somewhat liberated me. But I would not try this with just any man. I felt I knew he could hear me and even then it was a risk I chose that was worth it. I think if it did not go well, it would have been still worth it since that unspoken piece would always be getting in the way.

Allen

Well, I admire the author of this book, Martin Brossman, and what courage he has taken on to make this happen. I actually wrote a poem about my former boss and read it at his retirement ceremony. He did not say much about the poem. But he still makes an effort to stay in touch. You see he did not do the same work I did on himself, so he is not as expressive, but we still had a great relationship. He shared once that his father was an alcoholic. If a man is willing to share one of his secrets002C it gives me room to share one of mine. I find that men's work helps me relate better to all men wherever they are.

89

Ike

I have been stepping out to tell my peers that they are important to me, and the things I admire about them. However, one of my shadows is that I don't fully acknowledge my need for mentor relationships, and so I tend not to connect with older men who could offer me that kind of support. I judge that I am missing something valuable because of it.

Damon

A former coworker was the most generous, forgiving, honest, caring, pleasant person I have ever met. Yet when I talked to him, I learned he had marital conflict at home and was eventually divorced. Even with all of the marital conflict at home and the worst boss at work, he remained a positive person who was always a joy to be around. I told him that he was the one man I most wanted to be like. He said it meant a lot to him. That was about the last time I have seen or talked to him. I did reach him on the phone once and he made it clear that his kids were visiting and he did not want his time with them to be interrupted. Did he need to break all ties to a past job? Was I not someone he cared to stay in contact with? I don't know. It still hurts a little when you open up to someone and they don't seem to connect to you.

Phillip

I admire men from afar, like Sam Keen and Robert Bly, because they taught me something about manhood. I wish I could say my father taught me these things, but he only gave me what he knew. I have come to pity him for what he missed. We both deserved better than that.

Don

Father, Brother, Lifelong Friend—Yes.

Alexander

The one I admired the most is gone. The other has decided to drop our relationship. (I am responsible for some of it, but he is unwilling to repair the relationship.) The other has become too busy for a relationship outside of his family, seminary, and career. Recently, his wife has put far more pressure for him to be at home.

After 25 years of marriage she is jealous of his time. He just started seminary, he needs his job, so friendships will have to be sacrificed, and I fully understand that. So, quite honestly, I am starting over from scratch. But I have in the past told others how much I love and appreciate them.

Darryl
My father for his dedication to family, and my pastor for his willingness to be transparent and share his human frailties. Though I did tell my father that I loved him many times before his passing, I don't remember ever telling him that I admired him. As for my pastor, I don't think that I've told him directly, but anytime I speak with someone about him I inevitably speak of his personal openness and how that keeps me coming to church and continues to draw new members.

Blake
For me, the friends formed before age thirty are the strongest, longest, and most meaningful. I guess I have made very few new friends as an aged man. Funny thing, I now travel a lot and find I can develop friends very fast—within just a few days. However, when it is time to move on, it is not a sad parting but one with expectation that we will meet again.

Jeff
I don't admire any men. I just haven't learned to trust them yet.

David
I most admire my oldest brother (he was mentally & physically handicapped).

He was honest about being strong. He was fair about being true. He was a dreamer about being real. He was serious about being funny. He was complete while he was searching. He was himself while we were together. He was with me when we were apart. In his loving heart I knew I was always in the center, and I knew what that meant to him. I miss him, now that he has passed.

Do you allow other men to contribute to you? Do you know how selfish it is not to let other men contribute to you?

Samuel

I remember going to lunch with one of the men who I look up to a while ago. Normally I would find some way to slip in paying for the check. It gave me a sense of control. Anyway, Bob asked my why it was that I felt the need to never give anyone the opportunity to pay for my nourishment. I take that same outlook into my life. I know that I like to help people. I believe that at some level everyone wants to be needed, so I allow and look forward to the opportunities where men in my life nurture me.

Ken

Yes, at times I let other men contribute to me, although I struggle with this.

Wilson

This is a requirement of mine, that I let men contribute to me! Somewhere along the way I realized I did not know it all—thank goodness! I am always open to learning from other men (young and old) and have found this willingness to benefit me greatly.

Anthony

I find it hard for men to contribute to me. I have a strong orphan pattern, that leads me to a place where I can sometimes either not see any contributions, not ask for any, not expect any, or just think that I am an island and that I have to figure it all out on my own. In the past 24 months, I have learned that this behavior of mine, while healthy to a degree, can lead me into a destructive dance where I grind down to sadness, loneliness and depression. (Wow, that's the 1st time, I have ever thought of myself as holding any form of depression—whether for a second or for a day—thanks Martin, big lesson there.) I now openly access and request feedback and contributions from older men in my community. I very grateful for each tidbit!

One of my attributes is that I'm comfortable (for the most part) receiving compliments and feedback. Sometimes a compliment may arrive post-process and I don't really get it, but I still respond thankfully—one of the modeling behaviors I totally support. I do see this invalidating in many of the men I work with in groups and festivals. This is one of my gifts. I don't look through many people. I am an observant, intuitive and empathic man. With these gifts, I discern and build a profile of a man and am eager and curious enough to ask pretty direct question. I've always been this way, as I was taught to engage people in conversations as an equal—one of my gifts I'm very proud of.

Jeff

I ask for help regularly but have a hard time receiving their gifts without feeling obligated toward them. True, I need to be grateful, but I tend to feel like I owe them more than I can give.

In the past I have responded thankfully but now try to say something humble even if I don't feel it. Whether we are humble or not, I think we need to model that fruit of the spirit to other men. With successful athletes, I see them slashing their throats at opponents, or pointing downfield when they make a first down, or taking a pen out of their sock to autograph a football for their stock-broker, so I believe that feigned or genuine humility is noble and is better than the alternative.

Carl

I did once; I contributed and trusted him. I was hurt by the distrust when I found out he was involved with my wife. That was a pain that I have never felt before, and never want to feel again. How do you recover from what you thought was a solid friend, who you thought was a true brother friend, who you thought you could take on the world with, shoulder-to-shoulder. It has been years but the pain at times is still fresh. So, I now open myself with new men who I meet at men's retreats and my wife does not know—men who know my heart again, and I, in turn, learn to trust them. I think I own part of what happened since I let my friend become part of the family and he crossed the line, as did my wife when I was out of town on business. Now I am finally ready to let other men back into my life, to contribute to me again and I to them. I realize it has been selfish that I have not let them contribute to me again, and I to them. We as men need to be validated by other men. It is the way of true warriors which our culture does not truly encourage.

Fred

Yes, I do allow men to contribute to me. I have only recently started doing so. I never knew that it was selfish to not do so until recently. I have felt better since I have started. I have also returned the favor. I usually thank them and if I forget, I apologize and I try to remember to say thank you the next time.

Ross

Yes, I do let other men contribute, but again it's mainly been recently. Still sometimes I find it difficult to ask for help or advice when the issue is very personal. I have experienced the gold in having a man I care about ask me for help, and have learned to let go of the 'old me' and to believe that a man I ask for help may also feel the same way.

Mark

This is a recent development that I am making a conscious effort to allow men to do, and for myself, to also recognize how valuable and powerful it is for another man to speak the truth and develop those skills.

Allen

This is a tough one that I forget easily. I am not sure I fully understand. That may be because it is something I block out as I spent so much time making sure I was self-sufficient and proving that I did not need anyone. I need to think about it more. For me, it's learning to ask for help; one should not have to learn this as an older adult, but the truth is I do.

Ike

I believe that "receiving" is an act of humility, a gift to the other person. I recognize that I have a hard time with it. I often deny that gift to others and miss the gift that it would bring to me.

Phillip

Other men don't know how they contribute to me. I steal their actions and thoughts, and ponder them in my private world. I am usually a moment's hesitation from giving back, and then it is too late.

Werner
Yes I allow men I value to contribute to me, especially younger men. I now realize how important this is.

Kyle
A recent male cancer patient of mine taught me something about this. He was a middle-aged man with an incurable spreading form of cancer. He understood and acknowledged the declining state of his body. He told me a lot of what he went through in gory detail. But, he charged ahead with his life as though it would never end. He made himself walk using a walker but couldn't do much from the waist down and didn't have feeling or control of one of his two misshapen legs.

Yet he wanted me to take him on walks that a few times lasted almost an hour. A very large man, he would be sweating after 5 minutes. The last 20 minutes would be in silent determination to make it back.

We'd go to various stores to get items on sale. At times he'd ask me to stuff one of his legs into my car since he couldn't wiggle it past the door.

He asked me to help make a mirror that he could use to see, while he was lying in bed alone, to clean his deep fistulas that would leak and clean other holes in his lower body, and to empty his artificial sanitary paraphernalia

I'm not sure the depth and extent of my experiences with my patient or how this comes out in words. He willingly and happily allowed me to help him and he would direct me candidly how to do it. This made me feel good...like I was now a fuller person. Maybe he was not a 'wise old man,' but I was learning something here. Something new. Maybe he was a wise man and he didn't know it. I remember first meeting him. I thought he was trivial and shallow and egocentric—all judgments of mine. But, to my great confusion, then surprise, I was the one who was trivial and shallow and egocentric. Tears. . . . . Thank you, my friend.

Alexander

Sure, I always listen, evaluate, implement, or discard. I think it is more short-sighted, stubborn, or even arrogant, rather than selfish. I mean quite truthfully, I am not offended if someone is not interested in my contribution. I think in order for something to be selfish, there must be an offended party on the other side. I am not sure it is an appropriate term in this case.

Damon

I often tell other men what it's like to be a single father taking care of the children with little or no support from the mother or extended family. They react with admiration and say that I'm doing the right thing. What bothers me is why I am the rare example of what should be the first priority for a man—to take care of his children and see to their well-being. I understand that some women see children as a meal ticket or want to be "kept women," but that is another issue. I want to see more men talking about fatherhood and how important it is to them.

Darryl

I rarely put myself in the position to have people contribute to me, and it's even rarer that I seek out men. I have had trust issues with the men in my life since my childhood.

Randy

I don't allow men to contribute to me. On a deeper level I believe that I do know how selfish that is, and, that I want to be selfish because I want to hurt them as they hurt me.

Blake

YES, I ask for help often! Can't believe how much I don't know after having lived so long. You would be surprised at how much you can learn by just being near other men.

Do you invalidate men's contributions by 'acting' as if you are humble or respond with a "thank you" which allows the acknowledgment to enter?

Andrew
If they are sincere, I reflect their sincerity genuinely.

Ross
I do accept men's contributions but it takes conscious effort. It is seldom automatic. Again, this is a recent learning.

Mark
Not at all. I practice listening and not judging. I don't feel that I have to reciprocate by responding with idle words like "I know" and "sure" or anything else. However, I do wait until a man has completed before I will tell him with genuineness, "thank you."

Roy
I really stopped discounting acknowledgement to me when, in a men's group, two men were working on their response to each other. One of the men in the group would always discount any acknowledgment, and he asked for more feedback on how other men responded to that, as he was becoming aware of how he did that. One man replied, "I don't give compliments very often. They have to be well earned, and when I do and the man just shrugs it off, I feel like just saying 'f--k you' to him, and never complementing him again." I could not get out of my head how I invalidate the other person—sort of like knocking a gift out of someone's hand when they are handing it to you, when I don't accept an acknowledgment. So now I make sure to face them, thank them, and do my best to let it in. This is still not second nature and takes effort to do.

Wilson
Over the years, I have toned myself down to "bold." I have no problem recognizing that someone has either acknowledged me or complimented me.

Ken

Sometimes. I am starting to learn to take in other men's contributions. I resist at times because it brings up the pain of not having that for so long. So, nowadays, I feel the pain and take the contribution.

Fredrick

Accepting praise is always tough for me. I laugh it off mostly, but I also have faith in the incredible subterranean channels of communion that exist between men. I believe this because I understand things my friends don't say–things I just know about them and our relationship. I sense that they feel it too. I love the eloquent silences of male friendships. I love that not everything needs to find verbal expression.

Phillip

I avoid them altogether. They probably wonder if I was listening.

Don

Yes–I actually recently thanked a male friend for all of the gifts of insight that I have received from him over the past 15 years.

Damon

Yes, I try to look them in the eye and say thank you, and let them know that I appreciate their support.

Werner

It has taken me some time to even notice that I was avoiding the acknowledgment. I also have learned that giving advice when not asked is usually counterproductive. I believe that my attention and just listening is a way 'to fix' most relationship stuff.

Blake

I sure hope I have never invalidated any man's contributions to myself or anyone else. Acting, putting on a mask, keeps others out–at your own request.

Daniel
A little of both. It seems to depend on the level of respect I have for the person.

Jeff
I always appreciate help. Usually, I don't expect it and I always feel (erroneously) that I don't need it. Help from other men always catches me by surprise, leaving me speechless and awed that someone cares enough to pitch in.

Do you 'see other men' or just look through them?

Samuel
I work with teenage boys and I have come to believe that in our core, we all want to be seen. I believe in connecting with the men in my life and letting them know that I appreciate them. That goes for the way that I 'see' them. I believe in letting them know that I see them as more than background, and that they are important in my life.

Carl
I think I have a deep soul and I look deep into the heart of each man I meet, wanting to know more and nurture a friendship that is lasting. But it is a two-way event. Men will look through you as I do at times also. Yet when I feel we connect as brothers, friends and warriors, then we have to go forward and hold each other accountable—take a risk as men. I also understand that the men I meet all have unconscious filters that they use daily. Even though their view of life in their window is clear, they bring a Values filter - a Culture filter and a Religion filter to our friendship as men. Those are real filters most men do not see or know of.

Wilson
I see other men, vividly, since I have been focused on becoming\being a man for so long. Sometimes, it is obvious who has not 'done the work.' Often they are shells of egos with little scared boys inside that you can see if you look in their eyes—using big fluffy words to avoid expressing anything of substance. Speaking in second or third person, their words reveal themselves.

99

All there is to do is have compassion, since I used to be just like them.

Andrew
On a good day, I see them. On a bad day, I don't see them, and I look right through them.

Jeff
I see other men's friendliness first and, later, their character. I wish I could see their character first, because friendliness is inferior to godliness and righteousness. Anyone can say 'hi,' but who will be transparent and honest enough to accept the consequences for one of their failures, or act justly even under persecution? I wish I could see that kind of righteousness more clearly.

Jerry
Today, I see other men; it takes practice and awareness, because I used to not even know how I was just looking through them! What a lonely place that was.

Roy
I remember how I used to look through men, or maybe I was scared that they would see my flaws and judge me. I remember how once at a men's gathering, a 75-year-old man stood up and said, "In society, people just look through me, but here, men see me." It is hard to express in words the feeling we all felt for him.

Ross
I used to see a bully, a jerk, a nerd, an angry man, an idiot etc., etc., etc. Now I try to see past his actions and to consider what may have happened in his life for him to be the way he is. The key for me is compassion.

Ken
Do you 'see other men' or just look through them? Sometimes one or the other. It depends. My old habit is to look through them as I scan for babes. It shows up easily, I feel bad about myself when I realize that I am doing it.

Mark

I look into another man's eyes when I listen or when I speak. I never look through him nor any other direction except into him. His words are sacred and his mask is off at times. No man deserves to be ignored or unheard when he is speaking or not.

Ike

I chose, some time ago, to consciously look people directly in the eye and acknowledge each one as a person, to not let people I meet be invisible.

Don

Yes, I see them.

Werner

I had no idea that I looked through men until I started to do men's work. I spent most of my time in the past looking for the approval of the nearest women.

Daniel

I find that many of the men I meet are unwilling to 'be seen.' There is an image that must be displayed and upheld, and often—since I find that image to be abrasive, unfriendly, or unattractive—I will choose not to look deeper. I will choose to look past the man who may be standing before me, because truly knowing him may make me uncomfortable. Knowing him may reopen sores or wounds that I have buried, and why would I want to revisit those times in my life?

Merlin

Let's define terms first: to 'see other men' means to acknowledge their presence and search for or appreciate their demeanor, personality or character; 'look through them' means not really caring about their demeanor, personality or character and acting like they are really not significant for you to get involved with. To answer the question then, I 'see other men' when some sort of subconscious switch is thrown. Call it instinct or experience in dealing with men, but somehow I know that this man is worth getting to know, even if the encounter with him may be only momentary. On the flip side, I look through a man when the switch isn't thrown. When I get that gut feeling that this guy is shallow and dealing from a place of insincerity, I shut down in some way and just go through the motions of getting involved with him as the situation dictates. I will use a fictitious example. Say I'm, buying a car from a dealership. The salesman quickly becomes very friendly and acts as if he's my long lost friend. Now, I know this guy is just doing his job and perhaps would not be nearly as friendly if I met him on the street for the first time. I would not be rude with the salesman, and perhaps may banter with him a bit and enjoy the encounter. But I would not spend the effort to really 'see him' and learn to appreciate him, since I realize this is an inflated situation and this guy would drop me like a hot potato when I walk off the lot without buying the car. To summarize, if that switch in my psyche doesn't click, I just play out the situation.

Alexander
I think you are asking a question of depth here. I think you need to do both. I think you need to look into, and through, otherwise you will have an incomplete picture of the people themselves.

Randy
Mainly look through, because I still want to resist them controlling me.

Blake
Both. I find that I look through other men until there is something that catches my eye. Maybe just a small thing, but something I have an interest in. That's when friendship building starts. If you ask, they will answer.

Jeff
It depends on how connected I feel with another man. I give only as much as I receive. There seems to be a fear of total openness and vulnerability—certainly not traditional male characteristics.

What Insights did you personally gain from this chapter?

What do you want to commit to or re-commit to out of these insights?

Remember!
"Insight   without   committed   action   is   only entertainment!"

Chapter 6
What Does It Mean to be an Adult Man?

What does it mean to you to be an adult man, and when did you decide you were an adult man?

Who were some of your personal role models who have supported you in distinguishing yourself as a man?

What does it mean to be a man who is in touch with his heart but at the same time strong, managing his responsibilities, and loving, and enjoying his life?

Do you have what it takes do be a man? How do you know you do, how do you know that you don't? What do you need to do or hear to be a man?

◆**Martin's comments on this topic**

◆These were the questions that were addressed in the first Men's Inquiry. I still gain value from reading them.

◆To me what it means to be a man is about who I am in my life and in my relationships. "Being a man" sunk into my bones by being with authentic men, receiving their blessing, and allowing me as a man to mentor, bless and appreciate other men. Being a man is also how I give my partner my strength, love, and compassion. I am able not only to give these things to my partner but also to the loved ones in my life.

◆Another aspect of what it means to be a man is finding our unique contribution in the community. An example occurred when I first offered my Men's Inquiry as a workshop at the Triangle Men's Center (originally The Raleigh Men's Center) annual retreat. It went very well and the men there gave me a great deal of acknowledgment for its contribution to them. In the end I realized my contribution to this community was the Inquiry facilitation skills I have, and it seemed I was the best man in that community to do just that. I had found my place among men. Its value is hard to express; I remember it like it happened yesterday.

◆To me, being a mature adult man is not the dread of unloved responsibility and burden with no real joy. It is a life path to travel on, one of mastering the inward experience of being an adult man in my core, connecting to my mission, and outwardly giving back to society.

◆There are three phases that often occur during this process. The first phase is receiving enough father and mother energy. For example, that doesn't mean a father being just a "buddy" to his son. He must be father first, and buddy second.

◆The second phase is the transforming experience of allowing and receiving sufficient blessings of a community of men, while working through the challenges of the community, so that a young man feels he has moved to the next level of maturing. This is what I believe is the positive aspect of the rites of passage in our history.

◆The last phase is finding personal mastery in relationships with a mentor. Without this, which is true for most men, full maturing is difficult to attain. The void is often filled with over-inflated egos as compensation, or just a passive resignation to life. After passing through the three phases of being a man, I can say without a doubt that they were necessary for me to experience. Sadly, most men in our culture don't have the opportunity, or don't take the opportunity to gain this understanding. You almost can see the absence of some part of this in the eyes of a man who has not had this opportunity. These phases may manifest in different forms for some men. I do not know if they are necessary for all men, but they have proven to be a monumental help to me and thousands of men I know.

◆To start on this path, you can begin by asking the question:

"What does it mean to be an adult man in the presence of other men?"

The Men Address Selected Questions

What does it mean to you to be an adult man, and when did you decide you were an adult man?

Allen

That is a big deal! I mean really a big deal! It implies a certain sense of maturity, responsibility, and masculinity. It is about going from having to be 'only self-sufficient' to working with others. It is developing a strong gentleness versus just wearing my feelings on my sleeves. A sense of place or being when you know where you fit in! In terms of balance, being able to be childlike one moment, and very mature the next. Versus being childish or overly serious all the time. It is getting in touch with humor and a mature concept of joy, joy almost as a spiritual concept. It is also becoming emotionally literate—aware of feelings but not dominated by them. It is having access to feelings vs. blocking them. It is knowing there is an appropriate place to be angry. It is being willing to break out of any backlog of sadness, anger, fear, or shame. It is like working through the emotional pain of war- leaving me lighter.

Laurence

Oddly enough, I think I finally felt like an adult man upon the passing of my own father. He died in 1995, when I was 43 years old and separated from my second wife. After the burial, my two brothers and I gathered at the top of the hill in the backyard of my parents' tiny suburban home outside of Philadelphia, the only home I had known growing up and where we had shared many an early childhood memory. We lit up some cigars and actually shared a pleasant moment together. While we mourned our father's passing, we knew his suffering was over and there was comfort in that. At the same time, though lots of negative things were going on in my life, I felt grounded and solid. Although as an adult I never relied on my father for a lot of advice or nurturing, I knew he was no longer there to provide it if I did need it. I was on my own. Even though my mother was still alive, I felt like the older generation had passed and it was now up to me to proceed with my life, with decisions about my mother and our childhood home. It actually felt good in that way.

Bob

I guess if I could answer this question, I would not be in such poor emotional shape inside.

Anthony

An adult man is a man that is responsible, has awareness, lives in the present and has a purpose. I believe I started becoming a man a couple years ago, and still believe that I am everyday becoming more the man I have described.

The main personal role model who has supported me in becoming the man I have become is an older woman. She is a teacher, a mentor, a guide, an experienced life and soul. She has seen the promise I held, has been patient with me, and has provided me with tough lessons and beautiful moments of awareness. I'm very grateful for her in my life and know that there is no other teacher who was meant to be with me during the last five years, other than her. I have added respect for her, as she was the one who headed me in the direction of the men!! This world needs more wise, educated, aware old (mother) energy in our women. She knew I needed something from other men and guided me toward that.

A strong male role model operating from his heart, in all areas of his life, makes my heart skip a beat! I know this thing, deep-down, from my own old soul's deepest yearning, and this will be the way forward for our communities. This male form means the world to me and is my highest goal, as an individual man.

I know I am one of the new men coming through—one of the early men to live a full-life in his heart, while at the same time, being educated and professional, i.e. mainstream. I needed to and still need to spend time with other men, younger and older, to be recognized, seen, and challenged and to give recognition, to see others and challenge others. I realize that this is not a one-way street and not just for me; this transition from boy psychology to healthy man psychology was a huge step for me. Also a huge step was my formal initiation on sacred land in NNSW (Australia) by older, more experienced men.

What does it mean to you to be an adult man, and when did you decide you were an adult man?

Chad

It's been a process, not an event or decision.

There's an interesting Quentin Crisp quote, "My mother protected me from the world, and my father threatened me with it." Part of my process of becoming an adult man has been to internalize both the protecting nurturer and the aggressive challenger that my parents represented.

In terms of my conscious pursuit of authentic masculinity and wholeness over the last two decades, there have been some important events, rites of passage, and initiations both intentional and circumstantial. Having an older man, about my father's age, place a hand on my shoulder and say, "This is my beloved son, in whom I am well-pleased," was an event that broke through 30 years of hardened armor plate over my heart and opened me up to the process of healing the boy in me, which is part of my work of becoming fully a man.

Confronting my father about his physical and emotional absence for so much of my childhood was such an event. Forgiving and accepting him has been a process. Rejecting my mother's cloying, suffocating, incestuous attention was such an event. Forgiving and accepting her has been a process.

Betrayals by immature men (some in their 50s and 60s—it's not about chronological age), betrayals and passive-aggressive attacks by boys in men's bodies—those have been events. As always, the forgiving and accepting has been a process.

I once heard a man say, "It is a rare and wondrous thing to behold an adult—there are so few of them." To become one of those rarities is my life's work.

Brad

For me, being an adult man means having a sense of my power and strength, and knowing its limits. For example, in an earlier email to the Triangle group, I mentioned acting on my sense of competence as a therapist to change my position from one agency to another, where I can work more consistently with clients. My strength and power is (in part) was contained in my ability to be an effective counselor. Even though I know this is the "right" thing for me to do, now having acted upon my decision, I feel a sense of loss and sadness at leaving behind some very good things, and possibly losing relationship to some very good people. My sadness reminds me of my need of others, of my incompleteness—in other words, of the limits to my power and strength.

Being an adult man means asserting my strength, knowing that whether it is accepted or not, the community of women and children need that example, as do other men so that they can take their place as strong ones for others.

When did I decide that I was an adult man? For me this was a gradual process over many years in which I overcame my reticence about my strength, overcame my embarrassment from resentful women about male power, and just simply stood in my own space. It feels so much better. This sort of decision, or option as I would prefer to call it, is something that needs to be renewed each day in me.

Roy

The real 'in my body' experience of being an adult man occurred after my first men's weekend. I now accept that this occurs in the blessing and company of other men. Being an adult man is the process of asking the question, finding men to risk trusting them enough to let them into your life. It is having the courage to let others contribute to you but not being overly dependent on them. It is about finding and breaking down the fear you have of real relationships with other men—a fear I never knew, and had not become aware of, until I heard the fear in other men in the men's weekend. I see it as a giant weight I let go of that no longer stalks me. Being an adult man is a process, not an endpoint.

Stan

I have absolutely no certainty about what it means to be an adult male, except that I have a penis and various other accoutrements, which distinguish me anatomically from a female adult, for sure. And I suppose that my body muscles give me an edge in strength to lift heavy objects or run at speeds faster than a woman who is the same age as me. But as far as emotions (fear, happiness, and sadness), outlook on life, hopes and dreams—what's the distinction? Only history and genetic blueprint that went into formulating my ego/personality makes me unique and different from any other man or woman.

It is in the history part of my gender identification where role models made a difference for me. My father was portrayed as a 'loser' by my mother, since he drank liquor like her father. And her father, according to her, was clearly a 'no account' who drank himself to death. Why would I want to be a loser or a boozer? I had no brothers or other kids out in the country to play with, and my grandfather was as grumpy in his way as my father was distant. The person I felt closest to and thus wanted to emulate was my grandmother. Warm and caring, yet with an underlying sense of duty to family.

I recall that I felt like a 'grown up' male when I first spoke the word 'f--k' out loud to another living soul. That dramatic first was in the presence of a fraternity brother in college while also puffing on my first cigarette and sipping my first drink of liquor (poured from a bottle of cheap Early Times and mixed with Dr. Pepper, since the coke machine was out of Coca-Cola). Perhaps I never fully appreciated being an adult male until I saw my newborn son for the first time in the hospital delivery room.

Fred

To be an adult man I believe, means to be loving, affirming, responsible, supportive and accepting, as well as humble, caring and being considerate of others and their feelings.

I don't really know if you decide to be an adult man. When I became an adult man, I felt that I wasn't ready. I did not have too many role models. I don't know if I have what it takes to be an adult man. I have heard so many misconceptions about what it takes to be an adult man regarding sex, emotions, being open and the like. I think what I need are more positive male friendships, more male contact and continuous affirmations. Most of all, I would like other men, including those I know to simply tell me "You're ok."

Benjamin

I needed a good role model to find out what being a man meant. My mother turned me against my father by the age of four. He was working full-time and carrying a full course load at the university. Also he battled chronic ear problems in pre-antibiotic days, chewing on a clothespin to ease the pain while he studied. In a way he abandoned me to her. In the case of my brother, their second child, Dad had more time for him as his school load had lessened. I was content to ridicule him silently and remain as distant as I could. Mother saw to it that I was distant. She and her mother painted a very unpleasant picture of my father. In my mid-twenties I made peace with him, severing my relationships with Mother and Grandmother, as I felt they had cheated me out of knowing a truly great man. I resented that very much.

I moved from New York City to a tiny town in North Carolina when I was 29. There I met two families where it was obvious that the parents actually loved each other rather than merely tolerating their partners for the sake of the children. This was such a refreshing atmosphere. Both families took me under their wings.

The men in each family, while quite different from each other, were the epitome of what I have come to think is the true Southern Gentleman. Each strong, masculine, content and assured with himself, yet gentle, able to reason and handle difficult situations without raising their voices in rage. They and their wives could actually argue without harming each other emotionally or belittling the other. This was a radical difference from what I'd experienced all of my life!

I remained in their tiny town for over ten years observing, enjoying, and being loved by them. I learned how desperate I was for masculine touch that didn't inflict pain, although they told me later on that when I first arrived any physical contact caused an instinctive cringe. From these two men I learned most of what I now know about being a man. They helped me, though they weren't aware of the full import and understand that I had what it takes to be a man. As a result of their patient love and example I am proud to be the man that I am: strong, yet compassionate; unafraid of being close, and of developing intimacy.

Thomas

I believe that being an adult man means behaving in a way that shows strong leadership as well as action. It means balancing selfishness with selflessness. Being a married man with children means providing the basics, plus demonstrating good judgment to obtain respect and dignity. I cannot say I will ever be certain that I am an adult man, and may never get there while on earth.

Barry

These questions are pretty large here and really make me think. For me an 'adult man' is one who is constantly in the process of coming into being. I have found it to be not a permanent state, but rather a state that requires constant awareness of falling back into patterns of consuming power, and correction of those 'falls' and entering again into the process of becoming. To me, if there is a process of becoming, there is also a process of leaving something behind. The adult man is the man who is leaving behind the attraction to use power as power-over, either in the sense of one who dominates, or one who allows himself to be dominated (either by women or other men)−dominating or being dominated are two sides of the same coin.

I feel the adult man is the one who realizes that not only is he not at the center of the world, but is also not at the center of himself. The man who wants to be at the center of himself is the one who is heading back into possessive dominance. The adult man is the one who is able to acknowledge and live with the center of himself being empty. In this way he is allowing himself to be a person who is open to the giving of others, and able to receive the giving from others−and therefore is able to give and be received by others.

So when did I decide that I wanted to be such a man? Well, it is an every day decision, so the answer is... this morning! It can be no other way. I repeat that being an adult man is not a permanent state, but a process of becoming.

Darryl

I decided I was a worthy adult male one weekend in March in 1993, during the *New Warrior Training Adventure*. Prior to that initiation experience, it didn't really matter what I said or thought about my "adulthood" or my "manhood" because my internal experience was one of such isolation, self-doubt and masculine shame. Before my initiation I was alone, fearful, posing, competing, judging, disconnected and looking to women for any and every emotional/relational need I had. Following the initiation process, I discovered a deeply trustworthy and connected community of men committed to reclaiming the sacred masculine and committed to training up for self-determined missions of service to the planet. I also discovered the possibility that I could rise up to become a man that I myself truly respected. I'm not perfect now, but the change in my orientation and my experience of myself as a worthy adult man changed very distinctly and profoundly through that experience in '93. (And I had already had almost 20 years of very high quality, intensive, experiential psychotherapy and personal development training before I arrived at the *New Warrior Training*, including a doctorate in Clinical Psychology in 1989.)

Clark
I know that I am a 'man' by hindsight. One of my men said this about me: "He doesn't always have the facts, but he never doubts what he says." I think my context around my words is more important then the exact information. People will always read my intention and my context around what I am speaking for. I will be tested, and in that moment, if I listen and tell the truth, I will know if I am an adult man. When I receive masculine communications—being criticized by a man and standing in the face of criticism and letting it in—I am being an adult man.

Joel
1. I was walking down the street one day and a boy accidentally bumped into me and said, "Excuse me sir."
2. I began to realize how hard it was to be a success, and what my father must have had to go through in all those years of struggle.

Don
That point in a young man's life when he is completely prepared to take total responsibilities of all of his actions—around 21 for me.

Randy
No longer spend most of my time looking for acceptance from my mommy and daddy through others. I take full responsibility for how I think, what I feel, and the actions that I take. I decided that I was an adult man when I gave up struggling with all the things that I didn't like, and started to focus, then take action, on making all my desires come to life.

Frank

To be an adult man means I am self-sufficient, a provider and protector for my family. I decided I was an adult man at many points in my life, as my definition has changed. I was an adult man when I went off to college and was on my own. Then I realized I was an adult man when I got my first real job and began providing for myself completely. Then I decided I was an adult man when I got married and felt the need to take care of my wife. I recently decided that I was finally an adult man after the birth of my daughter.

Rod

What does it mean to you to be an adult man, and when did you decide you were an adult man? I have pondered this question in depth before answering. I believe that was the 'missing piece' inside me, my unrest, so to speak, before I went through my New Warrior initiation. At that time, I came to realize that being a Man didn't have a THING to do with my physical body......my personal wealth.......my 'toys'......the beauty of my partner.

I am a Man......and I have a right to be a Man, and be respected as a Man. I now walk side-by-side any Man....Bill Gates.....Warren Buffet.....Governor Arnold.......and I am an equal to any of them. What a relief I found internally after coming to THAT conclusion at sometime during my training. The unrest is gone.....at least as far as THAT issue is concerned.

The battle now, for me, is within. And I now have many, many male friends who are fighting similar battles who I can ask for help without fear of being ridiculed or chastised as 'not being a Man.'

Ross

I decided I was an adult man when I made a series of decisions which profoundly influenced and undid everything I had believed, up to that point in my life, about what it meant to be an adult man. I was a mostly-dedicated, although divorced father of two children whom I allowed to be adopted by their stepfather (their mother's fondest wish) after years of defending my rights and the terms of the joint custody agreement. I filed for divorce from my second wife, a law enforcement officer who was so resentful of the time and money I had spent defending my right to a relationship with my children that (she admitted) she undermined my parental

115

relationship with an ongoing barrage of negative language to the children about their mother, even after solemnly promising me she would not do so. I closed a four-and-a-half-year-old business I had started with two partners and a sketch on a napkin, locking the door and declaring personal and business bankruptcy. All of this occurred within two weeks, about nine years ago.

All of that, after all, was what my own father did (except for the adoption, in a literal sense, at least). I have often self-loathed my apparent psychological need to imitate the behaviors I witnessed growing up. I feel a decent bit of shame for doing it so well. I've been mad at myself for not being able to do what I wanted to do and instead did nearly exactly what the men I grew up around did. A lot of people, particularly me, were hurt by it. It is the great contradiction of my life.

Carl

It meant true validation from other men. Look how we validate through sports—hugs and butt slaps. Touching is a manly way of validating in our sports culture. But try to hug a guy in public and watch out. I sometime shake a man's hand but if he is comfortable with a hug, so am I. Like some of my closest men friends and I don't give a darn anymore what others think. I think that is part of being an adult man. For me, it is giving up my fear of how 'I look'.

George

40 years of often man-hating feminism had to be overcome. I knew enough of what it means to be an adult man after making the hard effort to change and grow to being more grounded. I really bought into that stuff, that men were the sources of all the problems. Are women really powerless in all cases, do they really want to be professional victims? Of course there were plenty of men jumping on the bandwagon to impress women. It seems like everywhere I turned in the media and society I was kicked in the balls and accused of not standing up straight enough. It was then I started shaking off that social bullshit and decided that man had just as much validation or value as women! We both have responsibility, praise and blame for the society we live in and when we all own our part, the society will change. For me, it was owning my own part and no longer shouldering all the perceived shortcomings of men!

Dave

I'm still learning what constitutes being an adult male (i.e., a man). It feels trite to write this, but nonetheless, it feels right to say that, for me, being a man means being true to myself, whatever that self may be. Role models during the course of my life have included my male relatives and teachers, some of my work colleagues and friends.

John

It is hard to define being a man for me. I know that physically I am male and that I will always be male but the emotional part can be very difficult to define. I know that for myself, being a single man can be very rewarding by not having to conform to what is expected of myself as a typical male (being married and having a family, etc.) and how I am expected to behave and think. I try to look outside the box and try to accept that I have different values and beliefs and try to make a point of not defining another male (or myself) in this way.

Barry

This has been a difficult question for me to answer until recently. I believe that my generation has found it difficult to grow into manhood knowing what it is to be a man because the men of my father's generation in many cases model the going to work 5 days a week and going to the pub with mates after work. They then come home to dinner on the table and a wife who 'knows her place.' You tell your son that men don't cry and to model being aloof. This model no longer suits men of today in my judgment. For me, to be a man today means to be comfortable in my masculinity and to be able to express my emotions to my friends and family in a healthy way, i.e. not suppressing them or overdoing it. To be authentic and honest is very important for me. Being a man also means to treat my partner as an equal and also to know that we are different emotionally and physically. For me, part of my role is to be strong for her so that she can enjoy my masculinity, and also for me to respect her as an equal in our relationship.

I guess I really decided I was an adult man when I started making decisions about my life without checking to see if it was o.k. with my parents or if I'd done the right thing. So for me being

117

a man means to be responsible and accountable for my own decisions and their consequences.

Ken

I decided I was an adult man about 5 years ago or so. I am 50 now. Before that I called myself a boy often, and I resented what I saw as masculine behavior. To be a man means to have a purpose, to create something of value for the world, to protect the innocent and weak, to allow myself to be protected when I am innocent and weak, to behave with integrity, to explore my world and all its wonders, to be a role model for boys and other men.

Arnold

To me, being a male adult means being financially independent of your parents, and to be contributing, through your work, to the work of the world that has to be done every day. It also means to be honorable and responsible in your relationships with your partner or spouse, your children, your friends, colleagues, and business associates. It means to play some part, if you have the time and resources, in aspects of community life that interest you.

I don't know, for sure, when I started to feel like an adult man. The feeling comes and goes. It seems to be strongest when I am strongest. I think that I was starting to feel more like an adult in my early thirties. I finally dealt with the reality of being gay and to have relationships. I completed my undergraduate degree. I also started to feel more like I could really direct the course of my life, and make things happen that I wanted to have happen. I finally had enough confidence and initiative to take more responsibility to move my career forward, and to play more of an active part in community groups that I was part of.

One person who inspires me now owned the summer camp that I attended in northern Ontario when I was growing up. With minimal financial resources but lots of courage and good ideas, the camp got off the ground, and has influenced the lives of the people who went there. Another influence was a teaching assistant in a course I was in, when I was about 20, who took a personal interest, seemed to see who I really was, and offered lots of encouragement. Another professor, toward the end of my undergraduate work, actively coached me through a very complex research project. I was surprised and pleased at the end—I did it! This professor had also taken a warm interest in the work I was doing, and gave good guidance, but essentially, I had to do the work myself. I think that opportunities for solid accomplishment, and developing useful skills with guidance from an older person, not necessarily a parent, really helps to generate this sense of adulthood.

My father's role in my sense of being a man has been very difficult. My father died when I was six years old, and became a kind of mythical figure in my life, impossible to really know and impossible to live up to. He was gone, and therefore could offer no reassurance. My step-father is a down-to-earth guy who I did not appreciate for a long time. He is modest and unpretentious, and I saw little reason to look up to him. Although he was successful in his own modest career, my own aspirations were very different, and I considered his experience irrelevant to me. He is also very capable as a home handyman, and on that level leaves me feeling inadequate. It is only as a more mature adult that I appreciate him. I think that the lesson he gives is that being a man is well within reach for people of good heart, reasonable competence, and willingness to put forth some effort.

Consider the contrast between 'traditional roles of men', and a man who is in touch with his heart but at the same time strong, managing his responsibilities, and loving, and enjoying his life. I think that the idea of the ideal man being unemotional is a myth that crept into 20th century North American culture, perpetrated by the movies and TV. I am not sure that it ever actually existed. I remember seeing some of the postcards my grandfather sent to my grandmother from Europe, during World War I. He was quite open about his feelings in the midst of his endeavors there. I think that the ideal of the unemotional man is a concept for manipulating men by some of the bigger forces of the military and business. At the same time that this model of the unemotional man is perpetrated, when it suits them, at other times they play on emotions, with no shame, to accomplish other goals.

Fredrick

What does it mean to be an adult man? Wel,l for me, it was marked by two events that happened around the same time and which I can't separate. One was a big professional break-through and the other was marrying my second (and final, and current!) wife.

James

I don't think of myself as an adult man since I don't have children. Being raised Jewish, I grew up with the word MENSCH, which means being a man—being enough of a man. I often feel as though I'm not enough. When I help others, I feel better about myself. I can look to friends, who I think have good lives in that way, and am always looking for good role models.

Bill

A man must decide for himself the meaning of his life. A man must chart his own course in life, regardless of the opinion of others. This does not mean he should not give weight to the opinion of others, but rather decide if there is any merit in considering his own path. A mentor could help a youth on his path by asking the proper questions, listen intently to the answers and offer any needed assistance. A man must form his own opinions about important questions based upon thoughtful study of the issues.

A man does not allow himself to be an apostle or a satellite of another man unless he has decided that his purpose in life is to serve. A man is well-centered in himself, not easily disturbed by events, positive or negative, which occur around him or to him.

Let me tell the path I took related to this: I worked for United Parcel Service for more than 32 years. During that time I was a Teamster shop steward for 15 years. I represented about 100 people in the High Point facility. As you know, a shop steward works a regular job in the company, as well as representing workers on the job. This requires several additional hours per week as well as some extra expense. There are meetings with the company and the union officers to attend. There is no monetary compensation for this responsibility. A number of employees I represented were fired unjustly, but with my investigations and presentation in hearings about 85% were reinstated on the job with back pay and benefits. The more effective I was at representing the workers, the more the company harassed me and made my job more difficult. I experienced two divorces during this period. Both of my wives, my parents, brothers and others kept advising me to resign from my union position. I felt I was doing a valuable service for the people. The officers of the local union encouraged me often and let me

120

know I was doing a fine job. The workers often told me how much they appreciated me (they elected me five times). My family members never got to see what it was like on the inside and no amount of explaining could have informed them. It's just something one has to experience. I knew in my heart I was doing the right thing for me and for the workers. So I kept going. In 1996, I had trained my replacement for about 4 years, and I was planning my retirement 5 years later. It was only when all the pieces were in place that I resigned as an officer of the union and became just another truck driver. I trusted my own understanding, regardless of the opinions of others.

If I were in the same position today I'd do the same thing. The only thing difference is that I would be more centered, less vulnerable to the harassment. If I had been different from how I was, I could have been more available at home.

Joe
I know I was becoming an adult man when I started taking only advisement instead of orders from my penis.

Arthur
Being a man is something I can only speak of in terms of after my men's work. I can't answer this from the perspective of my whole life. As a boy, masculinity was modeled to me as alcoholic, misogynist, racist, & detached. Since my own initiation, involvement with men's groups, and my work with rites of passage for teenage boys, I have a sense of my role as a man—to be there, in service, in grief and sorrow, in joy and rapture. I participate in all my humanness, prepared to make mistakes and be wrong, and also to not shy from my greatness, and rejoice in the greatness and humanness of others.

Bob
A man is a builder; he sets goals and finds ways to meet them. He is proud, which mean he knows who he is but does not feel the need to brag about it. He is strong and perseverance. He gives and does not complain. He is fair. He laughs. My father is a good role model.

Fredrick

What does it mean to be a man? In the higher sense of 'man,' I'd say standing up for your personal Code, no matter what it is. Being willing to take hits for it.

Henry

To me, a boy is a man when he <u>puts</u> away childish behavior, like not taking responsibility for his actions. A boy is a man when he loves his wife and children as he loves himself. A boy is a man when he loves obedience to Christ as if it were written on his heart. There are no hard and fast rules, but there are more boys than men today, and some never reach that stage no matter their age.

What does it mean to be a man—someone who disciples me, my father, my pastor, and my stepfather. A man who is in touch with his heart is in touch with God and others. I have learned that no man is an island, and if he is, he may pretend to be strong and self-sufficient but by himself he lacks the strength to make a difference in the world for the good which is the true mark of a man. Transparent relationships are what bind us and make us and others better people.

Every man has the potential to be a man and I am no different. Some days are better than others for me when it comes to modeling manhood. To be a better man, I needed to be presented the gospel and know Jesus Christ and God in an intimate way. The all-sustaining word of God is what has given me the milk to nurture my growth toward manhood. I have not arrived at being the man I want, but that is what brings me so much joy about being a Christian.

Ray

I don't know exactly how to answer this question. I know a great deal about what a man is supposed to be, do, not do, accomplish etc. I know that almost all of this is destructive to men, their families and their communities. I know almost all of it was a disaster for me. I played out this role until my mid-30s, when I began to feel betrayed and hugely unsatisfied. I'm clueless as to who or what a real man (as opposed to the socialized male, above) is. The only saving grace for me is knowing that nobody else does either and that most men don't even know that such a male exists.

Although I played to a socialized male role for years, I also lived a highly personal life at the same time. This included my creativity, my intellectuality, and my attention to myself. In my 50's, I finally grew up, in my view. I gave up all socialized role-playing and concentrated on finding and expressing myself. I've been working on this now for about 15 years. I have no idea whether I'm a man now or not, but I sure do know who I am. As I've spent all this time and energy on myself and working with men, I've come to the point that being who you are is far and away the best thing to be. Being a man or woman or something else feels like an irrelevant goal to me.

Von
The definition of 'being a man' has certainly changed for me over the years. Having grown up with macho models of the John Wayne variety, it took decades and a whole new set of mentors to redefine and unlearn old models. My new paradigm includes the ability to openly share feelings, demonstrate compassion, and express spirituality, but always building trust and emotional capital.

Wilson
It means strength: strength of character, loyalty, honesty, fearlessness, openness.
To be an adult man means to be able to say you are scared without feeling weak.
This one HURTS! I would say 40-42 years old - when I took responsibility for everything that was wrong and incomplete in my life.

Evan
I first decided that I was an adult man when people started to refer to me as mister. Being an adult man means seeing yourself as being part of a community of adults that protects and nurtures the young, and has a special responsibility to use accumulated wisdom to make the world a better place.

Damon
To me being an adult man is when you finally stand up and take responsibility for your own actions. I used to party all the time, and still enjoy drinking a fair amount of beer, but when my daughter

was born there was a change in me that felt instant. That was the end of recreational drugs and the realization that now there was someone who was entirely dependent on me to be there and able to provide for their needs, from now well into the future, possibly until and beyond my death.

Benny
At the age of 18, I became a man in one traumatic split-second. My father was killed by a hit-and-run driver on Thanksgiving, one day after his fiftieth birthday. I was also hit by the car, but survived miraculously. I became the 'man of the house.' On second thought, maybe I hadn't quite become a man. I had a difficult time and gave my mom more sorrow with some of my problems of attaining my manhood. We fought over the length of my hair, my education choices, where I would live, and many more issues that seem so insignificant now.

Daniel
In our society, adulthood, regardless of gender, is defined by age and gives little regard to actual maturity. I personally would define adulthood as being emotionally mature enough to handle my own affairs—personal, business, life, etc. I can't say, though, that I ever decided I was an adult. I assumed I was an adult when I turned 18 because I was doing, or was capable of doing, things I saw the people I believed to be adults doing.

Werner
To me, being an adult man occurred when I learned to discern between the men I can trust and the men I cannot trust. When I learned to let the men I trust in. When I learned to let a male mentor into my life. When I learned how to stay true to my principles. When I learned how to cherish a woman. When I made my mission in life first then invited my partner to join me. When I learned to take responsibility for what I can change in the world. When I learned how important keeping my word and the intention of my word is. To me, being a man is a lifelong task that I am still working on.

Who were some of your personal role models who have supported you in distinguishing yourself as a man?

Thomas
My personal role models are few. Certainly, for many years, I thought it might be my father. But now I've seen too many bad decisions on his part. At a young age, I thought it might be my best friend's dad, but I realized he was a talented achiever yet a raging alcoholic at the same time. One major role model is now a retired senior executive of a Fortune 500 company I worked for. Probably my other role models would be professional football coaches from the 1970's, men I never met.

Allen
There are many of the men in AA who demonstrated recovery. My sponsor. Many of the leaders of MKP. I actually develop or find new ones even now. It's a work in progress.

Wilson
Several of the men in the Men's Groups that I was involved with. I experienced men that encouraged me with their words and their actions.

Tim
Other than my Dad, a man of remarkable kindness and integrity, there have been two father figures, both deceased, who taught me about what it is to be a man. One was an author, the other a manufacturer. Their lessons were simple: that I trust myself, that I share both my love and my vision with those I trust, and that I regard integrity as a lifelong and life-sustaining value. In short, my Jewish mentors led me to aspire to be a 'mensch.'

George
Teachers, counselors, it's hard to remember specifically.

Barry
Only a very few men: a singing teacher friend I had at the end of my teens, an American dream analyst I met in Los Angeles in the eighties, one or two other male friends, and of course, some

125

women too. Also, my present supervisor. There are some authors, too, who have been models for me: Graham Greene, James Alison, Johannes Metz, Rene Girard, and one who is more written about than writing: Jesus of Nazareth.

Ross
One of them was a boss I had whose leadership model was one I admired, and who became a good friend. Other than him I didn't really have role models that I can recall. I simply emulated or tried to emulate traits I admired in friends and other people around me.

Ken
Some of the MKP leaders, my boss, and my friends Craig, Peter, and Mike. And then there's Sean Connery!

Ross
I can recall no personal role models who supported me in distinguishing myself as a man. I think as a result of my general 'holier than thou' attitude, I either turned off, or intimidated anyone who may have been willing. There were men who opened doors for me professionally, which is largely the way I did distinguish myself, if that counts. I don't think they thought of what they were doing as mentoring me. Again, the cynic in me: they all had something to gain. I have outright asked for mentorship from men several times. I was never outright refused but I was never mentored either.

Benny
The life my father led has been an inspiration. Losing him as a teen, his memory inspired me. Maybe I put his memory on too high of a pedestal, but it did help me. My science teacher took me under his wing. He was always there for me, despite the fact I was merely an average science student. He found the part-time job in an iron foundry that taught me I wanted to go to college. Later, I knew that had been his goal all along. His wisdom still teaches me years later. My Scoutmasters were my early role models.

Daniel
I can't say that I remember any.

126

Frank

My father is one role model. He was always there for me and my brothers. He always coached our sports teams, and dropped us off at school. He built his business from scratch, working hard but still enjoying life. My other role model was my maternal grandfather. He was a first generation Italian immigrant who started a family of 5, worked and put himself through undergraduate and law school all at the same time. He built a tax attorney practice from scratch by knocking on doors. My father and maternal grandfather were very similar, except my grandfather was always distant with his children, and worked too much. He never found the balance between work and family like my father did.

Kyle

My high school swimming coach, Marty Astorian, was not just a hard guy. He was intelligent, and had a soft side I could just barely get a glimpse of. He made me work hard (for him), because I thought he really cared about me and the other boys. I wish I could let him know how I feel now. I looked him up when I got out of the military and it was good to see this now gentle old man. We fell into our unspoken 'man' roles and I wasn't able to tell him how I felt, even though I think we both knew about it. He was consistent. He was compassionate. He was tough and unyielding on me and showed me how to 'gut it out' and bear my pain... he knew there was always more left in me, maybe even a lot more left that I would not have discovered otherwise. I'm still learning from him 50 years later. It helps to think about him. I'm thankful for the provocation of the questions for this book!

Another role model was so complex in its affect on my life. He was my boy choir director and to my surprise on a trip we took together he came on to me sexually. The first night he got a hotel room with only one bed and then after plying me with some whiskey he made advances. I was eleven or twelve at the time. I rejected him easily. Physically I was big for my age and bigger than him. There is much more to the story. The man was a very talented musician and a sensitive person whom I liked and looked up to. He showed me many things about culture by taking me to the symphony, inviting me to his formal dinners, and many other things in addition to music. The first girl I ever kissed was his

127

daughter. He showed compassion and toughness in his dealings with the boys and men of the choir.

Yet there was a time, much later in my 20s, when I hated him for what he tried to do with me, and for what I imagined he must have done with other young boys. I came looking for him after the Service with intentions of doing harm. I'm glad I didn't find him. And now, 40 years later, these feelings are complex and mixed with a richness ingredient, and the hatred is gone. I find now I want to dwell on this topic more to see what else is there (in me).

Don
My father and an older male friend.

Darryl
Carl Griesser, the Executive Director of the ManKind Project. Rich Tosi and Bill Kauth, the founders of the New Warrior Training Adventure. Curtis Mitchell, Chair of the Executive Committee of the ManKind Project International. And most especially, the most natural of all peace and justice warriors, Wekesa Olatunji Madzimoyo, my colleague in multicultural work, now an educator in Atlanta. What each has in common for me is that these men show me how to stand in any fire, no matter how hot, and experience the fullness of my reactive emotional life, contain it, and choose my behavioral actions out of high principles and out of service to peace and justice.

Joel
1. My father.
2. An older man I met in college was a mentor to me.

Randy
My Marine Corp drill instructor—because he walked the talk. My great friend Jerry—because his listening for me has always been profound. My friend Bob—because he modeled unwavering fearlessness. And my mother—because she has always had the utmost faith that I am a great and insightful person.

Andrew
My maternal grandfather was a retired, high school-educated carpenter whom I visited for a month every summer when I was a

boy. He was a typical 'man's man,' the likes of which I didn't get exposed to very much. He liked to putter around, work with his hands, fix and build things. He was very unlike my father, who worked a desk job, read the paper, watched TV and couldn't fix or do much of anything, except gripe. My grandfather didn't talk or analyze much, but he was always into something. He happily tolerated my following him around and observing him. He took me fishing and taught me to fillet the fish that we caught. He took me into feed stores in rural Mississippi where old men in overalls sat playing checkers, and he'd proudly introduce me as his 'grandson from Baltimore' who'd come to visit him.

The most important gift he gave me was that of being with a real man of whom I didn't have to be afraid. (Life with my father, by contrast, was a constant holding of one's breath, awaiting the next outburst of fury.) My grandfather died when I was 13. He was long dead before the importance of his gift became apparent to me. As an adult, I still marvel and am a bit jealous when I see a boy with his father or grandfather and realize that the boy doesn't fear the man.

That's how simple being a 'role model' for a boy is: be yourself, let the boy be himself and let him love you without fearing you. Powerful stuff!

In contrast to traditional role models of men, what does it mean to be a man who is in touch with his heart but at the same time strong, managing his responsibilities, and loving and enjoying his life?

Wilson
This is the ideal man but I am not sure it is the desired man in our society. A man like this, as viewed through the lens of our current culture, appears threatening since he is not doing 'what is expected of a man.' Actually, he is doing more.

Fredrick
That's a delicate balance. I've struggled to honor the parts of me that don't want to cry, that don't want to express emotion. I know that sounds crazy, but I've felt so much pressure from women and from our very 'psychological' culture to be 'more in touch with my

feelings'—which often boiled down to role-playing fake feelings in a theatrical way. For me, it has been liberating to realize that I can be authentically in touch with my heart without necessarily spilling it all over everybody and everything. That feels mannish to me.

Allen
You sort of answered the question in the question. I think just reading the question is enough. It has it all.

Ross
An interesting question. I've never quite reached this place. When I was a teenager, a high school sweetheart inspired me to all levels of expression and romantic idealism. I wrote poems. I wrote lyrics to songs and collaborated with musicians to put them to music. I was, in a manner of speaking, a budding artist. I felt quite natural producing the material. When this activity was exposed to my family, particularly my father, his father and his brothers, it was, to put it subtly, disapproved of in no uncertain terms. It's really the last time I felt 'in touch with my heart.' Anytime in my adult life that I have tried to revisit those skills, to do those things again, I have been unable to reconnect with the sense of comfort I once felt doing it. In my subconscious I hear the disapproval like a dripping faucet in the middle of the night; to the point of near madness leading to the necessity of shutting off the water supply for the need of sleep and peace of mind. I manage my responsibilities for the most part. The bills are paid, etc. But I can never remember, as an adult, feeling as though I was '...loving and enjoying my life...' in a complete way. Certainly there are elements of my life I enjoy and love. To be able to say definitively though, that I 'love and enjoy my life,' I'm still waiting and wondering about that one. What is it like? What does it look like? What does it feel like?

Ray
It's more than the heart men need to be in touch with. I need to be in touch with my soul, spirit, heart, feelings, body, the natural world, the creative world, the whole community of man. When I'm in touch with one or more of these, it's not a matter of being strong. If I'm in touch, that's the world in which I move and principles on which I move. It isn't a matter of the socialized male

'strengths.' For me, it's a matter of focus and commitment, not power. From an outsider's perspective, I suppose this would look like strength, but it's not strength in the self-will/ controlling others sense.

Tim

Such qualities are essential. I discovered that when I was made a non-custodial father. Although I was reluctant to do battle with the mother of my children, I had to learn to be a loving warrior for their sake. By learning to function that way, I have taught them that love does not require one to be either cowardly or submissive.

Thomas

Especially in America today, it is hard to do. If I become too sensitive, say like Oprah's following might like us to be, I lose respect. If I am too crusty, I won't fit nor do I really benefit others. For me, it's hard to enjoy life at age 49 anymore. Seems easier to just stay in a routine.

George

He must be able to do it in a manly, not macho, way; he doesn't need to be a sob away from his hanky, yet he doesn't need to be a poker face concealing himself from himself, not to mention others.

Ross

To me you have described the attributes of the new age of men. These are the qualities I am working to make part of who I am.

Ken

It means not having as many friends in this part of the country where many men don't express feelings (other than anger). They fish and hunt, they talk down to women, and they like to watch reruns and sports on TV. It means I walk my talk even if I may appear different at times. It also means I have some really close connections with men (and women) as a result. It's worth it!

Damon

Since I have never been comfortable with the traditional role model, I have had to forge my own way in life. Only with the birth of my first child did I finally feel I had arrived in adulthood as a man.

Darryl

Here is one example: In my work I lead mixed groups of people engaged in intense dialogue and experiential learning while challenging modern racism and other forms of injustice. There is no way in hell I can earn the right, as a traditional white guy, to facilitate such dialogue and learning unless I show up as authentic, with integrity, and speaking a universal language. To be in touch with my heart means I have full access to the complete range of my emotions and I know how to experience them authentically WITHOUT acting them out and putting them on other folks. I mean, I get to be sad and say so when I'm feeling injustice and disconnection (either in the professional work or in my personal life). I get to be angry about injustice, not just on my own behalf but on behalf of others whose voices may not be heard. I get to model what it is to be scared or concerned when risks and threats are about. I get to be in my joy, my experience of being powerful, and in my peacefulness, and model for others the deepening expression of these gifts. I have learned what it is to experience and contain my emotions while staying present in a dialogue with people who are different than me. I still screw up a lot, but life is definitely a whole lot easier now than it used to be, having these specific abilities near at hand.

Daniel

I spent a portion of my adult life trying to fit the traditional male role as father, husband, breadwinner, etc. and I was miserable. I was doing what was expected of me even though it had little to do with what I wanted to be doing. Today, I strive for balance, and I at least try to work at things I enjoy. And though my work today doesn't bring the financial rewards I would probably make in another career field, I have a peace and enjoyment, and a sense of purpose that I don't believe I could find doing anything else.

Benny

I feel I'm definitely in touch with my heart. It's easy for me to share this and open up to a woman I care for deeply. However, I tend...okay, I bend over backwards... to not 'expose' my heart to

132

male friends. Recently, I've opened up to my best pal, which has enriched our bond. He, too, has opened up to me. It seems we find we can still be 'men' and reveal our feelings, our hurts, and our doubts. Wow! I survived these revelations.

Joel

I am not there yet.

Don

A man in touch with his heart recognizes that it's okay to be sensitive and in touch with his feelings.

Randy

For me, receiving this heart-practiced role model means that instead of just me following the disconnected mystery of someone else's path, that I get permission, through their honest expression, to develop other qualities about myself such as trust and respect. When I experience my role models sharing from their feelings, I get the complete beauty and awe of this man in front of me. But even more importantly, when feelings are modeled for me responsibly, then I no longer spend my time trying to fill in the missing parts of the puzzle, instead getting to see the whole human-truth. And when the role is reversed, when I am loving, strong, responsible, and enjoying my life role model, then what that means is that I can love someone, be myself, and be fully-effective all at the same time.

Do you have what it takes do be a man? How do you know you do, how do you know that you don't? What do you need to do or hear to be a man?

Ross

I don't know. I know of no authoritative or acceptable definition of "what it takes..." Can I function as an adult, hold a job, etc.? Yes. Is that what it means? Do I sacrifice and try to do good for others? Yes occasionally. Is that what it means? Do I try to act in a way that does no harm to others? Yes, and sometimes I fail. I don't know what it means, "to be a man..." I can live with myself usually, borderline mild sociopath that I apparently am. That should count. I may be too self critical to see the truth.

Barry

Do I have what it takes do be a man? Yes. And I believe my journey for the rest of my life will be to constantly strive to learn more about myself and to make myself a better man/partner/father/friend.

Todd

I am a man; I know this at my core. It only took 32 years to figure that out.

Allen

Being told you are a man, that you have what it takes to be a man, by men you admire. It's like the mantra in AA: I have enough, I am enough, and I do enough. It is declaring you are enough with the blessings of other men.

Ross

What I need to hear... I needed my father to recognize that I no longer needed him to help me live my life. I still wanted him to be part of it, but I didn't need him to help me live it.

Thomas

I know I am an adult male, perhaps too serious about things at an earlier age. I believe part of being a man is not having to hear anything to reinforce the thought. So a major part of being a man is being so independent as to not need anyone for anything. Then of course I feel isolated and alone. This is a good question; I need to think about it more.

James

Interesting the question would be phrased this way - do women ask if they're women?? The idea of being enough of a man is so deeply ingrained, it's like we don't even know what we're doing here. I was at an RC workshop (Re-evaluation Counseling), where a man got up and screamed: "I Am A MAN - A FULL COMPLETE MAN!" If I really knew that I was enough of a man,

I could relax, tell the truth, not have to prove anything, be more creative and loving, etc.

Carl

I wish I had started to go to more men's conferences relating to men's issues twenty years ago, when I was a young father and husband. I now only hang with men who validate themselves as true men of integrity, as I do for them.

Barry

The simple answer is no, if I mean that I must be the one who does it all. The answer is yes, if I am prepared to allow things to be done for me.

Wilson

I would like to think I do and I would like to think I am a man. I know I am a man because I am not afraid to reveal myself, even in a bad light. I am responsible for what I do. I do not act or speak in superficialities. I am not a man because there are still things in my life that I refuse to address, people I refuse to join with, and relationships I refuse to develop. I need to take responsibility for everything in my life and I need to hear from other men that my actions are visible and have had an impact on their lives.

Ken

Yes, because I am doing it now, through the support of men who I value and have let into my life. I still desire to have more integrity in my relationships with women, and around sex.

George

Yes, partly through the feedback of other empathetic men who also evidenced having been through tough "valleys of death."

Damon

For years, I never felt that I was a man—more like a wimp. I was not the macho type. As I've grown emotionally as well as in age, the macho thing is not important.

Darryl

This is a tough one, because it sets up an either/or. Also the question of "being a man" in itself is not useful in my judgment; only the question of being a mature, responsible man points me to the possibilities. It isn't really a yes/no question in my experience. What I know is that some days I feel and judge that I do have the makings of a good man, a man of integrity and service. Other days I know I'm a grown-up, 55 years old, but I feel crappy and judge myself harshly as being out of integrity either with my own values or my commitments to others. On those bad days, in the back of my mind, I know I am really as all men, and when I get back to my men's group they will laugh at me, love me, and confront me, and I will be back whole again. I can even hear them teasing me now about how hard I can be on myself.

What did you or do you need to do or hear to be a man?

To Hear: From men older and more experienced than myself, I have heard and still benefit from hearing: "You are a good man." "You are welcome here, with all your fears/doubts/anger and shame." "You are like us. And we are like you." "We benefit from you disclosing your personal struggles because it is our work, too, that you are doing."

To Do: Show up as accountable to other men—to act my way back in to integrity when I have broken my commitments to others or myself.

It is great to hear and do these things with the women in my life, and their compassionate responses do count toward my experience of being male and being a man. I have found that it is distinctly necessary for me to hear them from men, not only from the women who have been generous in my life with such words.

Frank

I have what it takes to be a man. I have a confidence that I can do anything if I apply myself. I need to have success when I try something to keep that feeling that I have what it takes. If I don't succeed, I have to be able to figure out why I failed to maintain that confidence.

Don

Yes. I know because I recognize that there is no such thing as always making the right decisions. Being a man requires doing your best, but more importantly recognizing when I don't achieve best or make mistakes and I'm prepared to take responsibility for that.

Joel

I know I am a man and that I have what it takes. I do have to constantly seek what my authentic core self is. My life is a personal inquiry, a journey. Like Odysseus coming home from Troy, I am adrift in a small boat in a large turbulent sea, not ready to come home yet. What did Nietzsche say? "Look into the abyss and you will see yourself."

Chad

I believe that moving fully into manhood is a process that requires, more than anything else, that I become conscious of my terrors —the infantile terror, the animal fear, the defensive ego, the grasping, clutching, wanting to hold on tight—whether to the momma, the lover, the home, the job title, the good salary, the youthful athletic body—whatever. And once conscious, to act in spite of, and in opposition to, what the fear tells me to do. When I do that, I learn something. I learn facing the fear and acting in spite of it will not annihilate me. I won't die for saying "NO." It's hard work. It's men's work.

I also believe that joy and sorrow are inseparable, inevitable, and essential twin pistons driving the engine of a man's soul. I try to avoid sorrow sometimes, yet my ability to experience joy can be measured exactly by the depth to which I've allowed sorrow to carve out empty spaces—clear spaces—in me. That may all sound like a lot of B.S., but it's been my experience.

Daniel

I guess that would depend on how you define "a man." Am I male? Yes! Am I strong, loving, dedicated, caring, passionate, and sensitive? YES! Am I fearful, self indulgent, and inconsistent? OH, YES!!

In our society manhood is often awarded by accomplishment or denied because of failure. This means that someone besides me

137

defines who I am. We may spend years of our lives trying to achieve a status or level of accomplishment that is different for every person we meet. I was never "taught how to be a man." I was taught that I should be tough. I was taught that I should not express feelings of sensitivity. I was taught that men don't cry. As I grow and mature, the question becomes less and less "what do I need to hear or do to be a man" and more "what do I need to hear or do to become a good human?"

What Insights did you personally gain from this chapter?

What do you want to commit to or re-commit to out of these insights?

Remember!
"Insight without committed action is only entertainment!"

Chapter 7
Constructive Rites of Passage

What are the relevant rites of passage for males in our culture today?

What are the natural and constructive rites of passage that occur today?

What are the elements of honoring and noble initiation into manhood?

What are the various Rites of Passage in life? Which ones serve us and how?

How do we create relevant rites of passage for our sons and ourselves?

◆Martin's comments on this topic

◆After reading Robert Bly's *Iron John* in the early '90's, I wondered if within our American society we had a meaningful rite of passage from boyhood to manhood. I started my search at about the same time I began my career as a Life Coach because I knew that if we could identify a *meaningful* rite of passage, the results would surely be useful, not only for me but also for my clients. But what I found was a major lack of evidence of this essential element. I also came to understand the anxiety that its absence was causing for my male clients and the problems it was raising for my female clients in their relationship to men.

◆Discovering natural and constructive rites of passage was as important to me then as it is now. I believe that men would benefit greatly from reconnecting to the noble initiation into manhood that was once a natural stage of growth present in Native American and other cultures. Drawing upon the fairy tale that describes the archetypal issues of men, Bly says only older men in a society effectively initiate younger men into manhood, and that both the older and younger need this process for their own emotional growth and development. According to Bly, a father is frequently too close emotionally to his son to provide this essential ingredient in his maturing. The assistance of other men in the community is necessary.

♦Our society has accepted initiation by peers: into college fraternities, athletic teams, or the dangerous and destructive initiation into street gangs—usually not true rites of passage. True rites of passage can occur only when "elders" interact appropriately with the young men who are to be brought into the mature association. The little known essence of the process is that the older men who participate in an initiation enter into a kind of initiation themselves. When the older men bless the younger ones, something grows within both the giver and the receiver. Initiation is therefore mentoring in a special way.

♦Throughout my years in men's work, I have learned that initiation takes many forms. Masculinity alone can grant masculinity and it can occur at any age and at many intervals. Too long we men have turned to women to initiate us into masculine maturity. In truth, it is really up to *us* as men. Meanwhile, many women are tired of trying to do a job that should be that of a man—introducing a young man into manhood. One of my clients, a single mother of a teenage boy, told me she felt great relief when she admitted she could not effectively mentor her son by herself. She was relieved when this burden was happily removed; she worked with me to find responsible men in the community to provide the mentoring role missing in her son's life.

♦Despite the wide influence of Bly's writing, today few major structured rituals or ceremonies are available to help make the shift from "boy" psychology to "man" psychology. Without initiation-type activities in our lives, there is no clear line in our hearts between being a boy and being a man. Yes, the Jewish community has the Bar Mitzvah when a young boy is introduced into the community of men in the Synagogue. Even then, for many this is more of a celebration and has lost its value as a true initiation. While there may be questions about what happens in that ceremony, it is important to know that being a man does not mean that we should lose the childlike wonder of life. Rather, we are inducted to learn to gather it to ourselves, to feast on it, to keep it in our hearts, and to share it as a mature man.

♦Once, years ago, initiation supported men in making the tough changes that life requires. With the disappearance of these rites, many men do not or cannot make the shift easily or gracefully from childhood to adulthood, although this does not mean in any way that all aspects of rites of passage in history were constructive.

140

Many men today do not get the experience and emotional or psychological support necessary to go from child to man. So now we have a large population of 35-or-45-year-old boys running around causing trouble for themselves and others. For many of us, there was no hinge upon which the transition could take place. The "shifting point" just did not happen. In its place we have a blur of emotion, confusion and mix-up deep down inside ourselves, like that of a mere youth stuck in an aging body. It's a feeling that deeply affects our perception of ourselves and others, sometimes throughout an entire lifetime.

Age makes no difference

♦A good case in point is Ron, a 70-year-old friend and who was a past mentor to me in learning how to objectively think. A few years ago Ron called to ask me if I could support him in "becoming a man." Surprised, I asked him what triggered this unusual request. He shared that his deceased father and uncle had appeared to him "just like they were in the room." He said he asked them if they were coming to get him, and they had answered, "No, you're not done yet. You know what you need to do." Amazingly, Ron said he knew exactly what they meant. He needed to work on his self-image as a man. His dilemma was that he still did not feel like a man. After talking it over with a friend and trying to figure out what to do about it, he called me.

♦Feeling a bit insecure before someone of his age and maturity, I wondered if I was the right person—if I had the ability to provide what he needed. Ron was an extraordinary man who had accomplished more in his life than I could ever dream of doing. He had lived through hardships that I don't think I could endure. But there is something about a simple, honest request that can grab you unlike anything else. I was aware that I would be on my own, since the only men's personal development programs I knew of were in the form of three-day weekend workshops, and those were not an option, due to his health. So even though I didn't know exactly how to proceed, we scheduled a time to meet.

♦At our first session, Ron revealed the hidden details of his life; how he had stuttered badly as a young boy and his friends constantly made fun of him. His father thought he was a wimp. Though kinder, his mother told him stories about the evil deeds of men. Ron took these stories to heart and vowed not to join the

141

ranks of masculine "badness." For most of his life, Ron said, he had rejected men for the evils they had done. I asked him to tell me a specific story of how he knew men were evil from his actual experience.

♦He said he had been on a battleship in WWII, in a remote area near China and that the sailors were planning to leave the ship and attack a village known for its brothels. They were intent on a spree of raping and killing the women. As he continued, I assured him I understood the horror of it. Being one of the smallest men on the boat, he said he knew he could not challenge the others through physical strength. He was the only Medic on the ship and realized the crewmen were dependent on him if they got injured. So he confronted the men leaving the boat, telling them to leave their firearms on the ship, and that if he heard of any deaths, he would not treat the men if they were hurt. He finished the story and said, "This is why I hate men."

♦Clearly, he was a courageous man but unable to see it himself. I said, "How did you miss your own courageous act?" I asked him to create a log and to write the story, this time as a story of a man with great courage. I told him he could pretend at first it wasn't him, if that helped. As time went on, he had story after story just like this, and I continued to have him rewrite his history, keeping the content consistent, simply changing his interpretation of what it meant.

♦At the same time in his coaching sessions, we also worked on his assessment of what type of adult men he admired. Gandhi was first on his list. To that he added other men who were clever, wise, and had the strength to adhere to their principles. All were men who were able to transform conflict into something greater than existed, with their intellect. I could see what type of man he was!

♦I asked Ron to write about *this man* as though he were building a composite of many men. His resulting model was an archetype that we called the "Warrior-Wizard." Someone who has the ability to stand up for what he believes in, to understand social dynamics in a way that others can't see, and to make things change in a magical way. "In reviewing the past, I asked, "Tell me how you have actually been a Warrior-Wizard, and how you would have lived your life differently if you had realized it previously. How would it change the way you live your daily life now?"

◆A few weeks went by. Ron reported that he was feeling better about his life and in general about being a man. However, he still had some mixed feelings, and unfortunately he chose to stop our coaching sessions when a friend's death took him out of town. A year later, I felt a strong urge to call him. His shaky voice on the phone told me he had cancer and might not live through the night. He was such a good friend to me. My mind went immediately to how much he had helped me personally, and to a project we had planned to do together—but that is another story. I realized it could be the last time we would talk and I told him what a great friend he was, how much he had contributed to my life, and that I loved him. He said I had helped him accomplish the mission his father and grandfather had asked him to resolve.

◆I hesitated to follow up at that point on the topic of "being a man," but since this might be our last conversation, I simply said "Thanks for letting me contribute to you in the area of becoming a man." "You're welcome," he said softly, "You know that's all been resolved. Our work together was quite helpful.l I now know I am man enough!"

◆What, then, are the critical components in male rites of passage? I surely do not want to suggest that there is some specific path that must be taken. I only want to offer some components to consider including when constructing any rite of passage activity.

◆First, there should be some experience that gives a man a sense of transition from one state to another with the support of other men. This is often referred to as a "ritual space." Second, a man needs to find a community within which to develop that ritual space. And third, the process must honor and welcome the man into the community of men in a way that gives value to both the initiate and the other men involved. It should give him the opportunity to see his unique contribution to the whole.

◆Our culture unfortunately offers little that qualifies. One valuable exception is *The New Warrior Training*, an intensive weekend designed to address men's issues that I have both experienced and recommended for men of all ages. It is especially effective when participants join the weekly or bi-weekly Integration groups that are set up to perpetuate the personal work. I did *The New Warrior Training* in 2001. I've recommended it to friends and clients and gratefully watched as their confidence and personal effectiveness, relationships, and work lives quietly transformed for the better thanks to the deep journey they have been on.

♦Authentic initiation is a powerful process in a man's journey of maturing, enjoying his own life, and enriching his family and society. The gold I have gained and continually see when other men gain from deep meaningful fellowship and trust of each other are my reasons for writing **Finding Our Fire**. It is a collective reflection on my own experiences as well as those from men all over the world who have courageously taken on their own lives.

The Men Address Selected Questions

What are the relevant rites of passage for males in our culture today?

Allen

I was not allowed to have the normal teenage rites of passage of rebellion. Then I went to the Navy which has its own version of rites of passage—they just missed the honoring part. It has too much of that flavor of abuse without the honoring. Even the primitive tribe that scars the young man also honors him; we just scare him. For me, it did not start until AA, and then the next level was the New Warrior training that went beyond AA.

Bob

Rites of passage used to be closely related to sexual maturity and I wish they still would be. That way, I think men would not be ashamed of the sex. As far as I am concerned, I think I became a man the day I decided 1) to accept responsibilities; 2) to take control of my life 3) to give back what I had received.

Fredrick

We have a sad lack of such rites in our culture. Most of mine were somewhere between stupid and flat-out dangerous. Taking a dare to swing out on a frayed rope over a river full of jagged rocks while high on cocaine is probably the classic rite of passage. I was probably nineteen at the time. There was definitely some authentic warrior-initiation stuff in that for me, but the idiocy and desperation of it speak for themselves. Maybe the deepest one for

144

me was the first time I really had soul-sex with a woman, but of course the paradox there is that this was not something I celebrated with men.

James
Relevant rites of passage would include those that nourish the contributions that each of us make to the world—be it in athletics, the arts, or whatever. Other rites of passage are: to be supported by the community for our unique talents, and to have the community honor us as individuals for that, and Music and Art are a big part of it.

Mike
My exploration of the issue of rites of passage occurred 5 years ago. I bought Robert Bly's tape, *Iron John*. I listened to it again and again, finding a deeper connection with the subject matter each time. The down side was that he (Bly) identifies the problem and does not speak to the solution. I joined the group at a local men's center in search of a deeper spiritual connection with men. For 5 months I went to a group which gave me times of hair raising, exhilarating connections. It was not enough for me, I wanted more substance.

I left feeling that there was no support to speak the same language that I was speaking. I felt as though I had had an awakening as to the problem and was searching for those in the solution. Moving away from either blaming women for my problems or expecting them to solve them has been a slow process. I have now come to the understanding that prejudice is the key word for me against both men and women. Prejudice is the general term for expectations, and generalities.

Today, I require men to provide the first line of support, and understand that I must develop that group—individual by individual. My past is filled with trying to relate to women and seeing men as competition or buddies. I don't feel like a man is a buddy anymore. As to rites of passage, I do not believe that there is an event horizon suitable to live in the integrated life of a man. When I cry in front of other men, when I tell a man no because it is wrong even when it will benefit me, these are examples of passages. Everything I do with me usually follows suit with women.

About 6 years ago I lived in a group home with men in Wilmington. I came to notice that when I spent time with the men some part of me was nourished, even though because of my preconceived ideas (possibly homophobia) I wanted to resist what I was experiencing. Then when I was out spending time with my girlfriend, I could feel my battery run down. Coming to the understanding that men were necessary for my health and development was a slow painful process for me. Nowadays, I rely on my spiritual fellowship as it is convenient, concentrated, and a part of my life pattern.

"Something there is that doesn't love a wall—That wants it down". . . . Robert Frost

Von

One of the important Rites is discovering personal passions, gifts and talents. Along these same lines is the notion of taking responsibility for one's own inner peace. In general, I find that giving back to society in some constructive manner consistent with these talents is an important Rite as well.

Ross

I'm not sure if this means what I have experienced, or if it means what I am aware of (as in say, Sioux Indian tribe rituals). I don't really know that I perceived a 'noble initiation into manhood,' In order to avoid emotional implosion, I ran away from home at 17. I drove an old station wagon I had from New England to Florida. I didn't disclose my whereabouts to anybody for 10 days. I was told this was a big deal by family members—that they worried about me. I don't know how I could galvanize the message I was trying to communicate to them if I hadn't waited the ten days. It ultimately didn't do much good though. I went back after five months. I did have to borrow $60 from them for a deposit on my apartment, however. At the time I saw this foray as a bit of an initiation. I had to get a full time job. I had to rent an apartment. I had to buy food, cook, clean, etc., etc. I wasn't very good at all of it, but I did it. One day I was attending my last semester of high school and two days later I was sleeping at a motel in North Carolina. A day after that, I was sleeping in the car at a campground near Disney World. A month after that, I was a full time employee, had my own apartment, and had sold off the car opting for a motorcycle which offered far greater fuel economy. So was I initiated? I don't know. I do know I made a lot of bad decisions during the experience, including a big one, to become romantically involved with my 'replacement' girlfriend who, less than six months later, I married. She and her replacement husband adopted my children. I guess all of that is an 'initiation.' I don't think it's very noble though.

I would say events such as a first job, graduation(s), marriage(s), birth of children, promotions, loved one death(s), etc.—all serve as passages, one way or another. I've often wondered though what things might be like if some of these traditional 'rites' were joined on equal footing by less traditional ones. I see things like righteous indignation and moral outrage as laughable. I'd like to one day see a culture where hypocrisy is not the norm and where lifestyle selection is respected as an individual choice instead of vilified to some degree or another depending upon an observing individual's or group's usually defective and self-serving belief system. As a recovering Boston archdiocese catholic, one thing in life I can be certain of is that no one has the right to proclaim or pass judgment on another because no closet is clean or skeleton-free. Hypocrisy is a major pet peeve of mine. Creating rites is not something I've experienced, unless you count subtly tempting my children to face me after no contact for nearly ten years. They are both now of age and can make that choice. It is my belief that they must. I hope I'm right. The question of manhood and what it means came into my life when I was 19 years old. I was in Spain as an airman in the US Air Force. My life spirit kept me an independent soul adversarial to military discipline and uniformity. Somehow I was able to keep this spirit intact avoiding undesirable discharge but not avoiding continual parades before my commanding officer for various offenses against the military. I lost and re-gained stripes so often I went to removing and then stapling back chevrons around the star on each arm.

Anyway, in this new but poor land and strange culture, I recall wrestling often with my values, wanting desperately to finally be sure of myself in all ways. It became obvious to me that the way to do this was to not have any fear. This, I thought, was my biggest, if not only, obstacle. So, methodically, I made a list of my fears on paper. Then I set out to test each one to find out if I was justified in having it. I thought at the end of my list I would be free and mature and self-assured. It started with my fear of fights, drugs, and women. So, I went out and started fights, and took drugs, and then came the women thing. That was the most perplexing. I didn't know how to go about testing it. For example, I went into a cabaret in Zaragosa and sat at the bar. I spotted the prettiest looking woman in the large mirror behind the bar and simply gestured to her. In my sternest face I pointed my finger at her and then pointed to the seat next to me, and then looked away. In a second she was sitting next to me waiting for my next command. Then an empty feeling suddenly came over me. I didn't have a clue what to do next. It was embarrassing when she stormed off recognizing my bluff– a setback.

It was hard to get a date. Hard for me to ask. I watched some other men who were good at it but I couldn't tell why. When I finally did get a date, her sister had to come along to chaperone, even though my date was 35 years old. That was Spanish custom. I took her to a party and got her and her sister drunk, and her sister diverted with someone else. When we got into a room alone I could not get her 'things' off easily and in desperation had to chew off all kinds of straps and bands and materials. I recall my mixed-up feelings about whether what I was doing was alright.

So, in 1963, there came a time when not getting dates and being afraid to approach young, single, pretty women started really bothering me. I had an active imagination too and had no problems pleasing myself. I thought of the amoeba's sexuality. The parallel was revolting.

So, at age 20, this led me to a deep examination of my concerns around sex. I was alone in Oslo, Norway, being dropped off there (not in uniform) due to some contrived military purpose. I spoke no Norwegian and found not a single person there who spoke English. There was no such thing as credit cards and I had very little money. It was cold and evening was setting in. I found a cheap hotel and then quickly went out to find some food. I was there for about 4 or 5 nights and had to steal a lot of what I ate. But I had with me several bottles of Cognac that helped me through my loneliness.

On the second night came the culmination of forces of loneliness and confusion and depression about my sexual orientation. I had to know. I had to understand. And now was

148

the time. In the dark hotel lobby, around a low coffee table were three chairs. I got paper and pen from the night clerk and sat down in one of the chairs. I began to write. Soon, I switched to another chair. I wrote an answer and offered more dialogue. I went back to the first chair and continued, then the second chair again. I recall thinking that there needs to be an objective third party to police the dialogue lest it become indulgent, flattering, trivial or some other inference. The three of us continued all through the night. And in the early morning hours it was finished. I understood myself better.

Now at age 64, I look back on my life of struggling to understand myself and the man I am becoming. I am okay in myself and my sexuality now, although I am still learning and open to the new. I have imagination and feelings that I honor as harmless and imagination is not under my control, but my behaviors are under my control. I don't feel this is dangerous because I have confidence in my abilities to know my boundaries and behave in appropriate and moral ways.

Wilson
I don't think there are any. If there are, I have not found them yet.

William
As for the idea of Rites of passage, I would like to expand on the statement: "Change the world one man at a time."

Yes, the Warrior weekend training is a start. It opens some doors and a man has a chance to get in touch with himself. He is the only one who can do this, change his life. The door is open and it's up to him to carry on. This is where the I-Groups come in.

Example: I was on a retreat with an MKP leader and his son. His son was going through some heavy stuff, he was 18 yrs old. The next time I saw his son I was on staff and he was going through the weekend. He did some great work. The next time I saw him, we were on staff together. You would not think he was the same young man. It made my heart full to see a young man change that much. Thank you MKP, New Warrior. If only they had something like this when I was a young man, I would not have had to go through all the crap I put myself through. You noticed that I said all the crap I put myself through—before the Warrior training I would not have said "I," I would have blamed all my problems on someone else.

That brings me to my experience with New Warrior...I was raised in a dysfunctional family, I guess you could say. It was during the depression; my mother was divorced and raising me alone—very strict. I had an uncle who was always beating up on me. I developed a great big temper that got me into a lot of trouble. I got out of high school in 1940 and the war in Europe was going on and Japan was moving around. To get away from home I joined the Navy. I wound up on a submarine and spent six years in the Pacific. Submarine sailors learn how to drink booze early. Wel,l after that I was in love with the bottle for thirty years. Sorry this is taking so long, but I want you to know the background. Finally, I got rid of the booze habit. I was sitting in an AA meeting one night after three years listening to all the same old stories when I realized after three years I had to get out of this negative atmosphere. You see most people go to AA and they get sober, but they go to meetings and don't do anything about improving their lives. They keep telling the same old negative stories. So I was sitting there one night and decided I had to work on the spiritual side of my life. I started to really work on myself and thought I had come to issue with every thing in my life, until I went on the Warrior weekend. One day my wife and I were watching TV and the Donahue show was on—it's a talk show. There were six or seven men on there and they were talking about a men's group called New Warriors. They were on for two days. I looked at my wife and said that sounds like something I should go to. I called one of the men who was in Dallas, Texas and he told me there was a new group in Washington, D.C. that had just started. In November 1992 I went. I thought I pretty well had all my shadows in control. Isn't that a joke? I am in a great space now. I was 72 years old when I took the training. It's never to late to find your real self.

When I came back to Roanoke there wasn't a Warrior I-group for miles. I started working on men, introducing the New Warrior concept. Over the years, 25 men have gone through here and our I-group now has ten members. I am really sold on New Warrior Training. I received a call from a man in South Carolina a few years ago and there were a few scattered Warriors Men in North and South Carolina. He wanted me to come down to put them through the eight-week protocol. Went down and did it on a weekend. As a result we have a full scale Center. It sounds to me things are happening "ONE MAN AT A TIME." There are a great bunch of men doing a GREAT job in the name of New Warrior.

I owe much to the MKP New Warriors. I am still going strong at 85. I am in a good space, spiritually, mentally, emotionally, and physically. No more anger, fear, judgments, resentments, or reactions, I stay out of the dark and keep in the light. Change the world one man at a time...YES, as we raise our consciousness to a HIGHER LEVEL things will change. LOVE is the answer; it is the GLUE that holds it altogether.

My mission is "TO LOVE MYSELF AND OTHERS UNCONDITIONALLY AND SEE EVERY SOUL ON THIS PLANET UNITED IN LOVE, PEACE AND GOODWILL."

LIFE IS GOOD...GOD BLESS YOU ALL...HOPE I DID NOT CARRY ON TOO LONG......

Carl

For some men it is the special age when you get to go on the annual hunting or fishing trip with men / warriors. Boys look forward to the passage into manhood on a weekend with men.

Barry

Initiation into manhood is about experiencing the Hero's Journey; the descent into darkness and separation, the ordeal of doing battle with the demons or wonders of my life, and the ascension into power, fullness, glory as the sovereign of my life.

When I think of Rites of Passage I often think of the crystallizing experiences I've been through that have had the biggest impact in changing my perspective or worldview. Here are some that come to mind:

The first broken heart–I remember thinking that I would never recover from the pain. And I did. Marriage – For me (having been married and divorced twice) this was a sure sign that I was an adult, making adult decisions. In some ways it was just the beginning of growing up. Moving away from home–Making a life of my own for the first time. First Divorce–For me, first real chink in the armor. Life isn't perfect. Claiming my manhood/confronting Dad–Writing the letter to him and telling my truth was probably the biggest transformational event in my life. The first public

151

failing–Mine was an affair with a married co-worker, which became very public and caused quite a commotion and pain for many people I cared about. I learned that I wasn't perfect, but that I was still loveable. And it taught me who my friends were. It was the best lesson about integrity I have ever experienced. Starting a business. Male initiation–My warrior weekend was a profound experience in claiming my sacred masculine energy. Not sure there are other initiations available to most men that are as pure in intent. Death of a parent–Mom died 5 weeks after she was diagnosed with lung cancer at age 64. I couldn't have imagined the impact it would have on me or my family. It was the single biggest wake up call to my own mortality, and the pain of that transition will be with me for a long time. It has fundamentally changed the way I view my life and life in general.

I don't have children, but I can see how important the father/son relationship is to the maturing of a boy. I remember the first time I was allowed to spend the night with a friend, the first time I pitched a baseball game, the times my Dad was there for big events like graduations, or the really painful events like the breakup with a girlfriend. Rites of passage don't always look like rites of passage from the outside–which is all the more reason why it is so important to be mindful all the time.

Roy

For me the 'relevant rites of passage' was the New Warrior Training. I know there are other programs like this but don't know of many of them. If I had not done it I would not believe it existed. I also don't think it is the only path by far; I hope there are many. I do know that men seem to need it more than women.

What are the elements of honoring and noble initiation into manhood?

Ken
There aren't many true male initiations around these days in our society that I know of.

George
It seems we have succeeded in repealing many of these initiation features; men need them to grow, watched over by the senior "elephant" elder males. I wonder if this isn't what gangs are attempting to do since the void exists.

Arthur
The elements of rites of passage from my years of experience in working with young men on this issue is: Separation—from women, especially mother, but also from worldliness, time constraints and the comforts of home. Transition—Story/Dance/Chant, Risk & Challenge, Spirit & Honoring. Last, Return—to community as a new person, to be treated with more respect and to assume more responsibilities.

My culture presents rites such as graduation, marriage, divorce, getting a drivers license, a funeral, baptism, confirmation. From a male perspective, I find the appropriate rites today are marriage & becoming a father, although I see that they could be handled with more conscious regard. And in the context of a boy passing to manhood via an appropriate rite of passage, that these future rites for this man would naturally hold more reverence and meaning.

Creating relevant rites of passage is thankfully happening—the work I have done with the Pathways Foundation and the "Pathways to Manhood' program has been a huge part of my own journey. As I see what we do, the main area of improvement is that we get more men and boys from the same areas doing these camps together so that the community of men holds well after the camp. That these boys have at their disposal 12 or so other men, with sons they passed through this gateway with, who they can go to and draw from. The work we do on the camps is staggeringly beautiful; really vital in the father/son relationship and for this reason alone the work is worth it. However, as I have said earlier, much more could be gained from fathers and sons that already

153

know each other doing this work or at least from an area that is close to each other. Quite a number of the camps I have worked with have fathers and sons from all over the country who will probably never see each other again.

Community awareness is vital. Mothers, especially single mothers, instinctively know this work is so important. It is more the men who are 'okay' who seem hardest to convince. The greatest success in the community area seems to be coming from schools where there is this existing community. This can pose its own set of issues, but is far preferred in my view.

Carl

If you have a brother who is hurting, and even as an adult male has not felt honored or had a noble initiation into manhood, honor him with that weekend–one man honoring another–and telling him how great that he is a man's man. Validate him.

Ray

Identifying the elements of effective Rites of Passage would take me a lot of thought. Mostly I know what I don't want in it–all the typical male socialization stuff. Actually I'm not so sure that there should be a Rites of Passage to manhood. As I said in my last response, being a whole person, grounded in your self, is what every man and woman should be headed for. If we all knew ourselves and were true to ourselves, I don't think male and female would have the significance we give it today.

The default Rites of Passage I may have gone through today are the following:

Going to first grade. Going to middle school. Getting your driver's license. Graduating from High School. Getting your first job. Getting various diplomas. Qualifying for professional licenses. Renting your first apartment, and buying your first home. Getting married. Having kids. The first time you're fired. The first big disaster in your life. A parent dying. A spouse or partner dying or becoming seriously ill. Grandchildren. Retirement. Somewhere in there – starting or buying your own business.

I don't see much in this list that says anything about learning who I am, to make relationships (all kinds) work, to build and/or protect a community, to connect to the natural world, what life is really about.

I don't think there are any "natural and constructive rites of passage" in today's world. Most of us, men in particular, go through the events on my list without thought and without any conscious effort to find out about the issues in the preceding paragraph. For many men, the only rites of passage they really pay attention to is how much money they have and how many people they can control.

Years ago I wrote a novel which had a Rite of Passage in it. The young man was surrounded by the older men in the community. Each older man told the young man what he or the community expected from the young man during his life. Then he was initiated into the sexual world by one of the sexually experienced women of the community. I haven't thought about this passage in years. When I wrote this section, I remember it climbing on to the computer screen without any forethought of mine. Looking at it now, it seems a good idea. Maybe instead of just sex, the community of women should tell him what they expect of him too.

Actually, I think that Rites of Passage dangerously oversimplify the process of becoming a wise person. It implies that it happens all at once, that it can be given to you, that once you have it you can never lose it. Becoming a wise person requires a kind of process similar to going through corporate performance evaluations ... regular evaluations, the setting of goals, the identification of problems, the curing of the problems. Most of all it requires mentoring over time. How do you package all of this into a process that's practical and works? Even if we could figure out this answer, how could we sell it to boys raised in this culture – who demand immediate satisfaction, believe absolutely in money and power, and believe that life is only about benefits not responsibilities?

The difficulty of this task, though, doesn't excuse giving up on the effort. If we don't find the right Rites of Passage, nothing will change for men or for society. We'll just let loose another round of socialized males. It would be interesting to gather a group of men together for a weekend and see what Rites they could come up with.

Roy

The elements of a Rites of Passage is about the community of men (other than the father) taking the boy/man out of the ordinary world and bring him through some process that has a risk of failure (may not be real) and a challenge to it. This process involves blessing, appreciating, and identifying the boy/man as a man now—that now it is time to pick up the tools of being an honorable man and take that out into his community—giving him his place among men. It is a doorway not an end point, it is real, I felt different and that difference did not go away, and if I had not experienced it I would probably attempt to justify that it does not exist.

Dave

I don't see that we presently have a noble initiation into manhood in our society, so I see nothing to honor. Just getting to 21 years of age with some semblance of a right to be alive, midst all the male-specific shaming and sarcastic male-bashing around us, constitutes a Herculean task.

One important rite of passage for me – and one which I have noticed other men experiencing – constituted coming to grips with fully acknowledging and accepting the degree to which I was deceived and exploited, i.e., manipulated into believing falsehoods about myself. I dare say this rite of passage will become increasingly common in the next couple of generations of males. Only when we reach a "tipping point" and men begin in significantly large numbers to say "no more of this" do I think we will be able to begin to develop new rites of passage.

Jeff

Rites of Passage: The elements are training, correcting, rebuking, and teaching with the word of God. Define Rite of Passage. It doesn't exist in the pop culture that is American culture. In American culture, early success in athletics, sexual conquest, and pursuit of wealth and prestige at work are the benchmarks for success and passage. The Rites of Passage in the Christian world are birth, acceptance of Christ as personal Savior, marriage, fatherhood, and finally mentoring other young men. It is something we don't do in isolation but with the fellowship of other men and God.

Laurence

For me, it still represents some combination of the old notions of trial by fire or a quest of some kind, one that tests a young man's physical, intellectual, and emotional strengths. After completing the assigned task, one assigned by older men, a ceremony acknowledging the young man's experience is held. Everyone "passes" the test, whatever it is, but the most important thing is the lessons learned in the quest or journey towards wisdom. These should be supported, nurtured and honored by the older men. For me an outdoor activity of some sort always comes to mind. The Order of the Arrow ceremony in Boy Scouts is one and one through which I gained a measure of my manhood. My college fraternity initiation was another important event for me. It's very important, however, that the youth go through this experience with men he respects and admires.

Allen

I am not sure the order is correct but here of some of the components I think are important: Some type of adventure, acknowledging the ordeal, honoring the basic person then honoring their unique qualities, some type of 'naming process' in which the young man takes on the new name. You see the military take them down to the base level but not bring them back up as anything unique. They must make you part of the mass. In real work everyone is honored just because they are human. Make sure they get that. Then honored specifically for who they are!

What are the different Rites of Passage in life? How and which ones serve us?

Ken

About the different rites of passage, I am not sure, maybe: High school graduation, first beer, first sex, pubic hair, driver's license, first job, marriage/partnership, children, college graduation, divorce, promotions, 40, 50, 60,?

George

To me the different rites are the milestones of father, coach and mentor.

Dave

What are the different Rites of Passage in life, I am only going to write about one I feel is important, one which I never got, and that is a talk from my dad about the proverbial "birds and bees". Clearly, puberty is a physical transformation from boy to man. A lot of stuff is happening and I think it is a duty, no, an honor, for every father to walk their son through that. Outside of the educational value, to me, that talk is a right of passage and acknowledgement by the father to the son that he is (going to be) a man. I never got it but do hope some day to have the honor of bestowing it myself.

Roy

The passage from boyhood to manhood, into fatherhood and then retirement and creating the next phase of life for yourself. If you don't support young men through the first, the second 'just happens' and then there is the not planned for. For me my passage from boyhood to manhood happened late in life with the New Warrior Training. I will tell you after experiences with this work I get angry about how little we have done in preparing our sons for war. I am sure many older men in the military are aware of this and do their best to help younger men. I think we are going to see years of backlash for not doing that.

What are the natural & constructive rites of passage that occur today?

George

Boy scouts, Bar Mitzvah for Jewish males, and other male ritual endangered species.

Bill

Rites of passage are personal accomplishments as passing some test. Manhood is not conferred upon one, but comes from satisfaction inside. A young man must find an area of interest, and

158

then perform to his best ability. Of course it is always better if the young man is supported and affirmed by a respected adult male. For me in high school it was both academics and athletics, in both of which I did well. I continued participating in athletics in the Air Force. I studied Kung Fu for about eight years, which continued my process of growth. About that time I began studying eastern religions and writing poetry. But I can't say I had matured until I resigned my position as shop steward. Retirement in 2001 also was a rite of passage. In retrospect, I would have to say that each step along the way has been a passage out of which I have grown and matured. It would have been a less bumpy path for me if I had a positive, affirmative male mentor, but you play the cards you're dealt.

A young man can participate in athletics, learn to play a musical instrument, go to an outdoors school, like Outward Bound, master a skill or craft, such as wood working, excel in academics or just get a part time job while he continues his education. There could be combinations of some of the above. Whatever his choice or choices it must be something challenging from which he can derive personal satisfaction. This sense of accomplishment, if reinforced by a respected adult male can usher the youth into the next stage of growth. A spirit of camaraderie with men his own age and respected adult males strengthens the effect of the process.

Roy
Birth, purity, falling in love, graduating form high school, then for many college, finding God, first job, marriage, fatherhood, death of loved ones, retirement, our own death. But they are not enough to build a solid core to be effective, mature, and fulfilled.

How do we create relevant rites of passage for ourselves and sons?

Carl
Mankind Project and The *Wild at Heart* boot camp (a Christian men's development training), or even the *Promise Keepers* (though viewed as controversial by some) are several rites of passage for men. Both offer opportunities for other workshops to go deeper

into yourself as a man for true self discovery. I think you have to work hard to find them and even harder to create them.

Roy
The first is having the courage to have an open discussion, like this, about it.

Allen
This is a big problem that we don't have well answered. The main one I know is MKP. But how do we create it outside, how do we create it in society? This is a critical question that I don't have a clear answer for but hope we all will keep asking.

What Insights did you personally gain from this chapter?

What do you want to commit to or re-commit to out of these insights?

Remember!
"Insight without committed action is only entertainment!"

Chapter 8
Your Mission, Terms and a Game Worth Playing

What are your core principles and values and how do you live from them?

What keeps you awake to the beauty and passion of life?

What do you 'lose yourself' in something, that leaves you feeling fulfilled when you are done?

What gets you in touch with your dreams, possibilities, core values and principles?

What is the human soul? What happens when you ignore your soul?

How do you hear, honor, and communicate with your own soul, with your own self?

How are you doing as the guardian of your soul and what would you be willing to change?

Have you taken the time to embrace an adventure for your life that is challenging and meaningful for you?

What gets and keeps us conscious, in touch with, or present to our core values and principles?

How can commitment to our mission and core values give us freedom?

What is the value of having core principles?

How much time do you spend unconsciously seeking out the approval of women vs. truly figuring out what you want your life to be about first?

What is your personal mission? What have you committed your life to?

What game for your life have you created that is worth playing?

What gets you passionate about life?

Do you notice what really gives you fulfillment and do you make sure to set aside time to do that?

◆**Martin's comments on this topic**

◆John Eldredge in his book *Wild at Heart* hit the nail on the head when he said that most men have either made their meaningless work or their relationships into their great adventure. Healthy

161

women don't want to "BE" your great adventure; they want to be invited to be part of the one that you created. They also don't want to be married to a man who is married to his work, with themselves completely excluded. Of course this does not apply to all situations, just use it a something to explore. They say most people spend more time planning a big vacation than really thinking about what their life is about. Who are you beyond your work and relationship? What is your mission?

♦Often businessmen have written impressive mission statements for their work but it is not derived from passion. It does not make them want to get out of bed or feed their soul. One time when coaching a client, I made reference to the mission that Martin Luther King (one of my heroes) had and the man said, "Yeah, but look what happened to him." My answer was that King was more alive while he was alive and continues to live longer than most men who have lived twice as long. Creating and exploring your mission is a process that is always evolving. It is more like finding your own path by trial and error and letting other men contribute to you in order for you to discover it. It is a process of taking risks along that path, allowing other men to support and strengthen. This does **not** exclude the supporting assistance of women, which is equally of value. I use the example of men supporting us for this is the biggest challenge we often face and makes one of the biggest differences.

♦Some men resist and complain, "My life is all about my children." What a cruel thing to do, not only to the children but to oneself. This often leads to living 'through' your children so that being a model what you have suffered will be inherited by your kids. What greater gift can you give your children than a loved life that you invite them to share?

♦I have learned and deepened my mission and resolve in the company of men, discussing challenges within this context and discovering ways to upgrade all of it….both for me and for them. This inspires me even more. A mission does not have to be "BIG and NOBLE" but *meaningful* and *inspiring* to YOU!

♦The most significant issue that must be addressed is to identify what your core values and principles are. What are you saying YES to, and what are you saying NO to? They go together.

♦If you don't have something to say no to you, likely you will not be able to say yes when you mean YES in a powerful way.

◆What is the part of you that you will not compromise? Have you thought about that? Have you written it down? What are you saying is the core of YOU?

◆What can your family press up against and trust will hold strong? This is not about just being stubborn, dominating or holding on blindly to some principle. I mean those things you have considered thoughtfully and wisely chosen to identify with as your core values. Making clear to yourself what your core principles are is fundamental, and allowing flexibility in other areas is essential. Above all, you must be willing to stand your ground in supporting your core principles. Holding your core values means you will not have to push back or acquiesce, but being strong when the time is needed, allowing you to be flexible in almost all other areas of your life.

◆True strength does not have to dominate or defend, it just is! With out something hard for the feminine to press against she will seldom feel safe and when she does not feel safe she will want to metaphorically 'kill off the male'. This shows up as constantly criticizing, nagging, and finding fault with everything the male is doing. For the woman, it's like dancing without a partner holding a solid frame, clear where they are going and looking out for bumping into things. The woman cannot play her part. Some people hear this as either permission to dominate or believe it will breed more "blind macho crap." Actually the having to 'act masculine' or overcompensate comes out of the deep insecurity that the core is NOT solid. The more we don't feel comfortable in our masculine core the more we need external props to try to fill that void.

◆Stand solid and strong. It is about having the courage to draw the sword, but the wisdom to know when it does not need to be used. John Eldridge best described it in the book <u>Wild at Heart</u> when he said; "You can't turn the other cheek if you have no cheek to turn.". The absence of these distinctions often show up in the man that feels like he does everything to "try to make his family happy," and, consequently, they seem to have no respect for him. The next work to be done is to allow your mission to inform your life and to then to live from your values with determination, love, compassion, and vision.

◆This is not a "one size fits all" philosophy but just take a moment and try it on. See if you can let it get past your attachment to the way things ought to be and ask what really works. If nothing fits let it go. If it really makes you mad then maybe there is some truth that you are not willing to explore.

◆The truth is that many people's lives feel empty and meaningless because they are! They are waiting for a pizza delivery guy to come to their house and hand them the meaning of their life in a manual saying something like, I am really sorry I am late. These people have suffered a lot over what does not work in their life but often have not created a game worth playing! A meaningful life to you is not necessarily convenient or comfortable. If your life feels meaningless than maybe you need to stop looking for someone or some sign to come to you and begin working on creating meaning for your life. You may find exploring these questions over time in the company of other men could be a wonderful start. Do you surround yourself with friends that don't let you hide from your dreams or do you have associates that help you justify why your life does not work?

The Men Address Selected Questions

What are your core principles and values and how do you live from them?

Allen

Integrity, stewardship, consideration, compassion are a few of mine. I think just taking the time to write your own out is critical. I need to think more about this. This is good question! As far as living from them, you have to remember what they are. It is about giving the change back when no one will know the mistake. It is most tested in the areas where no one will see.

Brad

What you mean by "core values". This phrase is open to a couple of different meanings: the first of them being cognitive, the other meaning is personal and arises from my inner self.

Many men choose their core values cognitively, and then find that their best efforts are thwarted by confusions, guilt, angers, shames, etc. arising from within.

The second more personal less cognitive, more emotional/spiritual sense of "core values" refers to that which lies within or under those very confusions, guilt, angers, shames etc. That is, I begin to apprehend what is at the very core of my heart, by listening and learning to what my inner world is telling me, even if I find it difficult to go there, even if that process is slower than the cognitive selection of what is most important to me.

The relevance of this I believe is that many men in my experience talk of core values in the cognitive sense, and often don't recognize that they are doing that. When the inner tempests come along, they then easily loose heart.

I want to suggest that you clarify which sense of "core values" is the one you want. Or you may have another sense altogether... still I think it would be helpful to have it clarified.

As a Christian, I do not identify core principles and values, so much as identifying a person, Jesus of Nazareth, as the one I follow. Therefore, I live in imitation of him, and assert that he is the center of my life, and that this center lies outside of me. This means that I am living in a "not-yet" situation: I mean that I am in a process of becoming, more and more like the one I follow, and that this presents me with an existential anxiety. This 'anxiety' leads to either slavery or freedom. It leads to slavery when I am tempted to grasp onto what is not my own, when I panic about not being complete, and instead of being in an attitude of receiving, I grasp and close my hand over what is now my possession. I am now the maker of myself, and have lost dignity because I am not cut off from my own developing future. (Notice that the grasping hand is shaped like a fist — possessiveness is a subtle violence.) My anxiety leads to freedom when I am content to be in a position of not yet, and still becoming. I find this position to be very much like a death: what is given today is but a preparation for what is given tomorrow, and must be let go of, before tomorrow's gift will 'fit'. My life is characterized more by infidelity to this vision than fidelity. However, the image of Jesus crucified stands before me as the truth in action of my infidelity. The crucified Jesus deconstructs my actions and reveals to me what are the consequences of grasping onto my life: the cross reveals me

165

'taking life', that is, taking the life of Jesus. Yet no matter the seriousness of my taking, there is a greater generosity in Jesus, who 'gives' even as I take. This immense generosity is gradually changing my heart, and enabling me to become someone who begins to imagine that behind daily death, lies love and freedom.

James
Core Values? Music and Art are the windows to self expression and the gateway. Having them honored by the community is the way to strengthen them. Being a part of a community where we make that happen is one way.

Wilson
My core values are belief in God, love, openness, honesty, reverence, and kindness.

Tim
I start with the golden rule and mix that with love and forgiveness and a prayer for patience. It works except when I don't pay attention to or remember this.

Ross
My core principles are honesty, fairness, integrity and authenticity. I try to live them daily and fail often in many small ways. Being conscious of those ways helps me to make choices in my life that are more conscious. However, I have done things that some people would judge worthy of exclusion from claim to either of those principles for life. I've certainly learned what it means 'to be human' in the sense that sometimes we do things out of a survival necessity; things easily judged as (and that are) selfish and inconsiderate of others. I'm forgiving myself lately with the rationalization that such events are fairly rare and fleeting. I know too however that I can never eliminate them completely. I just don't want to hurt anybody when they occur.

Randy
Fairness matters.
I keep noticing how, men are caught under the "Glass cellar"–trapped in dirty dangerous and low status jobs like the barman and bouncer serving me drinks and dealing with drunks at

1am, the taxi driver taking me home at 2am, the cleaner cleaning my office at 3am, the garbage collector picking up my garbage at 4am and the road-worker and builder who are already at work when I wake at 6 am. Now that I am a parent I realize that there is something really wrong with the traditional idea that fathers work, while women stay at home and play with the kids. I want to stay at home and play with my daughter, and I want her mother to pull her weight and earn some money too. I am a part-time parent, and I love it. Being a part-time parent is like being a single parent, but I refuse to accept the victimhood that the label "single parent" implies. I enjoy work, but I love being a dad.

Todd

I believe in rigorous honesty and in this perhaps I look to the legend of Diogenes as a role model. Reportedly this ancient Greek carried a torch, demanding of others "show me an honest man!" I resist the temptation to see the world in simplistic, black and white, us versus them terms, and thus I believe whatever we are; gay, straight, black, white, left, right, rich, poor, we all have ideas and feelings that merit respect. I guess I would call that belief my core values for they influence what I will do and what I will not tolerate.

Bill

One of the core beliefs of Hinduism, Jainism and Buddhism is ahimsa. This means, "Do no harm." This very idea brings one to a place of gentleness and respect for others. I believe in the ever presence of the Great Soul within everything. I believe in the ever presence of the Divine around everything. I believe that everything is part of the sacred Whole. So charity and compassion for others flow from these ideas. To put it another way: "We're all God's children; we're all here to help each other."

Dan

What are your core principle and values and how do you live from them? I could write a book on this question. In summary form: Principles: Absolute honesty with myself and with others; Make my own decision; accept nothing I'm told; See people as they are, not as someone labels them; Protect everyone's opportunity to understand their selves and give them the space and respect to express their selves; and Make my self the absolute center of my decisions, perspectives, hopes, etc.

How do I live from them? Constantly remind myself of my principles. Constantly demand that they be the basis of what I do and say. These were really hard to do when these principles were new discoveries for me. It was always so easy to drift back into what the culture, friends, family, bosses wanted me to think and do. After 15 years of effort, it's much easier now, mostly routine. When I hit a bad spot in the road, though, that's always a sign that it's time to lecture myself again and get back on track.

George

The way I am living from my core principles is Independence in league with others and realizing truth without incarcerating others.

Clark

Martin: Your questions are wonderful and you have inspired me to answer as many as I can in one pass. Reading your questions answers or leads to answers of previous or the next question. Thank you.

I live by a code of honor. A code made by men for men.
Commitment before ego
Honor the truth
Respect Confidentiality
Keep your word
Be a multi-dimensional man
Be prepared
Defend Humanity
Always be faithful to the men
Defend the Code
Never Engage in Battle with weaker opponents
Fight only honorable battles
Earn and Honor Rank
Be humble
Embrace all men.
Be an Example to children.

Now this code lives in my personal life's higher purpose:

"I support men to be the most outrageous hero they choose to be."

I belong to a organization called MDI (Men's Divisions International) In this organization we accumulate wisdom from all time and teach each other how to be the man I have always wanted to be.

I have the honor of teaching "Basic Leadership Training". How to trust your gut and act on it. How to lead men. How to be a good follower. How to plan your meeting and your life. How to have real fun. How to make a difference. How to live a full-filled life......... Basically, any question you have I have access to men who have the answer.

When I have given my best to teaching men and have allowed complete communication. When we both have taken in on many levels my teaching and their teaching me I have a sense that, "it is a good day to die." That's how I know I am full-filled.

Kobe

1) Don't do anything that may affect someone else without first having their consent.

2) If I'm going to do something, I do it to the best of my ability, or make a choice not to, or I don't do it at all.

3) If I make a choice to not do something, I'm okay with the choice.

Eric

One of my core values is compassion. It is difficult to keep that present in my consciousness, so as a reminder, I have put on the face of my cell phone the words "best they can;" to remind myself that all of us are doing the best that we can in this life.

Joseph

I believe we are here to serve God and that he guides us to do his perfect will through our spirit. If we are in His perfect will, life will not be easy, but we will find happiness. Our life should be a shining light and witness to others of His love.

Mack

An interesting question. I never really addressed that issue. In regard to principals/values, Truth and honesty are the dominant ones. I believe they are so fundamental to me that I never feel in conflict with them. In fact, in the business world, I believe they have also placed me at an advantage with my competition. They have enabled me to focus objectively on problems and their solutions. I believe it has also made others -despite their own motivations- to want to work with me without reservation. At the same time I have never chosen to be judgmental of others with different principals/values. I am simply behaving in a way natural for me as they are.

Al
My core principles and values probably stem from my Christian upbringing and Midwestern work ethic. I have been trained to always bend over backwards to help and to always make the world a better place.

Charles
I know it is considered old-fashioned these days, and not very popular, but I try to live on one well-known basic Christian principle: To God, and my neighbor as myself.

A long time ago, when I was 25, I went to see an old Methodist Minister I loved. I loved him because, despite being 50 years older than me, he touched my heart with a direct gaze which was enlivened with a sparkle in his eye that told me that he loved and rejoiced in my youth, my promise, and my new marriage.

I loved him for his worldy-wiseness. Despite his Methodism he showed me that I was not going to hell if I enjoyed a glass of red wine with him and his wife over a meal. I loved him for his courage in being among the first to demonstrate on the streets against my country's involvement in the Viet Nam war. I loved his sense of the mystical and the transcendent, so obvious when he was conducting services and especially Holy Communion. But it was also in his intense love of people. Maybe it was his 30 years as a missionary in India which brought him to a deeper sense of the "beyond".

I went to see him to tell him that I no longer believed in God and that I was leaving the Church. He looked at me with that twinkling eye which was, at the same time, one full of love and understanding, and said, "Have you got any love letters?"

170

His question threw me. What on earth had that to do with my loss of faith in the existence of God?

Newly married, I responded, "Of course I have love letters!"

"They don't mean much do they?" he asked. "They are just paper so you should throw them out."

"Of course not! I couldn't do that!" I replied.

"So", he said, "they are more than just ink on paper?"

"Of course!" I said, wondering how my loss of faith in God had anything to do with my wife's love letters.

He paused. Then slowly, softly, he said, "My boy, when you are aware that there is something beyond the merely material and physical, you know God."

I sat stunned. I left the Church, nevertheless, for nearly 30 years, but never once forgot this understanding of God.

By pure coincidence I was attending a Requiem Mass for a friend, after 30 years of non-attendance at church. It was in an Anglican Church which adhered to the Anglo-catholic tradition, nothing like my own evangelical Methodist upbringing.

Somehow, for reasons I will never understand, the use of incense, colorful and beautiful vestments, banks of candles and serene music, bodily movements in genuflection, the sign of the cross, ringing of bells and soul moving music evoked once more that conversation 30 years earlier, with my old Methodist Minister friend, who taught me that the physical could point me to the "Other", the "Beyond", indeed to God.

It went further at the altar where, according to belief, the "Other" became present in the bread and the wine. It became tangible that the "Other" or "God" was there right in front of me inviting me to take him and make myself at one with him.

Now I understood what he meant all those years ago when he said that when I sensed that there was something beyond the mere physical, then I apprehended God. The physicality of the Requiem Mass in its movements, color, smells, sounds - all appeals to the physical, transported me to the beyond, to God, and I willingly, for the first time in 30 years to partake of the "Beyond" making itself known it me in tangible forms of bread and wine. God himself, the Beyond, was knowable, graspable, understandable.

Now I think I know that because I can finally love God in this way, then, and only then, I can love my neighbor as myself.

But that means that first I have to love God first, then myself, before I can truly love my neighbor as myself.

In others, I try to see God, the transcendent, the beyond, the One who makes himself known to me. It is because of this I am able to see him in the physicality of someone else no matter how unlovely. In the physical world which we are destroying, he calls me to see himself beyond the physical, which is why I must respond to environmental damage...

Curtis

My core principles and values are to attempt to live my personal, business and spiritual life as close to how my God would have me live it. I feel that all of us, including me, come short of this goal and foundational principle. But in my heart this is what I strive to do daily. Hopefully I am directing my children by my actions to lead a life of integrity and not compromise, winning not losing, positive outlook vs. negative outlook.

Kyle

My core principles are actually in my core—wherever that is. I've got some connection with it but it's not direct, and isn't necessarily in words. For, example my core values are in my behavior.

Sometimes I actually am aware of my behavior. But, most of the time I am oblivious.

I have another set of values stored in my head that I use for public display (and self deception). These are the values that sound good. They are mostly rational and safe and rooted in 'the American way'. I am often confused and frustrated that there is stress from contradiction in me most of the time. My confusion and stress leeks into my everyday life and seems to be the cause of my lacking relationships, my self-limitations, dishonesty, and even violence.

Abraham

I am not a religious person. But I do believe in doing the right thing. I have not always done that but who has. The bottom line is be the best you can be.

Andrew

Many of these questions have to do with "core values." What follows is my gut sense about core values, not anything I've thought about deeply or for very long. Core values seem to be innate. They truly do come from my core, my gut. They're not anything I consciously "decided" to adopt.

The single biggest core value I've held my whole life is honesty. I have long had a deeply held belief that the truth has a power, majesty and inherent value that are bigger than what's popular or expected. Perhaps bigger and more valuable than my own life. As a miserably unhappy kid, I had a devil of a time with the everyday question, "How are you doing?" until I decided to treat it as an unfortunately worded substitute for "hello." Throughout my life, pretense and puffery have offended me in a fundamental way. My own pretense (ironically, I haven't been completely immune to it) grieves me to the soul.

For me, honesty is so core, so basic, that I don't see my honesty as something I have, but rather as something I AM. That's not to say I never lie. But doing so seems to diminish me, such that I feel the loss whenever I do so.

Joel

Spirituality and love.

What keeps you awake to the beauty and passion of life?

Allen

My guess would be, getting a taste of it, being aware of passion and beauty in life. Like when I notice the different patterns of cream in my coffee. Seeing beauty in my partner, different ways beyond appearance. It did not start until I first dug out my own emotional pain. It is being around people that keeps me awake to it and looking for other ways people stay awake to it. Hearing men read poems and writing my own poems. The more you work with it the more you see.

Dave

What keeps me awake to the beauty and passion of life is respecting and being mindful of my own limitations as expressed in an acronym I learned in Al-Anon, H.A.L.T.: I need to beware of becoming too Hungry, Angry, Lonely and Tired. When I care for myself and attend to these conditions, beauty and passion arise of their own accord in my awareness.

Werner

Making an effort to notice nature and what God created that is beautiful in the world. I have to say when I was depressed it was like having a filter that blinded me to these thing so if I had not done the work to resolve the depression I would not be able to see the beauty of life. This included anti-depressants.

Steven

I don't know so many things. I don't know what a soul is. I don't know what happens when we die. I don't know if there is a supreme being or energy of some kind that has a plan for me or for anyone. Maybe we are just animals on a planet that is destined to be burned up by the sun in five billion years. I don't know. But I do know that I feel more full when I write, or draw, or communicate honestly with someone, or remind myself to stay present and to operate out of love (as I believe it to be). I know it keeps me more awake to the beauty and passion for life than when I don't do these things. Is that evidence of a higher power? Beats me.

Tim

For me, passion comes from the beauty of an honest emotion, from the love of the gifts of nature, from artistic expression that pierces mind and heart, from the delight derived from a life fully felt.

Jeff

Your Mission and Terms Seeking truth, obeying God, and loving our fellows keeps us awake to everything beauty and ugliness, joy and sorrow, health and sickness, pain and healing. In short, we are awake for life. We are aware of our experiences. We get to experience Christ. Reading the Word of God balanced by sharing with others is the best way for me to stay in touch with reality.

Frank

What keeps me awake to the beauty and passion of life is the experience of loss. Sept. 11th, the death of a grandparent, news of the death of a child all remind me how special my life is and that I need to be thankful for it.

Another thing that keeps me awake to the beauty and passion of life is the vastness and greatness of nature. Gazing at the Rocky Mountains, experiencing a 20 knot wind on a beam reach in my sailboat, or feeling the rush of class IV whitewater all make me realize how small and insignificant I am, and that I should be more aware of taking advantage of every day of my life.

Finally, meeting a person who has sacrificed much to make a difference in others lives. Whether it is the parent of a disabled child, a person who has dedicated their lives to charity, or a person who has taken on a cause and is making an impact one person at a time, makes me realize that a successful life is a state of mind.

Henry

Feeling that what we are doing is worthwhile. Feeling that it has God's stamp of approval and will benefit mankind

Bob

If I had an answer to that question about my purpose, I would not be on anti-depressants. That being said, religion helps me finding a sense to my life, but I don't use it very well. I think maybe being in a men's group that explored this could help.

Roy

What keeps me awake to the beauty and passion involve living my mission and staying away from addictions like food. Keeping up my mediation, exercise, and other regular rituals that feed my life.

Ross

Art, music, good people, stories, literature, things judged larger than life, the 2004 World Series, sex, learning, realization, humor, high definition, change, the diversity of the internet, that so many choices are available to everyone, that sometimes it really isn't only business; it's passion. All not necessarily in that order.

Stan

I meditate, practice Hatha Yoga and exercise every morning and evening. I walk on nature trails during lunch time and on weekend mornings. I climb 13 flights of office stairs, 2-4 times a day. I record my feelings and the trigger thoughts in a journal.

Most of all I attempt to be present every moment. When my mind wanders, as it inevitably does, I gently come back to the task at hand or my breathing. I don't think experience or practice meditating makes one "better" at this. I found myself so distracted that I questioned if I had ADHD. I didn't.

Dan

Pay attention to beauty and passion. How can you awake to these if you're paying attention to your job, your status, your money, and your power? It's a minute-by-minute choice about what we listen to and pay attention to.

Anthony

1st question - Each moment that occurs to me, when I believe I have everything organized, planned, thought of and completed (my imaginary controlled environment) and a surprise appears! I see immediately my humanness reflected in the mirror and I have to sigh and laugh! At this time of my life (27yrs), I am growing at such a rate and seeing things new again, I am on a daily basis, invigorated by the change and challenge of living in a time right now. The people I meet, in particular, other men – guys younger than me, making a choice to slow-down and take a look at themselves and their behaviors!

Nature also helps me to maintain my openness, appreciate my life and all the experiences I'm grateful to enjoy. At 27yrs old in Australia, I live in a growing city, in a highly success-driven family, work and as a result, I find it easy to get caught-up in "life". What keeps me in touch is my commitment to remain true to myself and gradually bring activities into my life that slow me down, rather than speed me up. To me, the human soul encapsulates the unique gifts I bring in this life for the benefit of everyone I come in contact with. It is another part of me, separate to my personality, overlaid upon my skills, gifts and failings. My soul is my history, my intelligence, my curiosity, my wounds, my wisdom, and my belonging! I am thankful to be human.

When I reflect back on my first 20 odd years, I can see where at times, I consciously sought distraction, primarily distraction from sitting still. I see now, that each time I sit still, I'm inviting connection with my soul. Communicating with my own soul has been a sort of enigma to me. About four years ago, I came in contact with an old crone of a woman, who is a guide/teacher, who is helping me to develop my skills as a heart worker. As part of this development, I envision communicating with my own soul or understanding whether I am already or not, will come in time! (Albeit, patience too, comes in time!) I honor this part of me by continuing to unearth new parts of me by: maintaining contact and practice with my teachers and mentors, placing myself in places where I can and often am forced to experience. When it comes to developing myself and getting to the true heart of my being as a person foremost and secondly, as a man, I am highly committed. I can see where I have learned my tenaciousness (from my mother), but the intensity and commitment to which I apply myself to this path, may actually be what I'm required to learn about myself. Progression, progression…. I take no backward steps!

The above is my adventure. I seek to learn about myself. The more I learn about my functionalities and dysfunctions, strengths and weaknesses, the better I can be in this life and the clearer I am to do the work that I'm drawn to, currently Men's Work. I am consciously working towards the best I can be. The best I can be as a man in this world, is to change the world around me – in my relationships, personal & intimate, as a son, brother, future father, future husband (soon!) and future leader!

Two things keep me on the path - my conscience or inner knowing (my soul/higher connection to source) and the constant challenges I face from my closest friends, my inner circle; my teachers, brothers in my various men's groups and the lessons that pop-up everywhere around me. Commitment to my mission and inner values is a simplification of my life and what is important.

Bill

I like to walk or hike in natural settings as often as I can. It opens me up to the mystery of life all around us. Reading some

177

poetry or writing helps. It is important to keep ones heart open to see the miracles all around us. In fact I keep a log of miracles and blessings in my life. Then when I forget I can look over it to be reminded of them.

Von

I believe that finding one's personal mission is a life-long quest. Making conscious contact with God, and doing so on a regular basis via meditation, prayer, and/or participating in a faith community is key to achieving alignment with God's purposes for us, and understanding of that mission.

Arthur

My connection with the earth and contributing to her and the work I do with boys and men, is by far and away the most passionate and purposeful work I have ever done. I run my own business to put the food on the table etc, but I long for the day when this work pays enough to be a 'real' job!!!

I lost my way some years before I found men work and found much meaning and solace in a timber plantation that we began that is mix-species, will be selectively harvested, and is native trees from the area that will always be there yet still provide for some of our needs. My kids have planted trees there and I take pleasure in watching both grow well. My dream scenario is that one or more of my children will work with this timber in some fashion – either building themselves a house or working furniture.

'People and Planet' is a phrase I use and if you knew me ten years ago …. Well you'd understand the significance of this. I absolutely have felt lighter and freer for this undertaking.

My soul is the voice that answers me, usually from my belly, with honesty – too honest at times and there are certainly times when I don't want to hear what is there, but I get the need for discomfort and confronting my fears. I am staggered at how far I have come in hearing and following my 'feelings', which I reckon, are the souls language. Whenever things aren't going well for me it always comes back to how disconnected I have become from my feelings/gut instinct/soul.

George
What keeps me awake to the beauty and passion of life. Hope and Rebellion, often synonymous.

Fredrick
For me, it's creativity and meaningful work. This can be my aspects of my job or a side hobby.

Laurence:
Simply taking the time to stop and appreciate it. Getting out of our own heads, listening to and appreciating others.

Andy
My mission is: I create an awakened joyful planet by teaching joy through boundless creative expression. So, my mission is about keeping myself and all others awake to the beauty and passion of life. I do this through my creative writing mostly poetry. However, with the demands of work, family and so forth, I do not devote the time I would like to truly living my mission through my writing. I have a children's book ready to go should I finish it and a book of poems on the process of dealing with loved ones dying also awaiting completion. The conclusion that I have come to is that I do live my mission, maybe not to the capacity I envision, but through my daily interactions with others through trying to live a joyful passionate life bubbling over with my audacious authenticity. Paul Goldman, Joyful Spotted Owl disguised as an erudite Research Counselor at a University Hospital Smoking Cessation Research Program. Kansas City MKP

Carl
As a man I tend to follow the road of income and let my true passion in what God as gifted me the true gift I have and that is know through a passion to do something greater.

Horace
What keeps me awake to the passion and beauty of life is spirituality, and the EXPRESSION of that spirituality. It wasn't always that way. The experience that turned the tide was when I was in charge of the spirituality for the New York Men's Division.

I found that men are naturally spiritual. I became a "space" for them to fill in, and bounce off. I had been alienated from my own particular tradition, and found many men felt the same way. I came to see my own experience better by looking through their eyes.

I came to see men with spiritual commitments had a better chance, if nothing else, of coping with life's problems. They were better grounded. I found the men who took no comfort in anything above and beyond their own egos were far more troubled, and in the end inconsolable. This became painstakingly clear as time went by.

For some, not all, it was a matter of commitment. They had to let go of their doubt and intellectual considerations, and commit themselves to a tradition. It was a lot like the leap of faith they took in taking the weekend.

It didn't matter what tradition—only that the commitment was genuine and came from WITHIN the man. It couldn't be about looking good. Nobody could talk anybody into it.

I did a lot of work using the traditions of the American Indian, which I thought was fitting given their role in creating our culture, and their universality. It gave me a respect for that tradition that fills me with awe to this day—and I only hope some of the other men I knew at that time took away something similar. In my own case, I wound up leaving the faith of my ancestors, and formally converting to Zen Buddhism. I was ordained a lay monk five years ago after roughly five years of study with a Zen master. It gives me an entirely new frame of reference, and hope, when alone I often have none.

One more essential step I learned: a faith is not an intellectual idea. It can be, but that isn't where the power lies. It has to be practiced; rituals need to be performed. It necessarily involves one in the advantages and disadvantages of the collective, but that is what being human is about.

I find that by practicing faith I don't need to be so conscious of values—in the traditional sense. I don't have to "will" them, or flout them. They just happen. I am highly suspicious of moralists, and more than that of the hypocrites who masquerade as religious. This has been a spiritual revelation.

I also think art and the creation of community are an expression of spirituality. Art in particular has been sorely maligned by our

180

society as simply another source of riches and fame. It's sad, but the vast majority of people I've met in my lifetime are completely ignorant of this.

If they buy art, for instance, the only reason they do so is as an investment, and if they go to a movie, or (god forbid) a play—they only do that as escape, like television, they have no place in their lives for spiritual growth. THEY DON'T EVEN KNOW WHAT IT IS! They are so on the treadmill the meaning and value of life escapes them. They never enter the inquiry—or if they do they let some dogma, scripture, or person answer the ultimate questions for them.

The kind of fear mongering and suffering that passes for religion in this country and elsewhere holds no promise for me, but I am also aware that without my faith and PRACTICE I am vulnerable, and no less susceptible than the millions of people who today confuse morality and politics with spirituality. I am speaking here regardless of the tradition. I don't think "God" wants anybody to die in his or her name, and those who use their faith as a way to win votes are a step backward in the evolution of human consciousness.

What gets you touch with your dreams, possibilities, core values and principles?

Werner
What gets me in touch with my dreams, possibilities, core values and principles is being around other people who seem to love their lives. Also I hear myself in the compassionate listening of good people. I put myself in challenging situations that bring up these issues or look for opportunities in life when challenges occur to find this. Until I cleared out a lot of un-resolved past stuff I was unable to access and hear my dreams and even possibilities. Also it helps to minimize my exposure to news, which seems is hell bent on reminding me of all that is bad in life.

Wilson
For me it is the presence of the Holy Spirit in my body and in my mind. God's Word, the Bible. Taking the time to truly connect to God each day. Which I don't always do.

Warren

I think continually learning and not being static is what gives us a passion for life, or maybe the passion makes us want to continue to learn. Maybe it's circular–travel, seeing and hearing other points of view, frank discussion about real issues are important to this process. Learning new careers, new skills, gives us new avenues to explore, new people to meet, new domains to conquer. Maybe learning helps you overcome fears about people, about your own skills, and about what you can contribute to the world.

I struggle with getting in touch with values and principles. I feel like most of these are instilled growing up, influenced by society and my family. I think it's critical that each boy/man eventually realizes that he's got to think for himself. He is got to make his own philosophy from what he's learned and from what he sees and experienced in the world. Most importantly, all persons need to know that their view on any particular subject can change and it's OK. I think that goes to wisdom, knowing what you know and why and knowing what you don't.

Open-mindedness is so important to learning how to learn. I need to be confident enough in my own skin to be able to re-examine issues that arise. Was my earlier conception of an issue correct? If so, it should stand some scrutiny by myself, and my (hopefully) ever-changing world perception. This continual process sometimes makes me feel like I flip-flop a lot on issues. I sometimes feel like I have few real convictions. But when I imagine having convictions for everything, I get a little freaked out since I know there is so much that I don't know and don't want to be brainwashed.

Dave

Reminders of my core values and principles occur when I spend time with fun, nurturing friends and read inspiring books and magazine articles. Nothing distracts me more from them than television, which I only watch while using aerobic training equipment at the gym–without volume, simply reading the super-titles. Fifteen or 20 minutes of exposure is more than enough to be apprised of what's what in the "tick-tock" world to which the mass media would have me turn over my life.

Ross
For me it can be different things at different times. Riding my motorbike with mates along windy roads, looking forward to a date with my lovely lady, and watching my dogs play with each other or just staring into a fire while camping on the beach.

Tom
Awareness of the present moment. Recently it comes upon me when I'm in the presence of my children, or when I'm listening to a beautiful piece of classical music, or when I smell my wife's freshly baked bread in the mornings.

Kobe
Looking, watching and enjoying life. It is the intention of being open to possibilities. You have to take time for it, it does not just happen.

Kyle
Death. The awareness of my mortality. That this is the only life I know, this is it! If I don't live it fully I have no certainty that I get another chance. Someone said you will not be fully alive until you come to grips that at some undetermined time you will be dead, grab every day!

Abraham
I have a hobby that keeps me alive. I believe I am addicted to Nitrogen (SCUBA) Term. My Daughter is also a driving force I struggle with keeping that relationship going.

Joseph
Relationship with God and others. I mean real relationship with them. Looking into someone's eyes and seeing them and letting them see you.

Curtis
It's achieved by constantly attempting to become more and be a productive, contributing member of society. This doesn't mean you just champion social causes but for me it means that you don't totally dilute your creative, productive side and cave in to worldly pressures. Seeing the beauty and passion in small things that my

children say and do and small pleasures means that I don't have to seek a higher high than that.

Tyrone

SIMPLE, MONEY!!! Making money! Seriously I just don't know. I guess if I was truly honest to myself, to avoid the discomfort of not knowing I focus on making money

Mack

For me it is observing and interacting with beautiful people. One of these is my son. He reverberates with the physical beauty, love of people and life around him. I believe his principals/values are even stronger than mine and he is non -judgmental. Strangely he serves as my standard rather than I would presume to be his. Whether it is discussion of a technical or personal issue I always I feel I have gained the insight from him rather than being the major contributor.

Al

Knowing myself and accepting and embracing all the quirks that I have. Accepting what I am and what I am not.

Kyle

Complete self-exposure. Listening to others and self. Finding and dealing with fear.

Joseph

I take personal time to meditate on these. I go to a church where we spend much of the time teaching directly from the Bible. Association with business people who stretch me. Getting out in nature but I don't do that enough.

Mack

For me I believe it is principally observation of the kindness, cruelty, and activities around me. I believe I am not as successful in conceiving and getting in touch with this without the physical example. Through this observation I can reinforce and perhaps modify possibilities and "core" values.

184

Kobe

I don't know about 'us'. What gets ME in touch with MY dreams, possibilities, core values and principles are my children and my wife when I am listening for it and not just reacting to something.

Curtis

I think it takes work because what you need to do to exist and achieve in this world can really pull you in a million different directions. I feel you need to discipline yourself to dream and keep highest hopes alive so they are not compromised by the negative of the world. Reading and associating with positive minds and people who encourage you and don't think dreams are phony at any level or age is the foundation to getting in touch and taking action.

Joel

Decision making, as I move into things. Choosing what I cannot change and working to change what I can change. Making a decision then not second guessing it, then make another decision, and another, choosing, choosing life! It is an ongoing process.

Al

Taking the first step! Do something to intentionally explore your core issues and write them down, explore what you are or were passionate about and re-experience it, do something about looking for what is possible in a difficult situation and act on it. When I do this the rest just falls into place.

Roy

I find my purpose when I slow down and notice life, when some tragedy wakes me up, when I am out hiking and just notice how the light hits the trees, and when I capture a moment on paper. I don't hear it when I am just driven or just accomplishing something for the purpose of being busy. I heard once a man say when you meet God and are asked, "What did you do with the gift of life that I gave you?" most people will only be able to say, "I kept busy", then in the presence of God realize what a wasted life they had. No one on their death bed regrets making a few more dollars they regret not spending a little more time with loved ones, not taking the time to smell the roses more, not giving up their petty anger toward their brother so they could be related again, or taking the time to explore questions like the ones in this book, then doing something different out of the insights that they gain. On my death bed I want to look back at my life and be touched by the life I lived not be filled with regrets. I work to remember this and often forget it.

Abraham

I like talking with other people and understanding we all go through the same things in life. Hearing myself in others.

What do you 'lose yourself' in something that leaves you feeling fulfilled when you are done?

Chad

I can lose myself, get totally absorbed, get "in the zone" with almost ANYTHING. I especially love working with my hands, working or playing outdoors, building or repairing something. Writing, too, sometimes totally captures me.

I feel incredibly fortunate in this respect. Whether it is a result of hyper focusing because of my ADHD, or because since childhood I have been something of a loner and have always entertained myself, or because I am insatiably curious and hungry to learn, or because of something in my soul—I don't know. All I know is that I live a large part of my life fully engaged and in the flow.

It's the experience of suddenly looking up from something, and trying to move my body, and groaning and laughing in pain because I have been in the same position for who knows how long, and standing, stretching, and realizing I am starving for something to eat, and that I've needed to take a piss for three hours and didn't notice until now, and that I have no idea what time it is, or how many times the phone rang. All I know in that moment of realization, of coming back into the "here and now" is that I am happy and have been happily at one with my work or play for an endless, infinite instant.

Abraham
Teaching scuba is the biggest thrill. I could live underwater, just suspended.

Joseph
My business. I read extensively and play chess. Individual time with wife and kids and group time.

Mack
I have a constant drive to have accomplished something-which can be a blessing and a curse. I lose myself in driving forth to accomplishing even little tasks whose completion I find very satisfying. The curse is that makes simple relaxation and rest frustrating. My struggle is to convince myself that simple pleasures and rest are also rewarding and fulfilling.

Curtis
I feel that athletics and creative writing does this for me.

Al
I create. I am blessed with a career that allows me to dig deep into my soul and connect with the essence of what I am all about. Eventually, I want to paint.

Kyle
Running in the forest, being in the forest, being with the forest, being the forest.
Telling stories, sex, composing music, really helping another

Roy
Engaging conversations that seem to make a difference for me and the other person. Creating something new in my work, or in art. Being at the edge or the frontier of something. I could include exercising and pushing myself a little more. Walking in nature when I take the time to notice nature instead of talking on the cell phone, or distract myself by worrying over things that I have already worried over enough. Helping people gain access to their dreams and possibilities. Meditating, just sitting still and witnessing my own existence for ten minutes. Noticing my thoughts bubble

up, noticing what distracts me and gently bring my attention back to my breath in mediation.

Frank

I am able to lose myself in a hard run or a hard bike ride. Time sometimes seems to stand still and I am able to go above and beyond my preconceived limits. At the end of these types of workouts I achieve a very peaceful relaxed feeling that lasts for the rest of the day.

Tyrone

AGAIN, making money!!! I do enjoy making money but also enjoy getting acknowledgement from others. I really have not thought about this much and maybe I should.

Tom

Love, in any form ... being kind, rather than being right.

Kobe

Video games, playing the bass, raking leaves

Eron

Teaching, helping someone truly in need.

Joel

Making love, when it is love.

Werner

When I work in my garden is the only time when my 'driven feeling' goes away.

What gets you in touch with your dreams, possibilities, core values and principles? What is the human soul?

Bill

The soul dwelling in each of us is the Divine with-in. The Self with-in the self.

Every human is endowed with divinity; we are all children of the Great Soul.

Wilson

For me, it is reading God's Word, the Bible, daily and associating with people who do the same.

Henry

The most effective way of getting in touch with myself is to submerge myself in a natural environment; whether it is camping out, on a nature trail or walking on the shore of the beach.

Allen

We stay in touch by seeing out dreams, possibilities, core values and principles.

Tim

What gets me in touch with my dreams is; adversity and success, joy and sorrow, and working on creating a clear vision for my life.

Barry

In my case, having to guide and lead others, having to father my children. Also, sharing my writing with the world.

Dan

I can talk at great length about the 7-10 year process I used to find my core values and principles and learned how to trust them and express them. I used everything I could find from books to tarot to hours of journaling. The key for me was to use the techniques and truths of my creative life in every other part of my life.

Roy

Resolving issues in our lives, simplifying, and really committing to things that can change us in a good way.

What is the human soul? What happens when you ignore your soul?

Wilson

To me it is the combination of body, conscious mind, and will. The spirit is separate.

Don

I would like to comment on the human soul. I define the human soul as the spiritual being that makes us who we are and connects us to world around me. When I ignore my soul, I believe I cheat the world by not sharing my unique gift. Communication occurs through meditation and any other methods that get us to our 'subconscious'. I'm on the correct path and recognizing that I have a long journey keeps me focused and open to make changes. My guiding principle is 'harmony' and to stay true to this principle I have to acknowledge that 'everyone' counts, even those who are considered bad, maybe even evil by some. This means that no matter whom I run into or what situation I'm confronted with, the only thing that matters is how I deal with it, i.e. my behavior. Constant self-examination is what keeps me conscious. Not being afraid to review the past day and say, 'I failed'. This type of acknowledgement allows me to make changes along the way. I feel one form of freedom is to know how to live every moment and this type of freedom will come as a result of staying true to our mission

George
That which is left (and is there) after all empiricism is extracted.

Tim
For me it is the essence of who I am. It's knowing that I am alive, aware, a human being and a man.

Dan
Who I really am. The self that is core of my being, the unalterable truth about myself. The "beingness" that is me (as opposed to the "doingness" that most people recognize and demand).

Ross
It is the thing that differentiates humans as a race, as individuals, as beings. The soul is where there are no lies. The soul is where only the truth is seen. The soul is where real connection to others must originate and reside.

Roy

It is something I hear in the 'shadows'; being authentic in the company of other men lets me hear it; when I am on my own life path I hear it; when I am giving my natural gifts fully I hear it. It is something that seems to get louder the more I am in my body and living honestly. I think it is the real me that I am slowly learning to know. I think some people never hear their soul for they have not listened for it.

Allen

What you don't want to sell the devil or get on the long black train. It's something you can loose if you don't take care of it but I have a hard time defining it. I think it is our spiritual essence. It is what remains when our physical body is gone.

If you ignore your soul, you die inside and feel that way. You feel totally out of touch with other people and maybe all creation. It's being alive in that you heart is pumping but by all other means being dead. These look like good questions to ask in the company of men.

Fred

I think the human soul is as valuable as the human heart. Because the heart is like our life support system alongside our lungs, the human soul is like a compliment to ourselves.

When I ignore my soul, I feel miserable. I feel that there was something that I have forgotten to do or say. Even though I never really know or comprehend what it can be, I am pretty sure that it could have been something that was vital to do or important. I then struggle to figure out what it could be and wondering if we'll get any where in doing so.

Ross

When I ignore my soul I get caught up in the busyness of life and don't take the time to connect with myself, my inner boy, my friends or family. I stop living and just exist. You can then live only lies. Ironically, this is a choice made by many people, not just men. Sometimes it's a passive choice. Sometimes it's not.

Bill

I am, at any given moment, either consciously moving toward spiritual growth or away from it. One is either paying attention or not. If we listen to whisperings of the soul and its wisdom we are guided, if not unwanted events often occur. Some people never get it.

Even if life seems to be going well for some who ignore the soul, an empty unfulfilled feeling is manifest. I believe that we all have an emptiness in our soul, which can only be filled by a spiritual relationship with the Great Soul.

Roy

When I ignore my soul my life feels like the back of head was grabbed by a powerful hand and my face being ground into the dirt.

Wilson

I have experienced this; it feels as if there are only dry leaves inside you that get crunched every time you move.

Dan

I get snappy and unhappy. I feel deserted and valueless; I feel like I'm playing roles designed for someone else that benefits everyone else but me. I've learned in the last ten years that, whenever I feel things start to fall apart, the cause is always that I've drifted away from who I really am and started building purposes and goals out of what "others" say.

George

What happens when you ignore your soul, you implode or explode.

Fredrick

I get depressed and then somebody comes along and tells me that you have a biochemical imbalance in your brain. Then I get "OK," and then think that's all there is.

Joseph

I believe that a man is made up of mind, body and spirit, with the mind being your soul. If you do not feed this, you will tend to become stale and negative. I feed this through church, books and association in business.

Kobe

I believe my core values and principles are my human soul, and when I ignore that, I have no direction

Mack

This is very difficult for me. The term mind, body, and soul are commonly used. Which may be interpreted, as soul is all that is beyond mind and body. I frankly will look forward to other responses to help me here. I believe this is an understanding that could be very helpful to me.

Joel

The inner voice. Tragedy, and if I am lucky, tragic-comedy.

Randy

The human soul, in my opinion, is the eternal core of who we really are. It is the internal source behind why we seek beauty and connection with others. It is the energy that mandates that we feel and have compassion. It is the essence that tugs on our hearts to give again and again. It is what propels a mother to lay down her life for her child. It is what causes a man to work a lifetime for the benefit of the world. It is the passion that sends an athlete soaring through the air. It is the tears that fill a man's eyes when he bows a knee to propose. It is the air that fills a parent's lungs when their young child looks into their eyes. It is what holds up a man when he teaches his son that life is beautiful, despite his struggles at work. It is what speaks, through wisdom, to let go and allow change. It is the sound that reverberates from a man's body when he stands upon a mountain and screams, "I am Free". It is the thing that we all so desperately seek—this thing, is Love. And when it is ignored, every facet and every unique cell of life begins to undermine itself until Love itself is no longer distinguishable, thereby making Love no longer a threat.

Al

A human soul is the essence of a human being. It is impossible to ignore ones soul without tragedy of one form or another. Sometimes, its just depression, sometimes, it leads to murder. I believe that a person naturally finds essence though sometimes after a life of torment.

Curtis

You are a spirit. You have a soul and you live in a body. To ignore your soul upsets this balance and hierarchy.

Abraham

This one is so far out I need to think about this for a few days.

How do you hear, honor, and communicate with your own soul, with your own self?

Bill

Our very reason for being is communion with the Divine. When I pray or meditate or reach out to another human being I am communing with the Divine. The Great Soul speaks to me through my soul. I believe any act of sincerity or kindness is an act of worship or prayer. Viewing a beautiful work of art or some natural beauty or speaking kindly to a beggar on the street can be communion to me. It is important to keep my soul open for these sacred visitations and attending messages. I honor my soul and its communications by listening when a message is received and making a note of it then possibly meditating on it or praying about the message and acting on it.

Wilson

I communicate with my soul, through constant prayer as communication with God.

Samuel

I have some energy around this question. I have become extremely attuned to the way that some men choose to speak to themselves. I watch as men talk down to themselves, degrade and demoralize themselves. I talk to myself as I would to someone I

194

love. I hear men cuss themselves for something that they did but they would never talk to someone they love the same way. Talk to yourself and treat yourself the same way you would someone you love.

George
Respecting the religious/spiritual need of mankind. Not forcing my own view on them but living a life of example.

Tim
I trust my ability to listen, to still the emotional noise that serves as its shield.

Barry
One of the ways is when I am hurt or angry. When this happens I consciously stop and try to feel what is going on in my body. I try to understand what I am feeling in my heart. Why have I been triggered? What is it that has triggered me and what part of me has been triggered? Another way is when I sit alone in a park or by a creek and just be.

Fredrick
I need a lot of solitude to do that properly. It works best for me alone in nature.

Dan
I journal. I talk to myself. I do my writing and artwork. These last two are where I feel most closely in touch with my soul. It's the place and method that my soul talks most clearly to me. Even sitting down and pounding through a Scarlatti sonata can ground me like nothing else; I feel that my authentic self is really talking for those few minutes.

Ross
How? Self-talk I guess. Listening. My mind has its own speed, its own language. I own it of course but sometimes it seems almost distinct and disconnected from me. I've always thought that this phenomena was a result of stunted education and maturity. I never got to finish college. I never got to make the passage from teen years to higher education and then to adulthood

with peers. Once I got married at 18, I was essentially outcast from peers. I was too young (and looked it) for adults and too removed for age peers. Big mistake.

Roy

I get out in nature, just a local walk in the woods but I have to pay attention and enjoy nature for it to work. It is like I listen to nature as though it could talk to me. It sounds funny but it gives me a real experience of connecting to my soul. Also, listen to what I say when what I say moves and touches others—that is what I call sneaking up on my soul.

Kyle

Answering these questions. Running in the forest. Gardening, Meditating, Romancing with my wife. But, I know I don't take enough time for myself for this. I get lost doing the mechanical duties of life like working, eating, drinking, and TV.

Kobe

A beer, a cigar and a nice, quiet cool day alone.

Joel

Listen to the inner voice, not the inner critic.

Tom

I pray frequently, meditate infrequently, and go for one hour walks four or five times per week.

Mack

I tend to constantly mull over and examine issues to better understand them and if necessary take action. I particularly try to examine any bias I might introduce from an objective examination.

Chad

As much as the idea of the inner child has been misapplied, misunderstood and ridiculed, the younger parts of me haven't gone anywhere. They are all still quite alive and present, and more to the point, much more in touch with the reality of and needs of my soul than the 40-something man. And in a sense, they are the older parts of me, because 7-year-old Chad now has 40 years of experience of being seven. He is much closer to 1-year-old Chad and 15-year-old Chad than I am, and has access to almost half a century of material and life through the eyes of a very wise child. Yet my younger selves can only show me what my soul hungers for when I'm willing to play, to wonder, to take risks, to look silly or foolish.

For instance, over the last two months I've probably spent $100 on magnets. Most are neodymium magnets, small but very strong, of various sizes and shapes. Some are magnetic toys and building kits.

I have no need for these. I have no "serious application" in mind. And most reasonable people looking at my finances right now would say I can't afford such a frivolous, pointless and childish expense.

But what I know from experience is that I can't afford NOT to have them. Playing with them, experimenting with them brings out the kid in me and somehow feeds my soul. I don't know why or how. I just know it is providing something that I need, and that somehow the experience of the magnets will inform what I do as an adult man in the world. I may never know how and frankly don't need to. In the meantime they're fun to play with.

Curtis
I think it has to do with what you choose to let in your five senses, what you retain and who you associate with that keeps you balanced in this area.

How are you doing as the guardian of your soul and what would you be willing to change?

Wilson
I could do better especially at keeping my body a clean residence for my soul.

Dan
I've worked hard since the late 80s to find my soul and learn to live with it and by it. I thinking I'm doing a really good job with my soul right now ... not always consistently and as totally as I could

be—but millennia ahead of where I was in the early 80s and where most men seem to be.

Fredrick
Pretty good, I think. I'd be willing to entertain the way I define my duties and responsibilities. Sometimes I think I sacrifice too much for them—other times, not enough.

Tim
I treat myself with kindness and forgiveness and regard myself as being human. Change follows awareness, knowledge, and growth. I do not resist those forces.

Ross
I could do better. I like to think I am 'willing' to change anything. Execution of that will is another story. As much as I have actually had consciousness of many of my 'issues' I struggle to actually change. Always another obstacle. Always a reason to conform again. Again, I'm conscious of and working on this.

Roy
This is such a critical question that I had to think a lot about. You see if I am the guardian of my soul there is no room for my ego, for my inadequacies, for being the 'little me', just me tending the gift that God gave me.

Joseph
Spend more time reading and on personal meditation and prayer.

Kobe
I'm doing well—nothing unless/until my ignorance may call for a change.

Joel
I am too careful of it, I am afraid of it being hurt. I need to let go of the safety switch and live more fully.

Abraham

During my marriage I ignored my own needs for my daughter to please my wife. I found that I need to be true to myself to make a relationship work. It is nice to know after years of being told you are a loser I found that other women do want to be with and hang out with me. I like it!

Curtis

I think I am doing okay. I would be willing to change everything and anything if I felt it would be God's will for me. I hope that I follow that call.

Mack

I just don't know what to say; I really have not thought about this much and maybe I aught to.

Have you taken the time to embrace an adventure for your life that is challenging and meaningful for you?

John

In recent years I have done things I never thought I could do. Assisting in co-authoring an article was something I took great pride in knowing that I could help other men in some way. Also looking out for my strengths and attempting to acknowledge them was a bit scary, but I have found it can be a very exciting experience as well. It gives me the confidence in attempting other challenges I might face at a future date.

Bill

Yes! I took three weeks in February and went to Jamaica. My main purpose was to teach a basketball clinic for young boys. Because of the spirit which attended me, people stepped forward to make my visit very comfortable and enjoyable. I was able to visit some wonderful places, which I would have never found on my own.

Ross

No. I need to think about this concept. I've never really thought about it like that before.

Fredrick

Not often enough, but yes. I'm doing pretty well in that department this year – kind of a New Years' Resolution for me.

Wilson

Yes, my complete faith that quitting my profession will bring me even greater fulfillment and satisfaction and make a difference in other's lives. Finally going for what I really want to do

George

I use vacations creatively and meaningfully. I go to places that really feed my soul in stead of just entertaining me.

Todd

I grew up alienated from sports and physical adventure, and thus out-of-touch with a dimension of my own masculinity. In my late twenties I attended a Sierra Club meeting that sparked in interest in the great outdoors, and afterwards I made hiking mountains a regular part of my life. Then a few years after that, I became friends with a fellow of very modest means but who managed to make long-distance bike touring a regular part of his life. When I met him he had already done two trips across the United States and one down the west coast. I joined him for one trip across Washington State, and then took it upon myself to bicycle across New Zealand. For someone like me, a formerly overweight and sedentary child who used to live for television, investing time in pushing my physical limits has become a sine qua non of my existence.

Henry

Initiating and facilitating a personal development program for men, that is my next challenge.

Dan

Every new book and every new piece of artwork is a new adventure in my life. I've resettled myself several times and changed jobs and careers several times, most notably when my second wife and I gave up our Boston jobs and life and moved to rural Vermont to become craftspeople. Now, I'm in another big adventure — another job change and finding a new personal relationship.

Allen

For me it is the personal growth of recovery and to create new adventures beyond that—and my dream to travel around the world.

Joseph

I consider my business to be this.

Ike

I spent one summer taking on all sorts of challenges and crossing things off my list of "one day I want to do that." I ran two marathons. I learned to scuba dive. I took up rock climbing and climbed to the top of Devil's Tower in Wyoming. I went sky-diving. I learned to sail and did some ocean sailing.

In the end it gave me a confidence that I can do anything I want to do, I just have to decide to do it. Now that I am married and have a child, I look back and am very glad I did some of those things, as I would never do them now.

I have long term plans to embrace adventure. I have to do an Ironman triathlon sometime in the next 10 years, and sail across the Atlantic. Both of those will happen.

Kobe

Yes. Children, marriage, music, sharing myself with others

Joel

I have tried many, but have not fully embraced anyone.

Mack

I have not and I need to do this. My adventure was the most challenging and rewarding job of my life. I stepped forward from a rewarding professional- I thought challenging but conventional job- into one into a new world. It was a world of complex high cutting edge technology, mixture of science and human factors, high classification, combat, and military/civilian intense collaboration. Using science and technology in direct combat is the adventure of my life I need to and will take the time to embrace.

Randy

I have enough drama in my life so I don't seek adventures in the sense of excitement. My stimulation comes from being more and more awake in life, and by creating my thinking and my environment to be intelligent, pleasurable, and successful—this is my adventure.

Curtis

I feel I have put this off in my writing. I look forward to earning the right to run with this adventure. I have had this adventure in athletics, business and other areas but I keep striving.

Abraham

I think for the first time I will go for what makes me happy and not try to please others. Pleasing others is still part of my upbringing but I working toward what makes me happy.

What gets and keeps us conscious, in touch with, or present to our core values and principles?

Bill

My wife and I practice daily devotionals. I read and study sacred writings from many of the world's great faiths. I meditate. I pray. I practice gratitude. (Just to express thankfulness for hearing a cardinal's song or seeing a flower, can invoke Spirit.) Daily practice, attentiveness and expressions of Love help to keep me on the path.

George

Working with kids, particularly elementary school level kids who are suffering. Giving them real hope is the dream. Also, I think volunteer work is a great way to stay in touch with what is really important.

Ross

Sounding odd I'm sure, but my definitive answer is sadness and failure. Sadness and failure gets us in touch with our dreams and possibilities. I think we tend to set aside our dreams and possibilities to conform, to measure up, to get by. When these things serve to frustrate and not gratify we're forced to reconsider. It was an obscure Harry Chapin song from the 70's: ".and so you and I, we watch our years go by, we watch our sweet dreams fly, far away. Maybe someday I don't know when, but we will dream again, and we'll be hap-hap-happy then, until our time, just drifts away..." Depressing yes, but designed as a poignant reminder to avoid losing your dreams. I now know what he meant.

As for principles, I see that as a slightly different issue. I act on my principles all the time. It surprisingly gets me into trouble quite a lot. I'm not sure my 'principles' are all that well conceived. I tend to hold people (including myself) to standards they find impossible to achieve and they grow to be resentful of it and as a consequence, also of me. It's how I was treated. I'm working on not doing that.

Barry

For me a big one is weekly meetings with my men's group. They (the men) help me to see things that I do or have done or that have affected me and that I may have otherwise been unaware of. The weekly meetings provide a time for me to reflect on my integrity and to be accountable if need be, to reflect on how I am feeling and why and to do any work around issues I may have.

Roy

Doing things of service that demand my attention are fulfilling, to me. Meditation and prayer. Just slowing down and noticing the blessing that already exists in my life. Letting life move me.

Tim

Sufficient time each week to remove myself from sycophants and narrowly mired individuals.

Dan

Be conscious of what we choose, of every little thing we choose. Pay particular attention to the little things; I found that it's always one little thing that starts my path away from my core values—"it's nothing;" "it doesn't mean much;" "who cares." Like pennies, the little things add up. Better they add up on my side than on something else's side.

Kyle
Engaging with people.

Joseph
Association with the right people, study and mediation of the scripture, and prayer.

Kobe
I don't know about 'us', but what keeps ME in touch is my children and the relationship I share with them.

Mack
I think we are put to the test every day of our lives. I think it is incumbent on all of us to take the brief moments necessary to address the day in these terms. I have not done this. I will try to set aside a few moments to reflect as a test. (I have been able to discipline myself on daily meditation-this could be a brief add on.)

Joel
Spirituality.

Curtis
It is the books you read and the people you associate with. It's also the book you principally read.

How can commitment to our mission and core values give us freedom?

Randy
These days I'm cynical. I still believe in truth and making a better world, but I have been squashed. I'm smart. I've worked hard. I've done all the right things and now I pay half my after-tax to the mother of my daughter. They say this is to support my daughter, but I can do the math, it is really to support her mother.

Nothing would make me happier than to live with my daughter. But it is her choice, not mine. I'm only the father after all. Where did I lose my beliefs? My honor? My ideals? Here's a hint. Poor people struggle. They are stuck in dead-end jobs where they have to keep their boss happy. Successful people are comfortable, they can afford ideals. They can be gracious and generous. I realized that I had no rights around my daughter, only responsibilities. I've done everything right. I had a brief relationship with a 37 year old lawyer. We broke up. Then I was told I was to be a father. I said great, I want to be a dad. But she's now got my daughter and gets half my after-tax each month. My daughter was to be brought up by her mother who I was forced to support by law. But my involvement, my part in bringing up a happy and beautiful and well-balanced girl, my love... this was all tentative, all based on her mother giving me access, based on her mother letting me love my daughter. I'm dad, but my relationship with my baby daughter is only based on my ex's good will. I'm a good dad, but I have no rights, only responsibilities. This is when I lost my ideals. So I need to think more about how commitment to my mission can give me more freedom. Maybe I need to really re-look at what I am truly committed to and how I can find some freedom in that.

George
When a man realizes that his masculinity is a matter to be struggled for and fought for, often fought for within, freedom is availed.

Ross
It gives boundaries and guidance. It is the essential reason many people turn to religion. They are unable to gain guidance from another source so they commit to a religion's 'mission and core values' or an even company's for that matter. But I wonder sometimes if it is freedom that is sought, or if it's forgiveness, or safety. I think people need a way to frame themselves and their lives. Some do it as individuals, some do it as group members, some do it as zealots. It's the identity thing.

Wilson
Commitment to my mission gives me freedom through the synchronization of all facets of myself.

Dan

I no longer sway toward every voice and pressure that comes down the road. I no longer feel obligated to live according to someone else's expectations of us. I no longer waste time and energy rushing from here to there as fads and the needs of others change. I keep my eyes and energy moving in one direction, making a whole lot more progress than we used to. I get to make choices that are good for me, satisfying to us. Things go best when I remember that freedom always comes with consequences and responsibilities. I can't blame others or other things for my choices or the consequences I face. Sometimes this has been the hardest part of my commitment to my soul and its core values. Also, I feel society, by and large doesn't like this kind of commitment and often extracts a price to let us live our own lives; these too can be tough to handle.

Henry

There is joy and fulfillment in feeling that you are carrying out your life purpose.

Fredrick

How can commitment to our mission and core values give us freedom? Everything else is slavery.

Tim

How can commitment to our mission and core values give us freedom? How can it not? With out it I would be just riding every emotion that bubbles up!

Ike

Commitment to my mission and core values gives me energy; focused enabling energy. That energy pours over into the other areas of my life. My life is rewarding to the extent I am interested in it. Being engaged in what I believe is worthwhile gets me interested. But it's more than that, my mission as I understand it is my closest connection with my creator. The more I get in touch what I am here for the more I understand my uniqueness, my value and my potential contribution. This is the antidote to being "stuck" in my old habits, self limiting thoughts and inaction, in mediocrity. Connecting to my mission calls out my best qualities and moves me into action in ways that serve to keep me inspired, humbled and engaged.

Joseph

If our goals are based on God's perfect will for our life, we will be happy and find true freedom.

Curtis

It's shows that despite the pressure of the world, daily negative news, and through the battlefield of all of the pressures you don't compromise what's important and actually free your mind to create.

Mack

We all benefit from simple clear missions and paths. Following these should the most rewarding experience. I think the important thing is to enjoy this freedom every day.

Kyle

I don't like the word Commitment because like Promise, it is in the future. How can this be turned around to be in the Now? Why do we teach our children that they must commit to something? Have we really examined deeply this issue? Let's say someone is driven to do a certain deed but remembers a commitment and changes this deed. Doesn't this bring internal conflict which is manifested in stress and work and confusion? In my life I say I will do things to my customers or family and I often keep my promises. To me these are trivial matters as compared to my personal values or to my marriage. My wife and I make no promises that we will love forever... no commitment to fidelity... We are extremely happy in our lives together. It is a light-weight relationship because of this and many other things I'm sure.

Does self responsibility or responsibility to others come from commitment? Or, could there be something else in us from which responsibility springs?

Kobe

For me, staying focused on my core values frees me to always be aware of my surrounds in a way that is not possible if I'm not focused on my core values. In other words, having a focused direction in life, rather than always 'searching' for one, frees my experience of life. It allows me to view life freshly.

Joel
It allows one to live fully in the moment.

What is the value of having core principles?

Joseph
Proper core principles enable one to be trusted. Following them makes the decision making process much easier and avoids guilt.

Kobe
For me, freedom

Roy
It took real work to figure out, hammer out, my core principles. I did it as an adult and wrote them down, then worked to see how they fit in my life—adjusting them so I would not compromise them. I believe my lack of awareness of them and just assuming I know them is what helped destroy my previous marriage.

Joel
Keeps you even and out of trouble.

Curtis
It's a rudder for your life.

Mack
Core principles are direct, clear and simple. They are easy to follow and easy to assess the results. It is easy, in fact, to make a daily tally of achievements.

Werner
Having core principles makes it clear where to be flexible and where to not be flexible.

How much time do you spend unconsciously seeking out the approval of women vs. truly figuring out what you want just your life to be about first?

Joseph
My wife's approval is important to me, but a secondary driving force.

Randy
Probably more than I should.

Mack
I must admit that that I first assess what I want to undertake and do within my principles and values. I truly believe these are compatible with my wife's values.

Werner
I had no idea how much time I spent seeking the approval of women which never really made them happy and is different from cherishing your partner. I learned this from examining myself. I now have a mission for my life and invited my current partner to be part of it, she has her own mission and I enjoy that.

Curtis
From the time I was a kid probably way too much!

Kobe
I'm through seeking the approval of anybody, unless I'm on a job interview

Joel
Too much time. My mother was smothering and fearful that I might grow up and leave her. It has been a lifelong struggle to find myself and be free.

Abraham
I spent too much time seeking woman and making them happy—while forgetting my one needs.

Roy

I think this is a very important question for if you spend too much time seeking the approval of women then you have no life for them to love. It is funny, trying to do one thing and getting the opposite results. Great questions. I have spend a lot of time and when I was doing that I was NOT seeing women as equals but a mother substitute.

What is your personal mission? What have you committed your life to? What game for your life have you created that is worth playing? What gets you passionate about life?

Joseph
Through business helping others to be successful and influencing their lives.

Kobe
To quote another, 'I am of the opinion that my life belongs to the whole community and as long as I live, it is my privilege to do for it whatever I can.' GBS from Man & Superman

Joel
"I am looking for love, in all the wrong places". I want to come home again, find the ideal mate and live happily ever after. It doesn't feel worthwhile but seems to be the only game in town for me. Wanting to be in love, finding my authentic self and core seem to be my passion. I really need something outside of myself and cannot find it.

Abraham
I am working towards and getting a plan in place to do what really makes me happy.

Curtis
I probably don't have it written down. I need to. I will. This is an encouragement to do it.

Mack

Never considered these!!! I have a mission for my business but not for my life!!! I'll answer but I will be working a long time on this later—because of its potential VALUE TO ME!!

What Insights did you personally gain from this chapter?

What do you want to commit to or re-commit to out of these insights?

Remember!
"Insight   without   committed   action   is   only   entertainment!"

Chapter 9
Allowing Contribution & Mentoring

Do you allow other men to mentor or contribute to you? Do you know how selfish it is not to let other men contribute to you?

How do you mentor other men?

What is the value of being in mentoring relationships?

How do you bless younger men in your life? How do you accept the blessing of other men?

How do you lead with compassion and strength? How do you allow men to contribute to you?

What is your relationship to authority? How does that relationship serve you?

What are other ways to relate to authority?

How do you know when to trust a man to mentor you?

◆**Martin's comments on this topic**

◆One of the times in my life when I experienced the gift of working with another man to be mentored in mastering a skill was when I choose to study Massage Therapy. Along with formal classroom training I wanted to work with someone who I felt was one of the best in the field and had qualities I admired as a professional and a man. I choose to work with Scotty Young of Carrboro NC, someone I had known for years. Scotty used to work in construction then moved over later in life into massage therapy and was known as being very good in his field. I had been involved with men's work for a few years by then and saw extra value in my own personal development by working with him. I remember being advised in choosing a mentor it is best if you can find someone that you not only admire for their skills but also who they are as a person. I was told you will know it is the right one if you also are a little serious about working with them due to your appreciation of who they were in contrast to your own current skill level. Scotty said he had never worked with just one student before but was open for it. I have to tell you there was a part of me that was intimidated about working with him because of my own skill level. My discomfort was not because I did not trust Scotty. I would meet with him once every two weeks and learned a lot, he would work on me but also have me work on him along with giving me assignments to work on different types of people to build up my skills.

♦One of the principles Scotty taught me was how there is often a correlation between long-term muscle tension and memories. When he would work on me, sometimes a memory or emotion would show up and sometimes not. For example when he was working out a very tight muscle in my shoulder I remembered a car accident I had had where the seat belt had hurt my shoulder badly.

♦One day, quite a few months into our work, while he was doing "deep tissue" work on my chest. I felt deeply overwhelmed with many emotions. I could not stop the tears from coming. He encouraged me to go deeper into the experience and to verbalize what was going on. The feeling was a fear but at first I resisted admitting it. Knowing I would not get free of it by keeping the feeling inside, I told him I was afraid. I was afraid if he really new what type of person I was that he would judge me in a harsh way. He kept one hand on my chest, paused, and said, "Its ok. I see the man you are, what you do and admire you. I wept for quite a while, deeper than I ever had. I experienced deeply grieving and not being alone. There was an almost joyful quality to it. It was like going through a tunnel that left me with out the fear any more. By expressing it fully it was done, complete, vanished.

♦This freedom transferred eventually to all areas of my life. I had not realized how the fear of rejection from men I admired was so great, so unconscious and was directly tied to a core need to get the admiration and "blessing" of a man I admired. After that event I started to see that fear of rejection and need for validation in the eyes of other men constantly cropped up when meeting other men, especially those I admired. I am in no way recommending that you need to do what I did to move through your issues, just pointing out the extraordinary value of the connection that can occur during mentoring between men. Mentoring with other older, wiser, capable men seems truly to be an important piece in our maturing process.

The Men Address Selected Questions

Do you allow other men to mentor & contribute to you?

Ross

I have tried. I have approached men for mentoring and not been very satisfied. Maybe I have a mentoring 'standard' they can't live up to or maybe I just don't understand the activity very well.

Barry

Yes I do let other men contribute but again it's mainly been recently. Still sometimes I find it difficult to ask for help or advice when the issue is very personal. I have experienced the gold in having a man I care about ask me for help and have learned to let go of the 'old me' and to believe that a man I ask for help may also feel the same way.

Steven

I do try and mentor other men, and allow myself to be mentored. To me, mentoring is just having compassion for another man while sharing my own experiences and ideas. It can look like encouragement, feedback, guidance, or whatever. It sometimes looks like tough love, a kick in the ass, holding him accountable. And like all relationships, I believe they exist to teach me about the relationship I have with me. Do I mentor me?

Samuel

I have several men who are acknowledged mentors for me. It has taken some effort to find them and cultivate the relationships. These men I formally asked to help me step up in my life. Then I have men who are committed to being in my life and helping guide me through life's adventure. I would hate to be a man who had not made this effort.

Benjamin

I would like to share a story of how I have let men mentor me. Two men who sensed a wounded soul when they became acquainted with me took me into their families and made me feel

215

worthwhile. I don't think they were aware how closely I observed how they handled the celebrations and disasters of life, but I learned well. They lived exemplary lives and I emulated them. Rarely did they need to give me advice formally, as I could learn simply by observation. And they loved me, along with their wives and children.

The debacle that was my life from age 18 to 29, which seemed irredeemable, has proven to be very useful in mentoring others now. Because of what I experienced then I find that I can now listen well and without passing judgment, while not attempting to "fix" the men who seek their problems or me out. In one Internet men's group of which I am a part I am the oldest member (65). Many of the guys call me "pops" or even "daddy" or some variation thereof. I am gratefully overwhelmed that they do seek my opinions, although I'm careful not to tell them what to do. In some cases I have on request stepped in as a surrogate father. Though I have no children of my own, this is quite rewarding. I've discovered parenting skills that have surprised me.

Before I allow a man to mentor me I must know his character, his reputation, and his skill and wisdom in the area in which he will instruct. Also I prefer that he be a friend.

Dan

I can't think of any relationship in my entire life with a man that I would call a mentoring one. Maybe, though, there were some possibilities that I missed or ignored. That's more than possible since I spent most of my life having to mentor myself and protect who I was. Mentoring can't work when you know that the things that have the deepest meaning for you have little meaning or a negative meaning for the people around you. There's no one you can trust to pay real attention to who you are and your needs; all you've experienced is people who want to force their expectations, their perspectives, their demands on you—make you like them.

Wilson

Do I allow other men to mentor me? Absolutely. I do not know it all. What fun is that?

Carl

I openly ask - I would not have done that just a few years ago. But today I am a 'warrior' and I can ask for what I want from another 'warrior' with their permission.

Dave

My physical survival and sanity have depended upon other men's mentoring me, so, yes, I allow them to do so! And, yes, I mentor other men, especially, at the present, a couple of them who are almost young enough to be my sons. I find that I draw to me those who find something valuable to learn from the way I behave and the things I say—and I feel honored by their attention. I am mindful of their vulnerability in their relationships with me, and I consider myself honor-bound to respect it and guard against needlessly hurting them through, for example, an impatient demeanor or inadvertently making them feel "lesser than" myself when it's simply a matter of their accomplishments being lesser than mine. Their gifts of admiration and openness to learning from me are precious.

Charles

To me mentoring and trust go hand-in-hand. I have been talking to a lot of our group's members in private recently about some issues that, on the surface of it, look as if they don't have anything in common.

However, on reflection, there is one common thread that runs through what they all have to say. That common thread can be labeled with one word: TRUST.

One member talks about knowing what he wants in life but that everything he does prevents him from taking even one step in the right direction. When I asked him a few questions, it seemed as if the central issue for him is that he doesn't TRUST what would happen if he made the changes he wants to make. He is, in other words, frightened of change. He lacks TRUST in his own judgment to make necessary changes.

Two other men have also been talking along similar lines. I asked one of them if there was anyone in his life that he could completely TRUST. I was thinking that if he had one or two trusted friends, he could confide his fears to them and invite them to mentor and support him as he initiated change in his life.

217

Neither man could name ONE person he trusted to confide in, to act as his mentor. They miss out on wonderful new experiences because of fear and a lack of TRUST.

Another three members have been talking about the LOSS of trust in a relationship. In one case, it has been the loss of trust within a marriage, and in the other two cases, the loss of trust in relationships with other men... when the words of love, support, or loyalty were not matched with the actions, where seriously made promises were easily and lightly abandoned. TRUST was the casualty (among other things).

Discussions with a couple of members who are bisexual married men reveal a particularly painful issue to deal with around TRUST. Most such men, it seems, entered into their marriages in good faith. They say that they had no idea, or very little understanding, of their sexuality at the time. The TRUST they have developed with their partners is a huge matter for them as they struggle to maintain their marriage vows. No one seems to have satisfactorily addressed this issue for them. As I said, it is a painful issue, and is worthy of a separate discussion of its own.

I am aware of other members who, having the opportunity to enter into close and sexual relationships once more after a divorce, are so powerfully affected by the prospect that they do not TRUST their own emotions. For some it is a frightening prospect which can prevent them from TRUSTING the process or even trusting that they can negotiate a satisfactory outcome. Many give up and miss out on deep, lasting and loving relationships because of a lack of TRUST that these can be possible without the sky falling in.

I suppose that, for me, the worst loss of trust would be if I lost trust in myself. For me, the ability to trust MYSELF is crucial.

It's a pretty hard thing to cultivate, this SELF TRUST, but it has been essential for me. Part of that self-trust includes the knowledge that even when I make mistakes, even when my trust is betrayed, even when people I trusted let me down, that even then I will STILL trust myself.

Who was it who said, "Feel the fear and do it anyway"? If memory serves me well, this was the title of a book I meant to read but never did.

The phrase seems to sum up beautifully how to go about developing self-trust.

If you make reasonable decisions based on the best information you have got, if you have developed a reasonable opinion of the person you want to trust, if you have consulted reliable and reputable sources before making up your mind, and if you still feel frightened, apprehensive, scared...... then maybe there is something for you to learn here...

All things being equal and if you still feel frightened, maybe you should "feel the fear and do it anyway."

Gary

Mentoring. A Big issue for me. My father was paranoid and very conservative in a very liberal city, NY. The message I got was to have no other male mentors to honor him.

It took years before I could fight off that message, and take on a mentor (likely around 50 years of age!). And HE needed to ask ME! But I wanted to be an officer in my local MKP community, and that meant taking on mentors. Even before that, I did Al-Anon, where sponsors are encouraged. There, one first needs to HAVE a sponsor before one can BE one.

Once I got a really good mentor as part of taking on an officer role, I learned its value. While he nominally was supposed to help me with the job I had, it really replaced therapy as a means to get at my core "wounds" and heal them! That first mentor is now a life coach I pay! (And he still mentors me in my newest position in separate phone calls). There's a protocol for how to be a mentor in MKP, and it's really helpful in my judgment: about not giving advice, men tee always initiates the call; after a period of time, it's good to end it, etc.

I've now mentored three or four people in my life, two formally. I have to say I got as much or more from mentoring as the other person, and as much as I did BEING mentored. One man fixed a piece of artwork at no charge that I hadn't found anyone who could fix for 25 years! Another man I kept suggesting he do therapy: he had what I could see was a serious clinical problem; but he'd had a bad experience with therapists, so he refused. After about 2 or 3 years, he made the kind of breakthrough he'd likely have sought from a therapist, and it transformed him!

My father was right about one thing: I did become a liberal after all!

219

Arthur

I have a mentor 13 years my senior. He seems to gain as much from our time together as I do. I think he can't work out why I asked him! I want him to tell me what he sees in me, especially the dark stuff that I can't see and also to keep an eye on my 'overeager' disposition. He often rings me now and says we need to catch up which I like. My patterns are to be the one that initiates so I feel supported in this.

Since doing this work I am not infrequently asked to help in matters of the heart and personal issues. I do get an ego jolt from this and try to be cautious in what I say and what is the intention behind my words. I amaze myself at times as to what I can do and how I handle these situations. This gift I have discovered is hard to fathom at times. Another of my patterns is to be critical – for much of my life the glass was definitely half empty and whilst this part of me is always here I do feel more positive and open to receiving and giving of blessings. I am complex alright!!

Jeff

Yes I allow another man to mentor me. I set aside a time for him and talk to him regularly on the phone.

Growing in Christ, which means becoming more like Him, in my relationships, serving and sacrificing for the good of my fellow men. I use my mentor to help check in on me and see how I am doing.

Von

I have been very fortunate to have been mentored by several wonderful men, before I even knew it was happening. One of my epiphanies was shortly after my wife was diagnosed with cancer at the age of 42. Although we were members of a church, we were not really connected to the community in any significant way. The pastor of that church spent considerable time with me personally, (probably more than he did with my wife). The net result of that encounter was one of my first appreciations for the value of male friendship. For the first time, I opened myself up to a cache of pent-up feelings and frustrations, and admitted the need for a spiritual dimension of myself. I ultimately rejected my prejudicial view of a pastor as a judgmental, out-of-touch, position, and accepted his earnest friendship.

Stan

About mentoring, my lack of trust in myself and other male humans continued through young adulthood well into mid-life and beyond. With the completion of college for our children and retirement after 30 year's of a rather unsatisfying career, I began to assess what I truly valued and what was lacking in my life. I began to realize that I desperately "hungered" for honesty in relationship. Relationship not with just other gay men, but with my wife, straight men and women, and my own children and grandchildren. I took to meditating. I took up the study of religious philosophies, training and practice in Shamanistic journeying, joined a local men's support group, and eventually found a good therapist. Fortunately that man not only understood the plight of gay men who had grown up in the predominantly heterosexual culture of the southern United States in the 50's and 60's, with its blatant homophobic norms, but recognized the hunger that all humans share for deep and lasting relationships. A men's therapy group in which kindness and honesty are championed now provides me with hope, at last, for overcoming my fears and allowing genuine feelings of love and connectedness (relationship) to surface in my life. A personal objective on my current path to relationship includes my ability to readily trust and access all human emotions, not just feelings of anger and sadness but those of joy and happiness that have for so long eluded me.

It is with gratitude that I now face each day. Thankfulness felt for all the men and women in my life, both past and present, which both helped create my world and save me from it.

Roy

Before the men's work I did I would ask for no recognition, accept none, and even avoid any situation where I might get recognized, then always be mad to myself that my work is never appreciated—how stupid is that. I just did not realize what I was doing! It was the company of other men that asked like a mirror for me to see this stuff. I said to one of my 'brothers' in a men's team once "I just want to be left alone, then I feel lonely!".

Fredrick

I had one male mentor when I was young, and I think that was enough to get me off on the right foot. He was kind of an uncle-

221

figure, even though we weren't related in the clan sense. He took time with me. We were both interested in astronomy and sailing, and he got me going in those hobbies. I feel an indescribable debt of gratitude toward him.

Dan

I try to convince them that the socially approved male roles and rules are not the only way for men to live, that they have options. When they accept this (which lots don't), then I lead them in a search for who they really are and how to express that. To me the skills, techniques, rule etc of living are all just so many conventions. They don't hold a candle to standing on my own feet and making my own choices. Conventions just take practice; finding who you are and learning how to express that takes intuition, creativity, and a great deal of trust in your self.

How do you mentor other men?

Ross

In the past I have done this condescendingly, as I was taught. I intend to do it again when I think I can without imitating my 'mentor.'

Randy

When I was the elected editor of my university's student newspaper, often I felt uncomfortable. I felt uncomfortable about the fact that 22,000 students could read my paper. I felt uncomfortable having to take a left faction - right faction position when I could see both sides.

But most I felt uncomfortable about the younger men and boys who wanted me to lead them. The volunteers who would turn up on deadline weekends to help out, wanting my time, wanting my leadership, wanting my mentorship. The pioneers were told to 'Go west young man". Young men don't know where to go these days. Sadly, neither did I. Years later I was at a party and there was a recent PhD graduate, a bit younger than me, talking about his inspiration. This man who had inspired this graduate with his ideals, his commitment and his audacity. His mentor.

I left this new PhD and went to the toilet and thought about what you think about in the toilet, girls and piss. Later that night he was talking about his hero again. Then he mentioned his name. It was me, D'Art, in an earlier life. I ran away. Did I really inspire and lead this boy to manhood? Or did I just enjoy being the show-off and the campus celebrity? Did he see in me something inspiring, or did his need for a positive male role model blind him to my flaws. Today boys see jerks on TV, and violent he-men on computer games. While positive role-models for girls abound, boys are left grasping for a way-of-being that isn't violent, but not weak and soft either. Yes I had flaws, and still do have them. But I added something to this young man's life and I'm proud of that. I'm not perfect, but is there any man who is perfect?

Bob

I wish I had a mentor but since I accept criticism with difficulty and since I am very demanding, I have difficulties finding one. On the other hand, I mentor a few young men, which give some sense to my life (is this my mission, maybe so?) and so far constitutes the one and only benefit of growing older. Young men are lost nowadays. They don't have any core values to identify to. With them I am what I describe as an intelligent macho and most like it.

Carl

I was just this past Father's Day that a young neighbor in his 20's wrote to me telling me what a mentor I had been to him through my word, actions and availability to him. He lost his father 12 years ago to cancer. I had not realized how much I had been a mentor until I got the letter a few weeks ago. It is hard to express what a great deal that meant to me. I realized how I have NOT personally thanked the men that mentored me and how we both miss out from me not doing that.

John

I look up to a man who can be themselves without having to compromise their values and standards. These are the men I have respect for and try to learn something from the experiences they have gone through themselves. Men who can do this are setting positive examples for me and hopefully other men who are trying to enjoy ourselves as we are.

Barry

I try to encourage other men to express their positive attributes and also let that man know that he is (was) having a positive effect on me and hopefully other men.

James

Mentoring - I haven't gotten much of that. Acceptance is the key. Until I feel really accepted by an older man, I will not allow him to reach me anything, and so, as a teacher to younger men, I try to listen and give that to them first. Then, I can show them things, I share with them my healing arts, and Real Estate knowledge. I was once on a trip in Europe, and a guy was talking about investments, and I didn't know until then that men could do that., I looked at him strangely, he said - that's what men do - share knowledge

Samuel

I actually work with a mentoring network in my town. We get to hang out with younger men who help keep us "old guys" young at heart. We help them weigh consequences and for the most part just listen, respect and admire them for the powerful young men that they are.

Brad

I mentor other men by walking alongside of them. However, I want to explain what I mean by that because it is possible that if I am blind I could allow the other man to fall into a ditch, and me after him. So there is a need that I have some sight to be of any value at all. How do I get this sight, or to ask it another way, how do I become insightful?

The straightforward answer is by being conscious at a deep level—that is, by sifting proposed actions (or beliefs/attitudes that lead to action) against what my deeper feeling states (drawing on past experience) tell me.

It is a little like the use of conscience, by which I mean that conscience is deepened consciousness, specifically to the point of being able to discern whether anyone, including the one I am mentoring, is going to victimized by what is being thought or contemplated. By victimized, I include the awareness that a choice of action may lead to the person being mentored becoming more himself, or departing/abandoning himself.

There is nothing absolute guaranteed about this, because mentoring is mentoring, a way to discern a helpful way ahead. If one is not sure about the proposal, then the risks need to be assessed. What is the worst that can happen? Let's try it and see—or perhaps too risky for the moment. Look at it later and reassess. Mentoring naturally cannot take away the fact that the choice belongs to the one being mentored. Mentoring is about allowing him to assess what is proposed or happening, and then standing back to allow him to make the decision.

Wilson

How I you mentor other men? Mostly through example, words, actions, consistency within the relationship.

What is the value of being in mentoring relationships?

Ross

It is an exchange, camaraderie. It feels very valuable. It seems real and uncontrived. Nothing is expected in return. All good things.

Samuel

The value of being in mentoring relationships is you get to connect with another man in a different way that you can anywhere else in life. You get to see the world through someone else's eyes. I think the best part is having a relationship that is void of judgments. I don't have to worry about being judged as not good enough. I don't have to worry about getting someone else's values pushed on me but still get the guidance that I need.

Dan

This is guesswork for me. Having taken 50 years to figure out that I'd made all the wrong choices and 10-15 years to figure out how to build a wheel that gives me the right choices, I'd say that the value of mentoring would be that you do the work when you're a lot younger and don't waste so much time getting your act together.

Fred

The value of being in a mentoring relationship is that as a mentor, you try to give direction when asked. At times, a person does not know whether they are coming or going or where to turn and that is where the mentors come in. If they do this well they also bring out skills in the person they are mentoring so they will be able to mentor others.

Wilson

If it is a good mentoring relationship, an outside, objective look at yourself from someone else's perspective.

Allen

It makes me accountable. It lets me connect with another man's life. I get to live my successes again. It helps me honor myself.

How to bless younger men in your life?
How do you except the blessing of other men?

Allen

Acknowledging that they are there and listening to them in a way they feel heard. Identifying with them, letting them know I have been in a similar place.

Wilson

Through prayer in both cases.

Ross

I give them time and I respond to them. I try to be available. Accept blessing? I'm not sure I've experienced the opportunity to do this.

Roy

Just by taking that extra moment to notice something they have accomplished and give them and honest acknowledgement.

How do you lead with compassion and strength?

Ross
When being led, empowerment (of me by the leader) is fundamental. I will follow only grudgingly otherwise. As a leader, I have applied this same principle with very mixed results. I've noticed some people don't really want to be empowered and they do not feel the same way about it. I'm not sure what the non-empowerment people want. Passion and strength is a possibility. It's easy to forget I guess that some people just want someone to look up to and not much more.

Wilson
I have always been in leadership positions at work, I found that a combination of compassion and strength is fairly easy to achieve - all it takes is an honest concern for the welfare of those under your direction. If you care about them, they will know it - they will follow you and you will help them grow even if it means discipline, at times.

What is your relationship to authority?
How does that relationship serve you?

Wilson
I have had to learn how to relate to authority. It took growing up and becoming a man to realize that authority is necessary and beneficial to me. Before, I always viewed it as a hindrance and took every opportunity to show up the authority - not a good strategy. I think this is also a part of being an adult man.

Allen
I am comfortable with authority now. I don't always have to fight it. I demand that they be in integrity in ways where I used to just assume they were not.

Ross
How do I relate to authority? It depends. Sometimes it's not good. Having been married to one for a few years, I don't care much for police officers. Mostly I desire/wish that 'authority'

227

figures respect me as much as I might them. This may be a problem with authority figures who presume I just need someone to look up to and not wanting empowerment and respect as I do. This can be threatening to certain authority figures. I've never been one to cede to authority very well unless I respect it first. I (will) do it. But I usually don't like it much. I don't believe a badge, a title, a license, a tenure, or a job role automatically entitles somebody to authority. Plus there is the nasty little complication that power and authority can be very addictive to the holder of it. There are really not very many people who handle it well. It's hard. I've had some interesting experiences with 'authority' people for whom I showed outward hesitancy to respect. One had a meltdown.

Dave

Increasingly over time, I find myself feeling comfortable with authority figures in the world around me. They're humans doing what they're supposed to do, and the ultimate authority, after all, is God—who I don't understand but feel comfortable with not understanding.

James

In some ways, men's work has enabled me to better support male leadership, as I am tired of watching male leaders get beat up all the time. On the other hand I do tend to go from one pole to another, in rebelling against the over controlling aspects of male leadership that I see sometimes. Men's work has enabled me to appreciate my nurturing self.

Laurence

Historically, my relationship with authority has not always been good. It seems that I vacillate between unquestioning loyalty on the one hand and the total rejection of authority on the other. In the former case, I found that there have been times when I didn't stick up for myself and didn't express myself enough. I think I devalued myself in some ways as a result. In the latter case, a total rejection of authority can result in other problems. In particular in my life, I found it hard to work for some employers, but didn't get out of the situation before it ended up being to my own detriment.

Fortunately, I believe I have learned a few things through the process over time.

What are other ways to relate to authority?

Wilson

I think the best way to relate to authority is to use it to help you improve either yourself or your situation. This is done through developed relationships and seeing situations through the lens of the authority. This broader scope opens many doors.

Fred

My relationship to authority is that I respect it. I obey the law and accept discipline when I fall short. I also do as I am asked by my supervisor where I work and obey the rules when I spend time at a social club in my area where I do spend a little of my time when I can.

Other ways to relate to authority is to accept it, let it direct you and use authority wisely. Accepting that authority is part of our lives and without it, where would we be?

Ross

Ways to relate to authority, at a distance or with cautious cooperation.

Roy

You need to decide if they are just and right, then assist your situation. If they are wrong and have gun to your head it may be wise to give them a sense that they are in control until you can figure out a way to change that. If an authority is hurting a loved one I will not 'respect' their position but do what it take to protect my loved one. I like the Quaker saying, "speak truth to power". If they are not true, let their lies be heard. I don't have any respect for authority which is never wrong or does not know how to own up to and clean up mistakes. This applies to most of the leaders I see in business and politics. I believe at the end of their lives they will face their sins. I think we have a lot of men who know how to "look good" but not to 'lead'. Real leadership has a humbling effect.

Laurence

What are other ways to relate to authority? What I've learned is to relate as openly and honestly as possible to the authority figures I may encounter in my life. Having learned to value myself, however, I can now do that from a position of strength and of belief in myself and my ideas. I won't "get along" with everyone, but handling differences in an honest and open way is much more productive for me and for any organization with which I might be involved. In a sense, I have chosen a path between the two extremes I once gravitated to resulting in more of a win-win situation for all involved.

How do you know when to trust a man to mentor you?

Wilson

This is very touchy. I am extremely careful about allowing another man to mentor me. He must have exhibited consistent wisdom, honest concern, and avoided speaking in clichés, opinions, or judgments. If he is willing to open his heart and be vulnerable, it is a sign that I can be vulnerable with him. He does not have to be an 'expert' but should be real.

Ross

I think it's a sense that the approach is sincere and seeing behavior over a reasonable time period that is consistent with sincerity.

Fred

I know when to trust a man mentoring me is when I am comfortable with him around me. This shows that he's not a threat to me or my security as a whole and there is no way he would use me or abuse me. I have had bad relationships where people have used me and abused my trust and that hurts me.

Brad

I have made good and not so good choices about this one. The basic question I ask is, has this man got a good connection to his life of feelings? Is he patient with himself? Has he the space within himself for me to cast my strongest feelings into him, and not be rattled by this, or have a need to retaliate (by becoming impatient, for example). Will he leave me free, or attempt to control me? Will he listen or superimpose his own thoughts/feelings upon me? Are there conflicts of interest involved?

Sometimes it is not possible to know before asking the man to mentor me. In all cases it is important to be able to stop being mentored by this or that man, if it is not working out. The other side of that is to estimate whether there is a deficiency in the mentor or simply in myself (needs discernment), or whether I am seeking a mentor who is so good, that he hasn't been born yet.

What Insights did you personally gain from this chapter?

What do you want to commit to or re-commit to out of these insights?

Remember!
"Insight without committed action is only entertainment!"

Chapter 10
About Fathers

What are the unique nurturing qualities that a man offers his children?

What are the distinctive ways in which the masculine nurtures that differ from the manner the feminine nurtures?

Are you a father to your children or just a wallet and a friend?

What type of son were you to your father?

How does holding on to resentment to your father hurt you and your children?

How do you honor the value of "fathering" in your life?

How do you let men support you as a man: a father, a son, and/or a brother?

What does it mean to forgive the father but not condone the action?

Did you accept your mother's interpretation of your father, or really see him for his true blessings and shortcomings on your own?

What is being too authoritarian as a father? What is being too much of a buddy as a father?

How does being to absent in your children's life affect them?

What does it mean to be a good father?

What is unique about the way men parent?

♦Martin's comments on this topic

♦Fathering is about blessing young men, and to do that you need to have the ability to *accept* blessings from older men. It is about helping our kids take calculated risks and their learning about consequences. It is about helping our children being able to deal with both failure and success. It is about knowing that how you give your attention to your children is a way of showing compassion to them. A father teaches best by demonstrating the person he is, and the acts of fathering make him into a better man.

♦We all can offer some father energy to young men just by giving them our attention, even if they are not our children. Bless young men that you know by just giving an honest acknowledgment of something you see them do or you see in them. The saddest scene is when you meet a man who has no heart-tie to his kids. In those cases you know there is a wound so deep in the soul that you don't know if they will ever see it or how they could heal it if they wanted to. Men's work will sometimes open the heart up; without an open heart men can miss out on some of the greatest gold in life.

♦Through the men's work I have been involved in, I have made a personal connection back to my grandfather, grandmother and great-grandparents as well. I was blessed to have a wonderful relationship with my own grandfather and saw him as a man to learn from. In working on this book I found an article I wrote about my grandfather in high school that I was very proud of. This is where I found the photo used in The Men's Inquiry live recording (which can be found on www.TheMensInquiry.com). What I remember now are my cousins Sally and Nancy making a comment that did not make sense at the time they read this article. They said, "Why did you not include the emotional content of his life?" I did not know what that was because I did not think that was important. As a young man, what was important to me was what he DID, that was who he was!

♦It reminds me how we as men learn at a young age that what you DO, not what you feel or have even experienced, seems more important. I thought I would share here a little from my article that I wrote in high school on my grandfather, Dr. Martin W. Brossman. My grandfather was a general practitioner who chose that profession because he liked how his father (Dr. Charles Brossman) had helped people and was greatly esteemed in the community. He was a veteran of WWI. During my great-grandfather's day animals were critical to survival to produce food and for transportation. I loved working with my grandfather on his property out in the countryside of Pennsylvania. He would talk to me about his life, sitting down after a day of hard work. I learned a lot about him this way.

♦It has been a wonderful gift and a good challenge to get my own father involved in the project of this book. After he survived a heart attack and built his health back up within the last year we have become even closer. I thought I would let him talk about his experience here related to this topic to give a unique perspective.

♦My father's comments: "My own father was the most remarkable, talented, well adjusted man I have ever known. At the

234

same time he was tough. He was the only physician I knew who was intense in learning – would spend hours reading the latest medical breakthroughs and techniques–and at the same time remarkably physically active and in perfect physical condition. He also had a terrific sense of humor and cared for all people—never judgmental. His love for us three children was so obvious. At the same time he expected us to be responsible, productive individuals. Even though he was intent on staying on top of the medical advances and practices he had no hesitation to repair a shoe or tar a third story roof. I considered him the most competent, versatile, well-adjusted man God could have created. I just loved being near him–went on calls as he visited patients, worked intensely at his side at our summer home, repairing the house, tackling the thick weeds and hiking over the mountains to enjoy the animals and countryside. With all this he was teaching us self-reliance and to savor accomplishment.

♦One incident remains vividly in my mind. I was in my early twenties. I did not enjoy working in hazardous areas at great heights. We lived in a high row house, some three stories plus. The roof needed recoating with tar. We had to climb out the second story window and up on a rickety ladder to the third story roof. We were at the edge of the roof with smoke billowing out of the chimney. I was getting a bit dizzy. We were building up flashing at the chimney and roof while looking down at the concrete pavement–it seemed so far below. Suddenly I realized, despite the love of my father, he was expecting me to be a self-sufficient individual solely responsible of working at the edge of the high roof in fumes and surviving was my problem alone!! I even imagined falling to my death below and my father saying to my mother later—it was too bad Martin fell- he should have been more careful!!! He was filled with love for us but self reliance was our problem!!!"

♦I am very grateful that my father is alive to help with this book even though it has been challenging for him at times. He worked in science advisory / consulting jobs that demanded long hours and lots of travel. For a while he had to live in New Jersey and he would drive home every weekend to Washington DC to be with me. I enjoyed working with him fixing stuff around the house, "hunting down" sales bargains in the DC area, going to Allentown, PA, to help and visit my grandfather's property and going to see parades or special events. I so distinctly remember when he let me come with him to work and help out with collating reports for a big presentation he was doing. It was important that we had fun but it was just as important to let me see what his work was like and what being an adult at work looked like.

♦Robert Bly says that even with a good mother and good father, a man needs more to mature fully. The core father and mother support system is the first foundation for a young man's maturity and the second part is the interrelationships with other men in a true give-and-take process, which is the essence of "men's work."

The Men Address Selected Questions

What are the unique nurturing qualities that a man offers his children?

Fred

The unique nurturing qualities that a man offers his children are affirmation, direction, self esteem, confidence, belief in oneself. Preparation for the world around them, courage, mainly for the son; to point him in the direction of true maleness and positive relationships and heterosexuality. These are all things I felt that I did not get.

I have always felt that my father was ashamed of me. I have always felt that he regretted having me. Why? Because my father abandoned me when I was still a child. He left town without telling his own family due to business problems that he was having and he did not even say goodbye or inform us that he was moving on. Even though I spent a brief time with him during those years, most of the time he never called me, never sent me a letter or a card. When he did call, he only did so to insult his own family. He also used his "born again Christianity" as an excuse to insult and judge us because we did not follow nor believed it was right. There were times that I felt like killing him for all of what he did because I felt that he deserved it because of all the hurt that he was causing the family. I felt it more because I was a boy and his son.

For many years, I have held on to my mother's interpretation of my father. Why? Because of all the hurt that he caused the family.

236

My father hurt my mother so much by cheating on her when she was pregnant with the three of us. It was not only with one woman, it was with lots of women. The worst part of it was, at one time, he used the very bed that he shared with my mother while she was away on vacation for his adulterous escapades. I hate it when a man cheats on his wife—because it affects the whole family, not just the wife but the children; present and future. Sometimes, I really don't know what to make of my own father because of all this hurt that he caused our family.

To be a good father means to love, accept, and affirm your children. You have to show that love everyday no matter what. Never put your children down when he/she makes a mistake. Simply forgive, forget and move on. A good father never stops his love, acceptance and affirmation of his children no matter what.

Eric

When I was age 12, I witnessed my Dad finally relent to the strength of my mother. Up to that point he would fight for his way to run things and set down the rules. He seemed so very strong to me and so much a man, albeit a violent and cruel one. But, something happened. I didn't know what to think of it but I lost something for him. On the other hand my mother gained stature even though, at the time I didn't like her small minded and puritanical ways. She denied anything ever being wrong and didn't want to discuss it. She would rather gloss over and pretend. I resented her for this and refused to relent myself.

There were times when I thought I might be able to talk with my Dad, like when I got home from the Service. But, this didn't happen. All through my childhood I didn't see much affection and what I did see was clumsy and abrupt. It's as if he would cancel whatever care he showed with some violet outburst. And so, I never got a handle on how to love him or honor him. What a shame and a waste. And I'm sad about it. I have some respect for him providing a living to raise a family of six even doing hard, low paying jobs as a welder. I feel sorry that he was so trapped in his life's box. I feel sorry he had such a hard and cruel childhood himself, stowing away at age 12 and bringing his 12 younger brothers and sisters to the US without a thought for their care. I am pleased I'm Dutch as it explains a lot about me. I like the mystery of my life.

My mother, whenever I went out of her mainstream thinking, would say, "Don't be silly." I didn't realize the weight of this on me until one day in my 50's I realized she never acknowledged me and my own directions. For example, that there is no God, or I'm not celebrating Christmas. So, my mother was in her late 70's when I wrote her "Dear Ma, I forgive you for not acknowledging me when I was a boy. I know now you had no intention to hurt me and wanted only what was best for me." She was hurt then angry. But, after a year she finally wanted to know more. And we had a beautiful relationship up to her death at 85. Because of this I was able to see and tell her of her most memorable act of love that influenced me more than possibly any other in my life. I would come home each day and say "Ma, I'm home." I thanked her, told her how much it means to me now for being there for me, anxious to see me and ask about the day. It was the gift of an old fashioned housewife, of strength and optimism and love.

In her 80's she broke through something and began to open up about her humble life to me. She became my most magical teacher, saying now she wanted to learn, but showing me things that turned my self-assured knowledge upside down. For a year she could not do anything for herself and she taught me about dependence and independence and how there is no such thing—only love. A parade of caregivers would come in to bathe, feed, move or turn her, change her, each with excruciating pain so she taught me about competency and incompetence and how there is no such thing—only trust. In silence she taught her care givers and me about grace and humility that I can't put into words. Finally, she taught me death is a sacred time to learn a valued part of life.

And when I think of how little she said during her last years I recall what she showed me during her last 18 months dying of bone cancer. I wonder if there is really anything meaningful to say in words. A lot of what I learned from my parents was what problems and human diversity were about. Somehow they stimulated me to want to understand myself and find what is real.

Charles
I am awestruck....
I have just belted home from Sydney, a day earlier than I had planned, to arrive at a city hospital after 10 hours of solid driving down the freeway to Melbourne. The reason for my early return

was the arrival of the most beautiful baby girl in the history of the universe. I held her tiny body in the crook of my arm a few hours ago, and marveled at her, just as I marveled at her father when I held him in the crook of my arm over 30 years ago when I was a 29 year old. She is my grand daughter and I love her already; he is my son and I love him more deeply than ever.

I kissed her so gently and welcomed her into my heart. I kissed him and told him I loved him more than ever. He looked at me, and told me he had a wonderful dad. He kissed me and hugged me back. My son and his child leave me awestruck. I am a lucky man to have so much love in my life.

Roy

So you ask what are the nurturing qualities of a father? To encourage risk. To give attention. And to have the courage to praise and say you love them. To break your own silence to help your child. This is it. To have the guts and courage to openly love. This to me takes way more courage than physical courage.

Brad

What are the distinctive ways in which the masculine nurtures that differs from the manner in which the feminine nurtures? What does it mean to be a good father? What is unique about the way men parent? I believe masculine nurturing can be summed up with one word: "Risk". The maturing man is the one who is learning to take life's risks, and is the father who encourages and enables his children to do the same. I think it important also to say that men can offer feminine nurturing also (when required), that holding, encompassing safety symbolized by the womb and breast; but specifically masculine nurture is at the risk end of the safety—risk continuum. This risk taking may involve physical risk, but more likely in Western society it involves emotional and spiritual risk. It involves the risk of leaving parents, of plunging into darkness, of letting go and being willing to die, experience grief, and emerge anew. This is why it is so tragic when a mother tries to stop the man from encouraging their children to take calculated risk for she is denying the food that the father has to offer and will do harm to the child. We see this aspect in a watered down form when for example, younger men will drive powerful cars in a foolhardy way, and 'risk' their lives. Is this really risking life in order to gain it? Or is it just a way of trying to avoid real risk by the attempt to show that I am bigger than risk and death, and am some sort of god that is above both risk and death? The two dysfunctional poles brought about by patriarchy are 1) the god-hero who is beyond the reach of risk and death, and 2) the man/father who is dominated by the need for security and his fear of living and its attendant risks. These are two aspects of the same coin. A father introduces his child into the desire to accept the risks of living probably in many different ways, but one way I would like to highlight. When a child experiences his fear of leaping into the risks of life, the father needs to be the one who can allow the child to cast into him (i.e. the father) the feelings of being afraid that the child has. If the father can accept this projection and feel it on behalf of the child, the child will see 1) that this feeling of fear is manageable and feel able without collapsing, and 2) the father can 'hand back' the feeling to the child in manageable bits so that the child can learn to 'take back' his own fears and live with them. I think that the man does this also for his spouse/partner. Alas what we so see and experience is a conspiracy in the genders to avoid the risk, the fear, the death, the fear of life, and so we become so safety conscious we end up with emasculated men, and dominant women.

Nick

What are the unique nurturing qualities that a man offers his children? I think nurturing is important. I often wondered where my ability to be sensitive and caring came from. Growing up, the definition of masculinity didn't include tenderness, softness and gentleness. These were not qualities men ever demonstrated publicly. However, somewhere in my maturation I learned to express and get in touch with the qualities that I was socialized to believe were from the "feminine side". After careful reflection, I attribute my innate ability to nurture to the way my mother nurtured me. "Nurturing," which is one of the most important qualities I have learned about being a father, I learned from my mother.

I remember the safety I felt being carried in my mother's arms while listening to old Roberta Flack and Dionne Warwick albums. The songs my mother sang and the hugs she gave comforted my spirit.

On the other hand, my father was the disciplinarian. He was strict and often impatient, especially when making clear to me the rules of his house. My father guided me and taught me important life lessons. He taught me to be true to myself, to believe in myself, and never to say "I can't." My father insisted on my sisters and me going to college.

Growing up, however, I thought my father hated me. He was mean and I felt I never did anything right in his eyes. He always seemed to give me the hardest chores. By the age of sixteen, I was paying rent at my parents' house, and even that didn't keep my father off my case. For a profession, my father was an entrepreneur, a general contractor and owned a construction company. Working for him was mentally and emotionally draining. I would get fussed at on the job site and then get fussed at more when we got home.

Retrospectively, I realize my father was simply preparing me for manhood. He was pushing me to be better than he was. Despite all the hardship of growing up in my father's house, I now know he wanted me to be the best man and father I could be, and his strictness was his way of helping me along. It was his way of loving me the best way he could.

It is the duality of my upbringing that has allowed me to balance my two roles as disciplinarian "father" and nurturing "mother" to my sons. Having the ability to be tender and gentle with my sons has allowed us to form the type of special relationship many fathers will possibly never have with their children. Why? Because we live in a society where men are taught to suppress rather than express what they feel. As a result, and to our own detriment, we never allow these important emotions to be revealed; we cheat ourselves of the chance to be fully real.

I believe that the ability to be nurturing, sensitive and caring not only allows us to develop better relationships, but it also shows our strength and embeds us even more deeply into our humanity. As fathers, it is important that we develop an emotional balance that will enable us to foster the best possible relationship with our children—regardless of what society says.

The best research shows us that our children unequivocally need "lap-time." They need to see us being tender and caring. They need to know we are connected and committed to them. And our children need us to be nurturing and sensitive to their needs.

Whereas breast-feeding is a demonstrative expression of a mother's bond, our ability to nurture and be sensitive is a demonstrative expression of a father's bond, both of which will likewise last forever.

The one that I think of most often is that I routinely see mothers being so invested in the care of their children that they unconsciously don't want to let them grow up and become independent. Over and over and over I see mothers "infantilizing" their boys by cutting their meat for them, telling them to put on their coats, telling them not to get wet, driving them when they could walk, warning them not to climb too high in the tree....

I have made a conscious effort to BOTH protect my children AND allow them the natural joys of going exploring, getting dirty, trying out their budding physical skills, taking chances (I have stood at the bottom of many a tree, saying, "it's okay, you can do it, I'm right here.")

Advice for moms: It isn't helpful to stay "Don't fall!" That just implants "falling" as a distracting construct in the climber's mind. Try out: "You have great balance!" And "You have such strong hands and smart feet!" "You can always find the best, strongest branch to stand on!" "You are such a good climber!"

Kobe

Females tend toward a more emotional nurturing of their children. By 'emotional nurturing', I mean to really try and understand their child's feelings and attitudes towards life. Men tend to nurture based on commitment and a strong stand for their child. It's the kind of nurturing that says, 'no matter what, I'm there for you'. I strongly believe that both nurturing is important to a child, and that one without the other may be less than effective or perhaps even unhealthy.

Damon

I guess men try to offer strength, protection and direction while women offer love, and contentment.

Frank

Men are unique in the way they parent in that they seem to let their children experience the difficulties in life more readily than women. I am much more likely than my wife to let my daughter experience the results of her actions, whether it is falling down while playing or getting frustrated as she attempts new things.

My wife paces her through everything, while I sit back and watch, let her struggle, then help her out when I see she isn't going to get it on her own. What no one but me knows is that I am watching her every move, making sure she has done her best before I help her.

Ike

I believe I have the opportunity to show gentle strength, conscious power, and true "noble warrior" qualities. My guess is that many women possess and model these qualities; I believe that my children will more naturally look to me for them.

Joel

His time and knowledge. I remember my father making me a butterfly net when I was very young. He took a clothes hanger, a broom handle, some cheese cloth and some masking tape and made a net for me so I could catch butterflies and look at them. He told me how the Indians in New England used fish as fertilizer for their corn and after we went fishing, we would use the fish parts in the garden. He told me that worms liked the rough surface of burlap, so we buried a potato sack and then harvested worms for the garden as well as for fishing. He didn't pass on a lot of wisdom on to me, but there was the soft gentle feel of his intellect in my life. I remember him letting me a close a paint can lid once, I forgot to put a cloth over the top, after a brief moment bordering on, "I am gong to kill this kid", we simultaneously began laughing.

Chad

Answering an earlier question, I quoted Quentin Crisp: "My mother protected me from the world; my father threatened me with it." I think that a father's willingness and ability to consciously do that—to embody the hardness, the impartial judgment, the challenges of the larger world—is central to what he can offer as a parent.

In How To Father A Successful Daughter, a wonderful book with a crummy title, Nicky Marone points out that girls and women often express anger by crying, and how they would sometimes be better served by a more forceful and assertive expression of warrior energy.

Shortly after reading that passage, when my daughter was maybe... 9? 10? We were riding mountain bikes up a long, fairly steep and very muddy and rutty single-track. Her rear wheel kept slipping off into deep ruts and she bogged down. After this happened half a dozen times she was in frustrated tears and said, "I can't do it" and started to get off her bike to walk it a hundred yards up the hill.

I said to her "Rachael, I have seen you outrun everyone on the soccer field. I have watched you beat every boy in your class in arm wresting. I have watched you make a 1,000-pound horse do exactly what you tell it to. Now you're telling me you can't get a 21-speed mountain bike up a hill? You are crying because you are frustrated. But that's not going to help. Getting angry may help. I don't care if you get angry at the stupid bike, the stupid hill, your stupid father, your stupid brother—who by the way is doing just fine getting up the hill—or your whole life. I don't care. Just quit whining, get back on the bike and get up the hill."

She stared at me with indignant anger, savagely jerked the bike up, and chewed up the hill. She passed her brother half way up and didn't stop until she was down the other side. Then she gave me the silent treatment for about an hour. But she got over it. I know my words stung. I know I sounded harsh and conditional. I also know that I care more about her finding her strength than I do about caretaking her feelings.

There is an idea that a mother's love is somehow superior, purer, more accepting, bigger, more heartfelt, more nurturing, than a father's love. I believe this is absolute bullshit perpetuated by mothers and by feminized men who don't trust fathers because 1) they have not worked through their wounds, anger and pain around their own fathers and 2) they remain unconscious of their mother's heavy influence.

A mother's love is no more or less conditional than a father's. Yet I also know that at times my love as a father may have felt more conditional to my children. I believe this is because my intent and commitment to equip my children with whatever they needed to face and thrive in the larger world is more important to me than my need for them to "love" me in the moment (i.e., to express warm fuzzy feelings toward me). Perhaps because I am less needy of their approval, love, and admiration than their mother to establish and maintain my own sense of identity, worth and self-image; I am therefore more willing to risk their unhappy reactions in the service of their development.

This isn't to say I have been a drill sergeant or taskmaster with them. Only that I seek to model the full range of responses to life, and to develop those in them, so that my son doesn't always have to be strong and assertive, or my daughter, soft and yielding. They each need to know how to be all of these.

Marcus

I can only speak from my experience. I had a strong affirmation of my parental nurturance when a team of child psychology experts concluded after an intensive evaluation of my ex-wife, myself and my 2 kids, that I was the more emotionally supportive and stable parent.

My experience is that I've focused on my children; knowing them, connecting with them through hugs, eye contact, and play from the time they were infants, and listening to them as they've gotten older. The fruits of this are that we have a deep bond and the kids have stated that they prefer my custodianship to that of their mother.

I'm not sure that the nurturing qualities I have with my kids are unique to men, I believe that women can set boundaries and can be loving nurturers. I know that I set clear boundaries and that makes my kids feel safe. I know that the way I play with reckless abandon brings them joy and gives them permission to let loose. I think that male playfulness is unique to males, especially because I've often gotten disapproval from women when I play in a way that my kids love and that I intuitively know is right and good. I am willing to be fearless with regard to hugs, gentle touches on the shoulder or head when appropriate, cuddling and eye contact. I judge that this type of ongoing physical affection is essential to the healthy development of my kids.

Brent

Here is something I wrote for one of the ministers at the Eno River Unitarian Universalist Fellowship. She gave a sermon on fathering on Father's Day.

245

"I must confess that I don't have the faintest idea what my purpose is or what's going on, and I never have. I became comfortable with that mystery a long time ago – that I would never know how any of these things fit together in any explicit way." – Gary Snyder

A written excerpt from the answer to the question, "what does fathering mean to me," from the perspective of a son void of a father.

I have father wounds. I am a 28 year old boy emerging into a man, one who learned from other men. I used to be a jigsaw puzzle hodgepodge of paper-clipped, super-glued, and paper-matched torn out magazine pieces of all the images of men who passed my field of vision from day one, and I still am. I have only mostly fathered myself, and at times, everyone, even my own mother. So, I can't really speak to being a father, mainly to being a son.

> What are little boys made of, made of?
> What are little boys made of?
> Frogs and snails, and puppy-dogs' tails;
> And that's what little boys are made of, made of.
>
> What are little girls made of?
> Sugar and spice,
> And everything nice,
> That's what little girls are made of.

Oh, boy. So where does this message send our men? I believe inside. I judge it first important that I differentiate my understanding between ideal father and real father. I believe there are both commonalities and differences. When I consider ideal father, I move in the direction of the sacred masculine. When I consider real father, I move more in the direction of the human being. I believe that one man can not be all men to me, and that the sacred masculine is received through the fathering from all men.

One way for me to get at what fathering means to me is to use language borrowed from the Native American Medicine Wheel. Fathering happens in all directions. It happens in the direction of Above (Sky), of Below (Earth), to the East, to the South, to the West, to the North, of within, and all of the space between. To borrow from mythos poetry, fathering happens in the realm of sacred masculine, that of the King, the Warrior, the Lover, the Magician as expounded upon by Robert Moore and Douglas Gillette in their book, "King, Warrior, Magician, Lover: Rediscovering the Archetypes of the Mature Masculine."

So what really is fathering? Well, I am fathered by the man who shows me his tears, so that I might know its okay to shed my own. I am fathered by the man who owns and shares his anger in a way that supports my courage, so that I might know what to do with my own. I am fathered by the man who expresses his joy, so that I might express my own. I am fathered by the man who shares that he is afraid, so that we may walk hand in hand. I am fathered by the man who shows me his pain; so that I know I am in good company. I am fathered by the man who shows his compassion, so that I might water my own. I am fathered by the man who shares with me about his shame, so that I might release my own. I am fathered by the man who plays. I am fathered by the man who works. I am fathered by the grounded man. I am fathered by the kind man. I am fathered by the man who takes good, good care of himself. I am fathered by the men who invited me away from my mother into initiation. I am fathered by the man who takes the time for his family, himself, and his friends. I am fathered by the man who has the courage to face his own emotions, his own power. I am fathered by the man who sets his boundaries. I am fathered by the man who shows me what it means to love and to nurture.

Dear Father,

In this world, will you do whatever it takes to come to a place to be able to provide this for me? And father, you and the sacred masculine part, will you encourage and support me in pursuing and providing it for myself? Will you affirm our commonalities, and will you affirm that we are separate and distinct? Will you stand

247

with me as I share myself in all of my glory, bold, naked, bleeding, shouting, kicking, screaming, vomiting, sweating, sleeping, crying, healing, eating, speaking, working, loving, connecting, and let me be? Father, I know that the potential for all of human existence lives in you as it does in me. And father, will you cradle me? Father will you hold me? Father, might we jump together in your big bed? Father might we play together? Father, will you show me the world? Father, when I have run out of a map, will you sit with me as I get used to a new compass and a new way to navigate? Father will you share space with me, so that that something that resonates within you, I might inherit? Father, will you simply sit with me while I cry and not move to make things better. Father, will you protect me, and stand courageously in the face of your own fear?

You know dad, I don't recall ever having celebrated father's day. So, I don't know the history of today, nor it's origins or even what the day might look like. I mean, I do have some ideas, and I imagine that on this day, Father, I am to honor you. You sit in the backseat, I'll drive. Take it easy on yourself. Here, let me put your feet up, and no, you won't be working today. Will you open your gift? I got you a tie, for the first time.

It's okay with me if you don't know; you taught me that. It is okay to be weak; you taught me that. It is okay to crumble; you taught me that. It is okay to be vulnerable; you taught me that. It is okay to feel anger; you taught me that. It is okay to be afraid; you taught me that. It is important to face myself; you taught me that. It is important to be open with giving and receiving; you taught me that. It is okay for me to be strong and powerful, and for others to share their gifts and power; you taught me that. And how will I ever repay you for all that you've taught me? Well, it doesn't work that way; and you taught me that too.

Where did you learn all that? Despite the warrior shadow one might see engaged in war and in division, where did you learn all of that? And, confuse not a boy for a man. Boys exist at all ages. Is there hope? Is this new? Does this need revisiting? The sacred masculine lives on. Might we as a world trust, love, and encourage our sons. Might we join in a collective fathering, a communal fathering?

Fatherhood is a cracking seed blossoming along the continuum of what it means to be. Fatherhood is poetic. Fatherhood is a concept, out there. It might be, at its extreme, a point of polarity.

On this day father, in the absence of your physical embodiment, I will set a place for you at my dinner table. Maybe you are out providing for the family, maybe you have left, maybe you are unwelcome, maybe you are engaged in battle, maybe you've passed, maybe you are missed, maybe you were never there, whatever the case, today, today, I will set a place for you at my dinner table. Father, what is it you want out of today? No, what is it you really want? No, what is it you really want? I encourage you to take it easy on yourself, to give yourself a break. If you never do another thing, you are good enough.

Fathering can be fathering alone, exclusive and inclusive. This is to say that father need not exist at the expense of mother. Fathering may exist in honoring mother. I am a 28 year old boy emerging into a man, one who learned from other men. Fathering is generative, exemplified by the sons in the congregation.

Clark

Writing personally, my father died 3 years ago and I have a picture of him on my living room credenza that I walk by everyday, and I almost always say the same thing to him, "Thank you for the lessons." I say this with love and respect. When I was 16, I used to think he was stupid. When I went to him on business issues he became brilliant.

The most natural form of masculine nurturing is the "whack" or "kick" and "rub on the head" for boys. My grandson spent Christmas with me. His parents would only talk with him so he dominated the whole house with temper tantrums and a screech that could pull nails out of the wall. After I told his Mom and Dad this was not okay and got their permission, I showed them a 100,000 year old technique of fathering. In the middle of one of his screech attacks I walked in and whacked him on the butt and told him I will be back in one minute to whack him again if he doesn't get control over his emotions. I visited him two more times when he saw me coming he said, "Stop granddad, I have control over my emotion." I then rubbed his head. Now this can sound like I want him to suppress his emotions—not true. He was using his screech to dominate his older brother. The screech would irritate the adults

249

and bring our attention to see what was going on, which usually was the older brother picking on or fighting with him. I told him he could turn his screech into a growl and that would not hurt the adult ears. The fighting between older brother and the 4 year old continued, with growls instead of the screeches. This is a four-year-old, so it's not like programming a computer, but everyone has a feeling of control over their environment, including my daughter and her husband. I am very blessed to be allowed to help in the raising of their kids. I love them very much.

What are the distinctive ways in which the masculine nurtures that differ from the manner the feminine nurtures?

Dan

What's unique about the way fathers parent? Unique in comparison to what or who? I know the sociologists like to make gender distinctions, but I find them meaningless. For me, the real question is how does each particular parent do his or her parenting? And, not parenting when you have children is a bigger issue for me than how any parent parents.

Allen

Providing the hard edge that without which the knife would never get truly sharp. The edge that honors in a very physical way. The slap on the back that the coach gives the young man, who is starved for that type of validation. But it must be done in an honoring way. It is the honoring wound. It is the giving the young man the challenge to find his healthy edge. The masculine nurtures in a challenge way that is need to be a whole person. Without it he is soft with out strength. The masculine helps break the ties to the mother as a little boy. He nurtures by showing the young how he works, if he can work with him. For me when I went sailing with my father. I was part of the process. I learned how to love sailing. In fact we were in a relationship together through that. I lost my love of sailing for a while when my father died and now it is back.

Roy

Masculine nurtures with attention and the feminine by embracing.

Joel

My mother kept house, put clothes on me, fed me and dealt with the tears. It was less of an adventure being with my mother, but growth producing. Father energy or nurturing is grounded more in setting an example. My father went to work every day, regardless of his feelings. He just went. Yes, this is an example of 'grin and bear it', but there is a place in life for doing things that are difficult because they need to be done. It is displaying leadership by example.

Ike

I believe that masculine nurturing is about making an inherent connection for children, that power can be expressed as gentle strength, not just aggression and dominance.

Frank

The masculine nurtures by letting one tough it out. The feminine nurtures by being right by ones side. The balance of both is key.

Brent

To me, the masculine nurtures differently by way of protection. I also see the masculine as firm, grounded, with boundaries, with courage. While the essence of the feminine is boundaries-less love, which also has its place.

Are you a father to your children or just a wallet and a friend?

Barry

I realize from being in the Men's Inquiry meeting how I have focused too much of being liked and my child's friend instead of his father. I have learned how to be a father first and set the boundaries second and I mean second to be their friend. Both can and should exist but without being a father first I was truly doing harm to my kids for the real world had big consequences when you don't honor rules and boundaries. I wonder if many men in jail were missing this growing up.

Allen

I have been just a wallet and distant friend. But as a divorced father mostly I was just a wallet. It's hard to rebuild that relationship for I did not want to give up the wallet connection – it was all I had. I am working on rebuilding that with my son but I will have given in if money is need to easily.

Joel
I have no children.

Brent
I don't have children.

Frank

A father. I will never be my daughter's friend until she is grown, then only if I am lucky. I fight every urge to give in to her every demand and satisfy her every want. The desire to completely spoil her is overwhelming. It is something I struggle with every day. But I am not raising a child to be my friend; I am raising a child who will be able to deal with the real world without my having to rescue her every time she makes a mistake.

Damon

I try to make every experience a teaching moment—Were they paying attention? What was their interpretation of what happened?

What type of son were you to your father?

Clark

When first reading this question, I sat, absolute blank as if there was no answer at all to this question. I then realized that this question had no answer because I was nothing to him. And that is when I began to cry. I asked: but how could this be, how could he feel nothing about me, how is it that he could not see me nor see himself without love for his child? This has been the unanswered question in my life. This has been what I've been unwilling or unable to find out. For perhaps the fear of finding out that I may have been the problem behind my father withholding his love, kept me from knowing the truth about myself. But the truth is: my lack of asking, my lack of knowing, and my lack of crying have kept me separated from myself. It was after this realization that I saw this question in a different context. I read the question again. This time the question revealed something entirely different. This time I received the question from his standpoint: how did my father think of me and perceive me as his son. This question came not from my self-absorbed child.

So I then remembered that he actually saw me as a sweet kid, a good boy. He liked that I looked Italian like him, he liked that I hung on every word that he said. He liked that I listened to him sing out of tune, he liked how I lit up when he sang "Oh Danny Boy." Oh, it's funny how our memories can be selective, and it's interesting how the first thing I remember is that in my father's eyes—I didn't exist.

Barry

The question about what type of son I was to my father reminds me about the letter I wrote my father. I truly started to resolve issues with my father and knew I was a man when I wrote my Dad back in 1993 on Father's Day. Here is the letter I sent him:

Dear Dad,

On Father's Day, instead of calling you or sending you anything, I wrote a letter to you in my journal that I never intended to send. Now I'm writing it again because I need to send it. About 2 weeks before Father's Day I bought 3 cards for you. They were all very sarcastic and not very loving. I guess it would be ok to joke about our relationship if it weren't so sad for me. I'm starting to realize that all my life I've joked about things that made me uncomfortable. I felt really weird about this past Father's Day. I know part of it was the anxiety I felt about not doing anything for you. But I couldn't bring myself to pick up the phone and talk about nothing. I wish I could call and feel like telling you how

253

much I love you and how much you mean to me, but I didn't feel like doing that. That's why I'm writing this letter.

I've wanted to do this for some time but I've been scared. I'm not scared of you physically anymore, but I used to be. I used to be terrified. As absurd as it may seem, what I'm scared of now is losing what little relationship with you that I do have. I'm not sure if I'm holding on to some illusions or if I'm aware of the good things you did for me, because there are some memories I'm very thankful for. In fact, the time I called you after Tanya and I broke up is a time I'll never forget. I was a basket case and you came over and we drove around and you talked to me. You told me about stuff that had happened to you, and I really felt loved. It was like I was hearing you talk for the very first time.

I didn't know it all my life, but I needed a lot more of that. That's why I'm writing you this letter. We may never have the kind of relationship I dream of having with you, but that's ok. I have to try anyway. If I don't try, then I won't be the kind of man I want to be, the kind of man I need to be. I won't be able to love the way I want to, I won't be able to run my business the way I want to, and I won't be able to be the kind of father I want to be, if I ever choose to become one.

I know that I've never expressed to you any of the anger I feel towards you. Not directly, anyway. I was reading my journal entry from when I was in Alabama for Memorial Day. Marc and I talked about how neither of us knew much about what being a man was about, or at least we didn't learn it from you. It was great to find out that I'm not the only one in the family who felt like that. What I did learn from you was how to avoid intimacy by not sharing myself, how to be afraid to try and fix things around the house, how to hold in all of my anger until I exploded in rage and scared the people I love. I learned that scaring people is an effective way to control them and that sarcasm is an effective way to hide my fears and anxieties. And most importantly I learned that ignoring my own dreams and needs is the way a "man" shows his "love" for his family.

What I didn't learn from you, but needed to, was that men don't have to be super-performers or super-achievers to be lovable. That it's ok for men to be mad, scared or sad and that men need to express those feelings. And that it's even ok for a man to cry. I didn't learn that a good husband really listens to his spouse, and when he can't listen or needs time for himself, he says so. I didn't learn that it's ok to mess up, it's ok not to be there for everybody else all of the time. And that life is not time spent on earth watching TV and watching your life slip away. Dad, it's ok to watch TV and it's ok to want some peace and quiet. If you'd have known that and been able to ask for it you might have endured less nagging from those around you and who knows, you might have spent more quality time with me. Not just teaching me how to play baseball, or how to throw a better curve ball so that I could make the all-star team. That was for you. But you might have taught me what it's like to be loved by a father, by a man, just by holding me and telling me that even if I couldn't play baseball or football, or make straight A's or whatever, that I still mattered to you, and that you loved me. So that on Father's Day I might have been talking to you on the phone, even if it was about the NBA finals, and I'd have been glad and thankful that you were in my life on that special day, and wishing you a happy one.

I've never been so scared to send a letter before, or so happy. I like the man I'm becoming, Dad. It's a slow process but I'm more loving, more confident, more accepting, more forgiving, and more peaceful than I've ever been. Sending you this letter is a big accomplishment for me. And whether you read it, understand it, don't understand it, tear it up, don't read it, or hate me for writing it isn't going to change that.

What I'd like is for you to write me back when and if you feel like you can. And tell me how you feel. I'd like to know what it was like to give up so much to raise a family. I'd like to know about your life as a kid, about your relationship with your father. I'd like to know how you feel about this letter. Anything.

I feel like I hardly know the man I've called my father all my life. I don't know how he feels, what his dreams are or were, what he's most afraid of. But I do know that I'd like to spend the rest of our time together on this planet finding out.

Love, Barry

Three months later he wrote me a 5 page letter. Just the weight of the envelope overwhelmed me. After 12 years it still tugs at me. Greatest gift of my life. From that moment on, I was on a new path. I truly believed he would read the letter and die on the spot.

It was 7 years later that I did my Warrior training, which was another big leap in my acceptance of myself as a man.

All of the things I need to hear to know I'm a man are things from within. For much of my life I let other people determine whether I was a man or not. I gave my power away to them, afraid of causing disapproval or hurting their feelings. Owning my power as a man is a process, one that may never end. I certainly feel loved and supported in doing the work it takes to become a man, but at the end of the day, it is a solitary endeavor.

This is the letter my father wrote back to me:
August 28, 1994

Dear Barry,

Don't think for one moment I have been ignoring your letter because I have thought about it every day. It has taken me this long to build up my courage to respond.

First of all I would like to talk about our relationship as you were growing up. Understand what I am about to say is not an excuse for anything I may have done or the manner in which you and your brothers and sisters were raised. I was raised and brought up in a society which was totally different than the society as we know it today. When I was being raised as a kid, it was a totally macho, male dominated society where women and children were things to be seen and not heard. At family gatherings in those days, meals were served in three shifts, with the men eating first, the women second and the children third. I say this to just give you an example of how things were.

When I got married and started having children I could already see signs in the changing society of children rebelling against parents and not showing proper respect. In those days, I, like you, did not know what a husband and father were supposed to be. I was young and of course totally inexperienced. For whatever reason, I honestly felt I had to behave in a totally autocratic manner if I wanted to raise my family in the proper manner. I realize now and have for a number of years, this was totally wrong. Unfortunately, I can't go back and do it over. This happens to be the biggest regret I have in my life. You do need to understand, you were not raised in the manner you were because of meanness

256

on my part. I honestly felt at the time, this was the right thing to do.

I had no idea what being a man was. I thought I did but have come to realize that was not the case. Having been raised as I was, it was not the accepted practice for a father and other men to really show and express love to children and for that matter to wives either. If you will just consider my relationship with Ma Ma and Pa Pa you will understand what I mean. This is how I was brought up, in a society with little communication and no openness.

I wish today I could be more open and feel comfortable in expressing my feelings. While I feel as though I have improved in this, my personality will not let me do it completely. Maybe time will allow me to do so more.

I have already given you examples of how I was raised as a kid. My only dream as a kid was to be a professional baseball player. When I was a senior in college, I was invited to go to spring training with Kansas City. This would have been at my own expense and since I was married and we were expecting you there was no way I could afford to go. I have realized for quite some time this would have been a waste of time on my part as I finally realized I did not have nearly the talent it would have taken to be able to succeed. As I recall, at the time I was extremely disappointed at not being able to go, but the responsibility of a family was much more important to me than a possibility at a dream.

As I think back on what it meant to raise such a big family, I have a hard time trying to pinpoint the sacrifices your mother and I had to make which I regret today. Since I have not known any other way of living, I just don't know. I suppose, without children, there would have been more time and money for vacations and such, but since I have never made enough money to be able to afford extravagant vacations I don't feel I have missed anything. Sure, we may have been able to afford a better house or car but I can honestly say these were not things which were a high priority for your mother or me. The one thing which does stick out in my mind was the worry and concern I had in being able to pay all the bills. Now that I look back on it, I feel I probably worried needlessly, but at that time I can still recall it being a major and constant concern. I suspect some of your brothers and sisters have

257

already experienced the anxiety and sadness which can happen due to lack of finances.

At one time I thought I would like to be a lawyer. When we first moved to Lake Charles, one of the lawyers I did business with told me if I got a law degree I could work for his firm. This would have meant moving to New Orleans and my continuing to work full time and go to law school at night. This would have taken many years and, quite frankly, I did not want my children to be raised in New Orleans. Whether or not this was a wise decision on my part or not, I don't know, and at this stage of my life I no longer concern myself with it.

At present, my main desire is to be able to continue working and earning money so we can finish raising Christine and Neal and get them out on their own. Beyond that I want to continue to be able to take care of your mother and I hope neither of us will ever become a burden on any of our children. You and your brothers and sisters have enough to worry about in our present society without any added worries.

Barry, I'm glad you wrote your letter to me and I'm glad I have finally built up enough courage to reply. I would like nothing better than for you and I to have a completely open and loving relationship. To say or think that I can be that way may be asking for too much. I still have a lot of the old me in me and whether or not I can change completely while I am still around is something I can't predict.

One thing which helped me to get up the gumption to write you was Laurie moving to Del Rio this week. I could not believe the sad feeling I had when I realized she was leaving. It wasn't because it was Laurie but because I realized my children were leaving.

Barry, there is one thing you can count on from me. I may not approve or agree with the lifestyle of any of my children but I will always love them.

Love,
Dad

Dave

I was and am a poor son to my dad. I wasn't bad in the troublemaking sense but I was bad in that I was disrespectful and dishonorable to him. I do blame myself but also acknowledge that my mother encouraged this.   They've been married (no, cohabitating/coexisting—big difference) for 40+ years.

Dan

These questions are overwhelming for me. I can only guess, on the slightest evidence, what kind of son I was and father I have been and am. Probably I was a kind of tough son to raise.

My father died when I was 27, only two years married and just a father myself. He had been only a distant part of my life even though he had been reasonably present. From my high school graduation until I got out of law school, our relationship had been very difficult because of all the bouncing checks he gave me and my colleges. As far as I knew, we shared practically nothing but our address. I recall no significant conversation with him, no doubt my fault as much as his. Thirty years later I finally knew enough about myself and people and could probably have had important conversations, but he wasn't available then.

Somewhere along in my transformation, I came to an understanding of him—at least my understanding of what I knew of him. He was a person who desperately needed the kind of mentoring I talked about in the last question. He didn't get it; he got driving, determined parents and wife instead. He didn't have a chance to figure out who he was and to express that. In so many ways I now understand, he only lived during his few brief times in Wyoming; otherwise, he was an automaton doing what his parents and wife expected of him. I think my sister and me were the only things he loved for the last half of his life. I feel so terribly, terribly sad for him.

As a father, I'd give myself a very mixed scorecard. I have three kids, now in their mid to late 30s. When they were young I was distant, the disciplinarian, wanted to be left uninterrupted. After the divorce (when the eldest was 14), I rarely saw them for the next five years. Bad fathering except for the fact that I was gradually getting my feet under me and finding out who I was. Thanks to my second wife, I relaxed a lot and learned to laugh and be more real. I was a better father then, even though I still didn't see much of them. During my 50s as I found and expressed more and more of myself, I connected more and more with my children, not more time (since they were into their own lives by then) but more honestly and more deeply.

259

Over the years each of my children has told me something about my fathering: at first they hated me as a father because I didn't do all the usual father things their friends' fathers did. When they were older, they realized that I had given them a very special fathering gift, far more than the Little League coaching and baseball games they'd wanted when they were young. They always knew that I had complete confidence in their ability to make choices and to cope with the consequences. I think they give me more credit than I deserve. However, in looking back now, I see that unconsciously I understood that each of them had a self that it was crucial for them to find and express and that my job was to get out of their way and to give them confidence in themselves. Each them has struggled hard and long to pursue their passions and it pleases me no end that they have each achieved their passions at last. If there is a secret to this kind of fathering, I think it is to refuse to respond negatively to the child's ideas. If there are dangers, point them out as things to plan for or consider, not reasons to flee from or give up their dreams. Get them to search themselves for the answers—then those answers are their answers, answers that work for them. With my kids, I've often discovered that what terrified me about some choice one of them was making was small potatoes to them or not even relevant for them. I still had to hold my breath and clutch the nearest table, but they plowed ahead full of energy and confidence and succeeded or coped successfully.

Willey

I just don't know how to answer questions about father and mother issues; I was raised in an orphanage till I was an adult. I used to have a good bit of pain about not every being adopted but that has faded in time.

Paul

I was and am a poor son to my dad. I wasn't bad in the troublemaking sense but I was bad in that I was disrespectful and dishonorable to him. I do blame myself but also acknowledge that my mother encouraged this. They've been married (no, cohabitate/coexist, big difference) for 40+ years.

Laurence

I was obedient, but sly. I didn't do a lot of "wrong" things, but those I did I tried to cover up. I think my father knew what was going on, but thought it best that I learned my own lessons. If I did get caught in a lie or a "bad action," however, I had enough of my own conscience that all my Dad had to do was to give me "the look" and I knew I had disappointed him and earned his disfavor. A prime example of this was when I cheated on my first wife, leading to a divorce and subsequent failed marriage to my second wife. I don't think my Dad cared much for my first wife either, but breaking the marital vows was not acceptable to him. The only comment he ever had to me about the situation was a memorable, "So you think you're pretty smart, huh?" I learned for myself the mistake I had made, but my Dad had seen it from early on. Should he have counseled me to take another path? I don't think so; I was in my mid-30's by this time, old enough to make my own mistakes and live with the consequences that resulted.

Joel

I was and am a good son to my father. There are stresses. I also found myself competitive with him.

Ike

I was a son that reflected my father. I was playful, engaging and powerful in the way that a child can be by being himself. I was also disconnected in search of connection, insecure, sometimes violent in words and actions.

Brent

I still am a son to him. Having just met my biological father, I am figuring out as I go. I will say, as a child, I was quite, obedient, got good grades, shy, scared, soft spoken, someone who wanted to be someone he was not. To my many fathers, I was starved for their attention.

Damon

I did what I was told and tried not to screw up.

How does holding on to resentment towards your father hurt you and/or your children?

Allen

If my brother could speak, that is his life. He turned his father hatred on his wife and I think he is living his life in relationship to his hatred of our father. It is also destroying his relationship with his son. I watch it get passed on to his children. I could have very easily done the same.

Joel

Lack of communication has always been the biggest issue between my father and me; I think I just accept it now for what it is, that is, the structure of our relationship. Holding on to resentment with anyone is contrary to genuine forgiveness or letting go. It is like hanging on to your end of the rope in a game of tug-and-war, after the game is over. It prevents you from enjoying the victory, or experiencing the defeat. You are essentially in a status situation, which prevents growth.

Ike

My parents divorced when I was in 4th grade and my father was largely absent from my then on. I resented him and put distance and judgment between us. I see now that I have transferred that resentment to many other authorities and "role models" and I have over-compensated for his "abandonment" with my children.

My biggest lack and the challenge to my parenting is the lack of patterning/modeling to be a confident powerful man in touch with my feelings and engaged in life.

Brent

Well, I know that holding on to resentment hurts my heart. I don't have children; however I know that my resentments hurt those around me. I am not fully present. I am afraid and closed to love. I'm not sharing myself with others, as they might want me to. I imagine my children would simply inherit my unresolved (and resolved) -problem.

How do you honor the value of "fathering" in your life?

Steven

I am not a father, and may never be. But I have come to realize that I need other men to see the father in me. I've been so blessed by many men who have acknowledged that part of me, and even thanked me for it. I've helped younger men do some powerful work, and been told that they wished they had gotten that kind of love from their own fathers. I've been brought to tears many times by comments like these. My own relationship with my father is the thing I'm most proud of in my life. Dad has showed up alongside me in this journey, willing to share and be a different kind of father. I am so blessed by that.

Allen

I have come to appreciate my dad, which is a long way from hating him. It was actually not until I got involved in Amway and learned how to talk that I realized that I got that from him. He never knew a stranger in the world. This was a great value for my success in Amway. By forgiving my father I was able to tap into his good qualities in me. Also, I can appreciate where he came from. His dad died when he was real young and he grew up with out any role models and did the best he could. Part of my recovery is taking what I liked and leave the rest. Honor and take what I like form him and choose to not take what I don't like. Like the constant women chasing he did. I got some self-esteem from seeing his struggle with self-esteem. I have the self-esteem that he struggled all his life to get and did not. I even got a book on our family history from him and read about all the great people in our family's past and I can see and take in what he could not. That is something I can pass on to my kids.

Henry

I honor the value of "fathering" in my life by trying to do the best I can with what I have to work with!

Joel

I enjoy the children where I work. I find myself giving to them and am protective of them. I also, look to mentor younger men.

Brent

I do men's work. I honor and bless men who have been on the planet longer than I.

Roy

I have learned the value of men appreciating the father in other men and look for opportunities to do so. To me it is one part of being an adult man.

How do you let men support you as a man: a father, a son, and a brother?

Henry

I let men support me by accepting their support with gratitude and reciprocating when I know it will be beneficial to them—even when it comes to giving or sharing the limelight.

Wilson

I let men support me—Absolutely, like a brother. It has taken two-thirds of my life to get here and only happened through my work with men and learning to let them help me.

Allen

I let men support me every week in my New Warrior I group. They support me as a man, as a brother, for they honor me and listen, challenge me, and keep me honest.

Joel

It is difficult. Since I was prevented from trusting my father as a man, I find myself isolating myself from other men who might be supportive to me.

Brent

I don't always. Sometimes, I allow them to pass the time with me, I let them be kind to me, and I let them experience my authenticity.

What does it mean to forgive the father but not condone the action?

Allen

I like to think I have forgiven him. For I have a lot of his action in me I had to learn to work on in me to get beyond. I like chasing women. It is one of the main reasons I took the New Warrior Training– to break my attraction to 'needy' women. I love sailing through my father, and forgive the beating and drinking problems for I know I gain by not doing that.

I forgive my self and, since we are so alike, I have also found I have forgiven him as well.

Darryl

For me, forgiveness came as the recognition that, for all his faults, for all of what he had never been taught or never learned, Dad was the one who survived and who didn't leave us, who tried over and over to figure out how to raise four very smart, rebellious and antagonistic children during the sixties and early seventies. Though he appeared to be the bad guy, the source of Mom's unhappiness, he was the one who stayed. She was the one who left by suicide when I was 13, not Dad. So, I came to value what he DID do for us, and that became my version of the story of our history together.

I resolved this one at about the time he came to live and die at our house, under hospice care, when my children were very young, so they never had to live through me carrying all that anger and hatred toward Dad.

Frank

Forgiving the father but now condoning the action means that one is able to recognize that everyone has their weaknesses and their failures and if you can look back and see that your father tried his very best, you can forgive the mistakes. No one is perfect.

Recognizing those weaknesses and trying to improve on them is the key to making sure one is the best father he can be and that one doesn't make the same mistake their fathers made. Of course, we all get to make new mistakes -with our children.

Kobe

To truly forgive is to forever give up the right to complain about that person, either to yourself, others or the person you are forgiving. Blaming that person for something in your life is a way of complaining. So, to truly forgive, you actually accept responsibility for your life exactly the way it is, and exactly the way it isn't.

Holding onto this resentment is just another wall between yourself and the person you're considering forgiving. You sort of give up the notion of a clean-slate relationship with that person. It also demonstrates to your child that perhaps it's healthy and desirable to hold onto this resentment. While holding onto the resentment may feel good at the moment (I mean, after all you're right and they are wrong!!), I could see that it can lead to a very shallow and meaningless relationship.

Joel

Forgiveness, in the truest Christian sense, is an act of letting go. You have genuinely forgiven another, when his or her action no longer adversely affects you. It is not condoning the action; it is that the action no longer commands your attention.

Ike

As I understand it, my father was the source of a primary wound to me. This "abandonment wound" has shaped my personality, my choice of mate, and many of the problems I have encountered in relationships. I knew his father and so I thought it was no mystery where his harshness and distance came from, but it did not start there. Last year my father told me that his father's father died when he was eight and a new man "took" his mother and he was apparently harsh and difficult. So the "beginnings" go way back. What is incredibly humbling is the impact that my divorce is that I am passing on some of those abandonment wounds. When I condemn my father I condemn myself. I want to stop that cycle and begin a new one of connection and healing. What is also humbling and empowering is that the energy I have to see people be connected, healed and engaged in their lives comes directly from this very same wound. That understanding gives me peace.

Marcus

I spent many years being angry at and blaming my father for things he did or didn't do. I'm sure I haven't eradicated all of the blame and resentment, but I've made headway. I now have an ideal father who lives in me. I can conjure a mental image of my Dad, smiling at me, blessing my life. I can remember positive interactions that we had more readily, and see loving motivations behind some of his behaviors that I'd previously judged as bad.

I'm a Dad, and it's essential to me to find the good that I can take from my father and carry it forward to the next generation. There are things that my dad did that I wouldn't do. I bless him for doing the best he could with what resources he had—holding the resentment ultimately would embitter me and draw me closer to the behaviors I don't want to repeat. I choose to forgive, not blindly, I will bring light to the darkness, look at what's there, and let it go, or reframe it.

Brent

Forgiveness is a fairly new concept to me actually, within the past couple of weeks. This question sounds like talking about the ability to separate the person from the behavior. I believe the potential for all people exists in all people. Mother Theresa, Gandhi, Hitler, Sadam Hussein . . . the potential for the human condition lies in me. The action of another is an action I could easily have been involved in, given I had taken a certain path. That is to say, the concept of forgiveness that most speaks to me is the cessation of harboring resentment toward or against another entity, in this case the father. In so doing, compassion and understanding is injected into the process, placing itself between my heart and the sense of resentment, giving the resentment back to the universe. An expression and release of my resentments, fills me with new space for compassion. I am figuring this out as I type.

Randy

I believe the only way to forgive is to truly understand. If forgiving statements are made without a gut-level comprehension of why this happened, then I as a child cannot separate long enough to be free from my father's violations. True forgiveness is seeing the real heart of the matter, and that is when the condoning or not condoning becomes irrelevant. At that moment, I as a child see that my father's actions were only a projection of his denial to see and therefore had nothing whatsoever to do with me.

Did you accept your mother's interpretation of your father, or really see him for his true blessing and shortcoming on your own?

Dave

I bought my mom's interpretation of my dad hook, line and sinker. Dad also made this easy by the way he acted toward us. Needless to say, our family was and is still extremely dysfunctional and unhealthy. Growing up in a household like this has really distorted my view of men, women, mothers, fathers, families unit...you name it. I'm 35 and have only in the past couple of years been trying to figure out what is healthy and normal...how I've been affected and how I need to change. I am not proud of the status of my current relationship with him. It is superficially fine but no depth at all. I don't know how to go about changing it.

Laurence

I always held my own opinions of my father independent of anything my mother expressed. I was fortunate to have two very good parents all things considered, though I didn't always communicate with them in the most constructive ways.

Bob

Many of my actual problems come from the fact that I have always considered I did not measure up with my father. I began to grow up and become a man myself when I realized that the image I had of my father was my mother's. What I know about corporate culture and the exterior world (politics, economics, etc.) I have learned from my father.

Wilson

I was a dutiful loving son to my father. He died when I was 15 so we did not get to experience a lot of turmoil, separation, or conflict. I have always longed for that fulfillment.

Wilson

I was fortunate in that I NEVER took my mother's view of my father into consideration. I completely trusted my experience with him even when I knew his shortcomings.

Ron

I grew up seeing my dad through my mother's eyes. He was overseas a couple times, and then when he was home I didn't see him much. He would be reading the paper or a book or watching television. I didn't even speak with him for many years, but in my mid-30's I sought him out and asked him to tell me about himself and his life, and he did. He died a year later. If I hadn't sat him down and asked him for his side of the story I would never have heard it. After that I understood how distorted my understanding of my father had always been. I got to know him after he died, by remembering him, by spending time alone with him, so to speak, without anyone around to interpret him for me.

Darryl

Mother died when I was 13, before she could really render much of a verbal interpretation to me about my dad. It took a very long time for me to see Dad's shortcomings and blessings clearly. My involvement in men's work, particularly the New Warrior Network and the ManKind Project, has been very helpful in my re-writing that relationship.   Today the only remaining negative spokesperson for Dad-as-Evil-One is my older sister. With her I just refer occasionally to what I am grateful for about the way Dad was, and don't take on all the re-hashing of what didn't work.

Joel

My "mother's interpretation" of my father was brutal, haranguing and lethal to my developing a positive sense of masculinity. It was hard to filter out her hostility and see him as he actually was. I am still experiencing him and developing an appreciation for the man. My mother's interpretation of my father was overwhelming to me as a child. It has taken many years to bless his true nature, and I still suffer from having him taken from me as a role model by her.

Kobe

I think I saw my father for who he was, but only after around 15-years-old or so. Before that, I tended to accept my mother's interpretation of my father, which was always very good. She was very supportive of him. It wasn't until after 15 or so that I started to form my own opinions about him (and life, for that matter). Interestingly, these opinions continued until age 30, when I forgave him and really started a relationship with him as a new person.

Tom

I reckon I've usually accepted my father's own projections... Indeed, I know that I have very rarely accepted my mother's views in this regard. And I often think that I should listen more "openly" to her opinions in general, but regrettably, for most of my life I've found it difficult to do so.

Ike

When I was younger I accepted my mother's interpretation as fact. I have not fully gained an appreciation for the blessings, or his humanness.

Marcus

I believe that I now see him from my own perspective, and I know that for years my perception of him was strongly influenced by my mother's story about him. My relationship with my Dad continues to evolve, though he died when I was 16. As I journey through my own fatherhood, I understand him more, as I do my own personal work, I see him in a different light.

Brent

Well, I grew up fairly confused here I had three step fathers, and grew up thinking that one man was my biological father, when in fact it turned out that another man was. Not only did I accept my mother's interpretation or lack thereof, I inherited her concept of man and father as part of my own identity, part of who I am, mostly I recall inheriting the bad stuff.

Frank

I never accepted my mother's interpretation of my father. My parents have a strong marriage, and I always saw them as "one person" until I was old enough to see that I was a lot like my father. Noticing that my mannerisms and my reaction to emotional situations were similar to my father made me realize that we probably shared many of the same hopes, dreams, and fears. That realization made me realize that my father, although appearing strong to me, probably had the same weaknesses I did.

What does it mean to be a good father?

Mark

Being a good father begins with recognizing that love begins at birth. Giving unconditional love to a newborn child who may only recognize touch, smell and other senses is different for a man like me to have accepted and still given love unselfishly.

I remember my first born like it was yesterday and remember how I transferred through this rite of passage into fatherhood. I looked into her eyes and saw myself only smaller and weaker. I saw the innocence of a child enter the world without fear. I saw my child for the first time and she saw me and knew I belonged there.

As my family grew, I had a second daughter, more beautiful than the first if only because I already knew how I would love seeing her enter this world, and knowing that I would love her at first sight. My love affair with my daughters has blossomed through the years and they are now grown, and one has married to start her own family.

Being a good father is not enough. A man must be a good man first and then he can be a good father. Since I am learning to love being the man I am, I know that I am a great father. This has come from the letting in of other men into my life. I cared (and continue to care) about my children's lives, their toys and their days, despite my absence at home while working.

I played and provided unselfishly and made a happy and peaceful home environment. I chose a mother who loved and cared for them unconditionally and complimented my personality. As they grew, I always marked the milestones like birthdays, sports games, school events, teacher meetings, family functions, vacations, quality home time and many firsts like teaching how to ride a bicycle and eat a pizza, take photos, write and keep lasting memories.

Many of these memories are reminded to me recently. I have uncovered my daughter's gift to me on my 42nd birthday which I am scanning and attaching. She wrote, "101 Thank You Daddy's."

Being a good father is one of many great commitments a man can accomplish in his life. The journey is long and winding and something to enjoy despite the possibility that it will be rocky and not always sunny and dry. However, the only thing which remains most important to me is my children's love and recognition of how good a father I am by them marrying the type of man that I am.

I remember a wise fat man tell me that "daughters marry their fathers." Well, I know this man was right, and if that is the only fact of life for any man out there, then there is no option but to be a good father. Love is the only driving force which will overcome all other emotions and desires. Love is unselfish and pure and giving it away only gives me more of the same.

I wish that I understood this at an earlier age so I could have taken in so much more that I knew I could have made time for. However, I am grateful that I recognize so much now and am living my life with passion and fury.

Being a good father forced me to be a good man, a good husband, a good friend, a good son, a good brother and just good. It doesn't stop at the limitation of any one-life role. Good is good, just like black or white.

Being a good father is wonderful and rewarding. It gives me a chance to grow up a second time around. A chance to experience anything I missed during the first childhood. As I enter my older years, I hope for the bonus experience of being a good grandfather someday. I will be ready to experience my childhood again and be certain to be a good father again.

101 THANK YOU DADDY'S (from my daughter)
1. For always changing my diapers
2. For seeing that I grew up all right
3. For teaching me not to act when I'm angry
4. For fixing the toilet seat
5. For writing me little notes.
6. For teaching me how to drive
7. For buying me a new car

8. For fixing all of my car troubles
9. For making me laugh at your stupid jokes
10. For introducing me to Johnny's pizza
11. For putting up with my crying fits
12. For teaching me how to relax
13. For helping me learn right from wrong
14. For trusting me
15. For teaching me responsibility
16. For taking me skiing all of these years
17. For always buckling my ski boots
18. For always buying lifesavers for the chairlifts
19. For going out to lunch with me even when you were busy
20. For having patience when I didn't understand something
21. For always getting me out of trouble
22. For not killing me when I got my first speeding ticket {or my second for that matter}
23. For standing by my side when I had to talk to the judge
24. For spending time with me even though you were busy
25. For making fun of the guys who had hurt me
26. For beating Donny at basketball
27. For reminding me of how I gave bear hugs
28. For taking me to the Big Apple Circus
29. For knowing when to leave me alone
3D. For noticing when I lose weight
31. For teaching me to think for myself
32. For never underestimating my intelligence
33. For helping me not have a nervous breakdown during my SAT'S
34. For getting me a limo on my birthday
35. For hiring good looking men to work for you
36. For making snowmen with me
37. For helping me build a birdhouse
38. For taking me on vacations
39. For introducing me to slammers {and tequila}
4D. For getting drunk with me on Super Bowl Sunday.
41. For helping me realize not to smoke and drive
42. For picking me up when I got homesick
43. For picking me up 4:30 in the morning on New Years Eve
44. For buying me my first pair of diamond earrings
45. For going through life making sure I was happy

46. For taking me to fancy shmancy restaurants
47. For surprising me at work when I really needed it
48. For standing behind 'we" on important issues
49. For being there to share my happiness when I got my college acceptance letters
50. For dealing with my insurance agent
51. For not breaking down the first time I shaved my legs
52. For letting me borrow all your clothes {although you didn't know about every time}
53. For telling me secrets mom told you not to
54. For teaching me how to jet ski
55. For not complaining when I put seven holes in my ears
56. For encouraging me to always be myself
57. For giving me long answers to yes and no questions
58. For teaching me to be optimistic
59. For buying me little surprises when I was sick
60. For buying me my first rose
61. For making sure I always had snow tires
62. For making me watch "Being There"
63. For giving me money to put gas in my car. ,
64. For never putting down my dreams and aspirations
65. For telling me of my childhood experiences
66. For getting me 18 presents for my eighteenth birthday
67. For knowing the difference between good friends and not good ones
68. For helping me be a good judge of character.
69. For helping me dig my car out of the snow
70. For making your famous soups
71. For not making fun of my obsession with Mr. Wilson
72. For wanting to take me drinking on my eighteenth birthday
73. For explaining to me my accounts when mom got fed up with me
74. For fixing the springs on my bed
75. For spending Sundays watching movies with me
76. For buying me my first pretzel in New York City
77. For writing me a "What 2 Do" poem
78. For not getting mad when I didn't set the table
79. For teaching me how to say "ok"
80. For not getting mad at me when I cut school

81. For teaching me that grades aren't the most important things in life
82. For camping trips we took together as a family
83. For having water fights with me in the pool
84. For raking the leaves into piles and then jumping in them with me. "
85. For taking me to my first Yankee game
86. For coming to watch me play basketball
87. For carving our initials into trees
88. For showing me where and how you grew up
89. For teaching me the value of a dollar
90. For bringing me to see the tree in Rockefeller center
91. For introducing me to Hamakashlema
92. For teaching me how to ride a bike
93. For saying stupid things to make me smile
94. For worrying about me when I wasn't home on time
95. For never really complaining about my bad habits
96. For letting me keep all my 6 million animals
97. For always making me laugh where it counts the most...in my heart
98. For still making me believe that one day I could be a princess
99. For walking into my life when the rest of the world walked out
100. For being my best friend
101. For loving me the way I love you

I just thought I would remind you of how thankful I am for everything you have done for me. These are just a few of the items. If I put all the things I was thankful for I would never be able to finish. I love you dad—HAPPY BIRTHDAY!

Love,
Suzy

Von

I feel I had done a lot of 'making it up as I go along' about being a father since my father died when I was 18, thus leaving a gap in my adult relationship model. Although I held no resentment towards my father, the model I recall growing up was that adult males were basically "drinking buddies", rather than nurturing parents. My father-in-law was a self-made man, with alcoholic roots and characteristics, which further delayed my understanding of a better model for fatherhood. Now, as the father of a 19 year old son, I work hard to demonstrate my model of adult male relationships. To reinforce this model, I have asked my current mentors to reach out to my son, just to ensure that he has another person or two to reach out to, should our relationship struggle for whatever reason. They have since provided him personal references for job and scholarship applications and also help keep me tuned in to what I need to be focused on, to ensure that he matures productively.

Fredrick

I don't have children, but I did feel a deep sense of connection with my father. Like most men of his era, he was gone a lot – that was and is the double-bind for men. To be good fathers, they have to be good providers. And that translates into being physically absent most of the time. In many ways the best thing my father did for me was to be a heroic figure. He built an airplane and flew it – a little single-seat bi-plane, like the Red Baron. He'd wear a leather helmet and goggles, and I was so proud of him when I was about twelve years I could have burst. I still love that gift. I just felt that my dad was a lot cooler than my friends' dads. I could sense they felt it too, which made it even better. It all sounds silly and shallow now, but, hey, I was twelve! It meant a huge amount to me then, and I'll always be grateful to my dad for that.

Gary

I am asking that question right now! My son is only 12 weeks old (I'm 56!), so the parenting thing is too new for me. But my father put me on a pedestal, ignored stuff he shouldn't have, and criticized mercilessly stuff he should have let go of. I'm conflicted: unwilling to accept my role as an "elder," yet much happier with my father than my mother in my life.

I was a goody-goody two shoes. In college even, I'd defend my father (at Yale, wondering whether to support George Wallace or Richard Nixon!). But the negative, prejudiced talk he'd confine to home (where he'd sound off and dominate the conversation), I'd take out on the road. It was tough.

At the end of his life, when he lost his memory, he also lost his prejudice! It was one of the most astonishing lessons I ever got from him.

And now I'm dependent upon him from the grave: as my own career went into the toilet, my inheritance from him is what keeps me afloat. Much irony from the young man who was so proud I needed "no help from anyone!"

Ronald

I do not have a son. I do not regret either being the father of a single child or that my child is a girl. I live at home in a world surrounded by women, (even the cat is female), and still believe that one of the most enriching parts of my life has been being a dad.

I am not my father, a wonderful man whom I admired and loved dearly. One of the most difficult moments of my life came as he lay on his sick bed and when it became clear there was no hope of recovery I was able to find the courage to request no further intervention for active care. Part of that courage came from him along with many other traits and characteristics of my being. Within a few moments he had left us.

One of my life's most meaningful moments happened simultaneously. The last words my father heard anyone ever say before he slipped from a semi into a full coma were, "I love you Dad." They were words I never remember him saying to me although I know that was how he felt. I cannot recall a hug or a kiss from him. It was the way he was. It is not how I am.

My daughter has come to know a father, a man, who can say, "I love you," who can demonstrate affection in a physical way in public and in private. Is it because she is a daughter not a son? Possibly, but I don't think so. I took from my father what he was and loved him for it. I give to my daughter what I am and am blessed she loves me for it as well. I did not see my father as perfect and certainly my daughter does not view me as omnipotent or infallible, but she loves me anyway. I hope she will be spared having to make the kind of final decision I made for my Dad, but I can think of no better end than to hear her say, "I love you Dad."

Arthur

I was reflecting on this recently when my 8-year-old seemed really disappointed at my not making his art class which I regularly help with for the last hour of school on Thursdays. I thought of how my father had never come near my school and never knew any of my school mates yet one generation later and here was 'that look' that I knew, yet I could name every kid in his class! One part of me was with the irony and humor of this, and another part of me could see that there was much of my own pain as a boy for the father that never 'showed up.'

So for me being there is important. Perhaps I overcompensate but I am a regular at school and I enjoy it. My business operates from home and I have great flexibility with my time. I truly value this.

I try to be as honest as I can with my kids—to do my best to own my stuff ups and apologize when I am wrong or have acted poorly. So I don't pretend to be anything I am not with them. My upbringing was strict and we could never play inside, or burp out loud, or get too dirty...... So I love a good indoor romp or a great burp or sitting in a pile of dirt!

There are times when my own parents jump out at me and take over, it's an eye opener. Controlling and authoritarian. I hate that part of me, yet know that hate is no path for growth. It usually surfaces when I am tired or I'm focused on something else and they get in the way wanting something else. Also it can appear when I feel as if they are not hearing me.

I would like to be calmer in these times. A true father to me is one who can remain calm amidst chaos – I'm working on that.

In my group other men have spoken about the hope of finding a deeper relationship with their blood brothers and I have an ambivalent relationship with my brother—we have never really hit it off. I really felt into this and am sure that my brotherly needs are met by other men and I am happy with this.

My relationship with my Dad has moved considerably. I have discussed much with him and whilst I would like more I realize that he has moved quite a deal from where he stood and I need to be patient and accepting. My work with rites of passage has his interest and he and my stepmother ask many questions of this and me, so that feels supported and valued to me.

Joel

To provide for your family and to be emotionally present.

Communicate, inform, guide, be there when needed and eventually let go.

Tom

I have been blessed with a wonderful father, so I try to emulate his ways (when it is appropriate) as much as possible. I am trying to offer love, honesty, support, comfort & shelter, and protection. I pray for wisdom and strength...

Ike

Being a good father means I am walking in my power and light and teaching my kids to walk in their power and light. For me, that means that I am celebrating who they really are and teaching them to own the responsibility for the impact they have on the world. On a good day I model that for them. On other good days, I have an opportunity to model "acting my way back into integrity."

Evan

In my experience as a father and son, and based on my observations and conversations, it is my judgment that we men usually find it easier not to over-identify with our children, thus giving them more space to grow and realize their independence as well as a healthy interdependence.

Brent

A good father listens. A good father hears. A good father touches. A good father holds his ground. I could go on forever . . . a good father is grounded.

Joel

To provide for your family and to be emotionally present.

Communicate, inform, guide, be there when needed and eventually let go.

What is unique about the way men parent?

Dan

I feel strongly that many fathers do not parent, or do not parent very much, because they aren't allowed to or encouraged to by the mothers, by their employers, and by our culture. Constantly told whatever they do is not enough, right, or useful. This was very much true when my generation were learning, or rather not learning, to be fathers. It seems different now, though I have substantial doubts about the actual realities. Being a father is also compounded by the enormous social pressure on men to be "men" rather than to be what their selves choose to be. I think that being a useful father is as much about knowing and expressing yourself as it is about how you do the parenting things.

Benjamin

This chapter opens so many thoughts that I can't possibly write them all here. A man offers to his children love and acceptance first of all; guidance in delaying gratification and in developing healthy priorities; respect for others; respect for property; respect for the environment; honesty; integrity; and how to accept failure when it comes. He teaches by example more than by words, though words have their place.

I hold only sympathy for my father, who was maligned when he hadn't the strength or time to correct the maligner, my mother. I hold regrets that I didn't discover what a great man he was until I was 25. At that age I rejected my mother's interpretation of him totally, and severed my connection with her and her mother. I bear her no resentment or hatred, as those emotions would be like cancers in my life. The severance was such that I did, without any remorse, attend the funeral of neither. I am convinced that Dad did the best he could under withering and constant attacks from his wife and his mother- and father-in-law. As it was, I learned a great deal of value from him in spite of that. In the past six years I have discovered the joys of fathering. I have several men fifteen to forty years younger than I who treat me like their father. Through my own near-disastrous mistakes, and through the caring example of two very fine men in my early thirties, I find wisdom and an instinct for parenting totally unanticipated. This capability is further unanticipated considering that my own father was prevented from fathering me. From the third-hand testimonials I receive, that seems not to be over-inflated. The self-appraisal is quite in contrast to the dismal self-image I once had.

What Insights did you personally gain from this chapter?

What do you want to commit to or re-commit to out of these insights?

Remember!
"Insight without committed action is only entertainment!"

Chapter 11
About Mother

How does resolving issues with your mother enhance your current relationship?

Has any part of you taken on the role with your mother of making up for what she did not get from your father? How do you get freedom from that?

What does it take to resolve issues with your mother? What specifically have you done to resolve issues with your mother? What does it mean to be complete with your mother?

How do you treat your partner like your mother?

What was your mother's image of your father and how much of that did you accept?

What is the gift that mothers give to us?

◆**Martin's thoughts and experience with this topic and questions:**

◆A man spoke up at one of the Men's Inquiry meetings on mother issues (included here by permission) and said, "My mother has a severe health condition and she is not doing what her doctor and my common sense says she needs to do to take care of herself. I asked her what she would do if the tables were reversed, and I had a serious health problem and was not taking care of myself. She got very upset and quickly got off the phone. I have discussed this many times with her. Even went to visit and just hang out with her. We would get along and she would agree to do something, but nothing would happen. I finally decided that it is time for me to let it go. I told my father I was no longer going to try to force this issue. I don't want this to overshadow the last times I spend with her or let it get in the way of just being with her."

◆Another man said, "My relationship with my mother, huh? Well, that's probably at the heart of my problems. My mother always was and still is critical of me. It doesn't hurt as much as it did when I was a kid. Dad split before I was born. I've learned to handle it better or at times just plain ignore it."

◆A third man said, "Where I get into trouble is that there is still a part of me that is seeking my mother's love and approval and when I don't get it, I blame myself and think that it is my fault. Rationally, I know this isn't true but it's hard to change this perception. I realize that my mother was not capable of giving me the love that I wanted and needed at that time and is probably never going to be able to. That hurts. It is also hard for me to accept. I finally figured out how I trash relationships with women by trying to get my mother's love through them. Do I love myself? Some days yes, some days no.

♦ "My big problem is what to do about this? In my mind, just letting it go seems like a cop out; like nothing happened and that my hurt isn't real. It also seems to let my mother off the hook, and no one seems responsible for my hurt and pain. I realize that Mother isn't capable of giving the love that I want and need but it just doesn't seem fair. Deep down I want someone to say that they are sorry for what happened to me and that my feelings are real and not imaginary. I'm tired of blaming myself and taking the responsibility for something that isn't my fault. If anyone of you have ideas I'd greatly appreciate them."

♦Another man responded. "Well your mother is what she is and I doubt she will change now. It is clear you are the only one still being hurt by holding on to this, I don't think your mother is losing any sleep over it. What if you just declared you got what you need from you mother and the rest is food for your own personal development. Sometimes our wounds give us our greatest gold or gifts."

♦He answered, "Well it has showed me the value of a mother's love by experiencing its absence. Come to think of it I may have not have become a teacher with out that; maybe I would have not taken that path without that wound. I always am an advocate that we look out and care for children. Show them their value and my students do well. Interesting."

♦Like the man said, the mother you had (or did not have) is the mother you had. You can not change what happened but you can change how you respond to it. You may find some gold in the wounds.

♦My own mother, now in her 80's, was a real pioneer for the rights of people who were persecuted. In her North Carolina women's college she was part of an honor group that studied and re-enacted politics. The best students won the right to go to Raleigh to role play the State Congress while the actual congress was not in session. She proposed a bill that "Blacks" should no longer be required to sit in the back of the bus, before the real bill was ever publicized or enacted, and when the news of her proposal showed up in a newspaper report. the KKK burned a cross on her college campus! She was called before the dean who told her they might lose funding because of her act. He said she was ahead of her time, threatening her expulsion if she continued with radical behavior.

♦I remember one time when my mother heard about something I was doing to make changes at IBM...I was creating a grass roots motivation of the employees in the service and support area. My mother warned me that I could get in trouble trying to make so many changes and asked where I learned this. I told her that I learned it from her! My mother had the courage to make a real difference in the world and was not always popular for it. I am fortunate that she is still with us at this time and hope she realizes what a contribution she was to the world and my life. Did I have problems with my mother, of course! Was I a lot of trouble to my mother, you bet! I can still remember her saying, "Wait until you have kids." My mind was so active I was always "getting into things." I also did my share of blaming her for things, but that certainly didn't improve my life. The more I courageously took steps to face my own issues, the more those past problems faded.

The Men Address Selected Questions

How does resolving issues with your mother enhance your current relationship?

Allen
Otherwise you will just find someone to play your mother or convert her into that. It is simple; I had to marry my mother twice in different women to figure this out. I wish I had this book three marriages ago!

Arthur
The topic of my mother is loaded for me! My father was unavailable and my mother then turned her emotional stuff onto me, the oldest and also male child. Dad was a minister and so

285

much is expected in provincial towns of someone of such standing. We had to be perfect! So behind closed doors was where we could be human, pity that for children this is not clear. So there was my shaming, and as I put it, 'emotional hijacking' from my mother. If she was happy, I could be happy but if she was upset then I had some dancing to do.

Her view of my father was not great as I recall, and in recent years my brother and I have recalled how she would say "You're just like your father!' She has been married four times and despite her success in the world, still manages to find men she can control and put them at the head of the table or behind the wheel of the new Mercedes, yet to me they look like a puppet on a string.

So for my relationships it has been difficult and a co-dependent dance for sure. Mum was and is very competent, yet has no sense of herself. She cares so much about what others think. So my expectations of women have been askew – they must be good housekeepers (mothers) and look good, yet be emotionally volatile.

I have noticed when my wife is angry something inside of me stirs and I have to do something. This is my greatest learning and something I have mixed success with.

Mum and I get on much better now. I noticed how some years ago I just needed to get away from her and wondered if in some way I was inadvertently putting myself through a rite of passage. I recalled how some African tribes had the son not speak to his mother for a year or more. I was curious about this. The following was suggested to me.

I wrote her a letter that was petty and naming and blaming and held nothing back. I really put everything into this. Then I sat with it for a while and was amazed at how acknowledging all this really bought up my stuff and for a few days I was an irritable pain in the ass. Yet I knew I had to allow this and while I used the EFT mantra mentioned earlier, it did seem to work. Once it lifted I did a ceremony in my back yard where I put on some appropriate music, lit a fire and sat with the letter, read it again then put it to the flame.

Then I wrote another letter that was more considerate and had nothing in between the lines—a letter she would receive. This felt good despite Mum not liking the letter at all and she sure pulled out all the weaponry. It was both a difficult time in letting her own reaction out and it was also a very enlightening time as I saw [things] happening around me. It took some time to settle down, things got worse before they got better — so much pain pushed down.

We finally had the epiphany that could have gone horribly wrong but for my wife stepping in and settling things down and leaving us together. I asked Mum if we could start over and that I'd like to tell my story to her as I see it and then she could respond as she saw fit. Well, by the time I had finished, Mum was crying and agreeing with me... asking questions.... and the one thing she said that I recall most fondly was in reference to my sharing that I had this thing that was missing in my belly, something was missing. She said that she has felt that way all her life. I felt like an adult speaking with her for the first time. It was a moment I had not seen coming.

We still have our moments but I do feel that she is far more accepting as to who I am rather than who she wants me to be. Addressing these issues with my mother has enhanced my relationship with my wife. It is as if I see her as her, and sometimes before, I would see her at times as my mother.

Blake

I don't know, really. I do know that my parents had a long and loving relationship, though I could sense that they were often deeply frustrated by communication problems and the self-sacrifice each often made for the other, sometimes fruitlessly—even to the extent, I said to myself a couple of years before getting married that I would never get married. I could see the frustration and yet it did not seem to be worth it. There were NO character issues, as in my own marriage. Both marriages have similarities. My dad was, like me, that reasonable, self-sacrificing, fair-minded etc. So was my mom. In my own marriage, my wife is more willful than my mom, and therefore we have much more conflict, but the underlying sources of deep frustration seem similar.

Aaron

I know this might be a bit of a bummer but you wanted honest and this is what is true for me about my mother. I was born in 1960, and I was raised by man hating women. I never knew my father, etc. Of course when they would realize I was in the room with their rhetoric, they would say, "Except for you, you're different." I still don't really know what they meant when they would tell me that. Was I a different kind of man, or not a man at all? I still wrestle with that. I know now that I am a good man, but I'm still not totally sure what they meant. I have a few ideas, but they are only guesses.

Well, in their view of changing the world for the better, I was taught that it was okay to cry, and express emotion. When I was pre-adulthood they all patted themselves on the back when I was moved to tears or when I could talk about what I was feeling. I would overhear them talking about how they were creating the perfect man. But when I became an adult, all the rules changed. Societiy's' views were changing as well. I found that women who were around men who cry thought these men were too sensitive, and yes, even weak. All of a sudden I was confronted with the attitude that I should be the strong burly man who could be sensitive to a woman's tears, but keep mine inside where they belong. So I started stuffing. I also started drinking, and dabbling in drug use. After a time the drugs left my life, but alcohol was always there when I wasn't supposed to share my feeling with those around me. It would work temporarily, but my anger and rage over the double standard always got the better of me. I would get very hurtful to those around me. I am not, and have never been violent, but there is more than one way to damage a human being. I became quite good at it. I spent my younger years freely expressing emotion, but when I became an adult that genie did not want to go back into the bottle.

To this day I am emotionally messed up. I try to keep my emotions in check, but they always get away from me. If I'm sad, I feel worse when someone sees me cry. People still make fun of me when I am moved to tears by movies or music. I try to only do it in private. I find it difficult to tell people when I'm upset without yelling & screaming and ranting & raving. If you know what I mean. With love I am either too passionate, or too distant. I can't seem to find a balance there. With society's views on inappropriate behavior these days, I rarely touch anyone anymore. My mother did not prepare me for the real world and think I missed something, not having a father or even a good man in my life to play that role. I am very lonely because I can't seem to have a decent relationship with anyone, male or female. That creates more uncontrollable emotion. Depression is a constant in my life.

Strangely enough when I'm not depressed I am extremely happy. I have tried prescribed mood stabilizing, I hate them!

As you might imagine I'm in therapy. I think about suicide a lot, but I don't want to do that. I just want to be normal, if there is such a thing. I pray that some day I will figure it out, and find a way to live with my extreme emotions. For you Trekkies out there. I feel like a Vulcan. Always trying to control intense emotions.

Thanks for letting me carry on. I'm feeling very shaky now, but it helps to say it and get it out. I am glad there is a place to talk about this.

Dan

Like any relationship, resolving issues with my mother would have taken my mother resolving issues with me, which she never made any attempt to do. Just before she went off the edge mentally, she still complained that I hadn't become a lawyer in Chicago, lived in our suburb, and joined the country club—when she was 83 and I was 50. She had absolutely no notion of me as an individual. I was only a symbol to her of a social status. As long as I enhanced her status—and I did until I was in my mid 30s — I was visible. When I stopped enhancing her social status, I become invisible to her and she believed only in the son she wanted me to be.

A large part of my life was always at odds with my mother's intentions for me. By the time I was 12, I'd become a past master at living my life when I could, and her life for me the rest of the time. By the time I went to college I just wanted to get as far away from her as possible and be a real person, and I did (although the last part took 35 more years).

I treat no one like my mother treated me. Everyone is him or her self. No one is a symbol of my expectations and desires.

"To be complete with my mother" would be a death sentence for me. The only world she saw or conceived was the one in which the "neighbors" and the "family" dictated everything. There was no place in her world for individuals, for real people.

My mother got everything from my father she wanted, or convinced herself she did. She pretty much pushed and pushed until she got it. Only once or twice did I ever see my father stand up to her. That was only when she became a danger to me or my

289

sister, not—let me hasten to clarify—a physical danger, but a manipulative danger.

My mother adored my father and thought that he was perfect; she played the grieving widow and wore her wedding ring for 20 years longer. Growing up, I had no reason to doubt her opinion of my father. By the time I was in high school, my opinion was straying very far from this opinion. After working in his office for a summer in college, my opinion was radically different from hers. Thirty years after he died, I found myself increasingly protective of and sorry for the non-life my father lived. The poor man never found himself—or was allowed to find it—and spent his whole life playing roles his parents and my mother imposed on him.

A voice says I should apologize for my clearly negative opinion of my mother—after all one shouldn't attack one's mother. "Should" is a word my mother used all the time, and a word I walked away from ten years ago. I have little reason to speak kindly of my mother in relation to me or to my father, and I'm not going to change this decision just to comply with social "shoulds."

Steven

My mom was orphaned at an early age, and I always noticed the sadness in her eyes. She married a man who, for many years, didn't know how to be available for her, which only deepened her sadness. I spent my whole life trying to make her happy, trying to get rid of her sadness and pain. I tried to do the same for every woman I was with. I thought it was my duty to save her, and then resented her when she didn't show the proper gratitude. It took me a long time to understand that my job wasn't to save any woman, and I had to resolve my mom issues to see that.

Wilson

When I resolved my 'Mom' issues while she was alive, I found that her judgments of my relationships left my head. No longer was I looking for a partner that met her requirements. I only looked to my requirements.

Has any part of you taken on the role with your mother of making up for what she did not get from your father? How do you get freedom from that?

Wilson

When my Dad died, I was 16. I refused to take on any of his roles for Mom and actually isolated myself from her. We pretty much 'went our own ways' at that time. I resented her for living and Dad dying—I even remember saying to myself, "I wish it had been Mom." Since I was a captive of what I did not address, my freedom did not come until later years when I was able to address my issues to Mom and make myself available to her, but now as an adult man with clear boundaries. She did not change, and it didn't matter to me if she did.

Tim

With my parent's divorce I seemed to look as the 'man of the house' to my mother. I felt uncomfortable when she brought her emotional problems to me. Like, "this is not right" but did not know what to do about it. I just tried to not be around when I sensed her emotional need of me. I now think of this as almost emotional incest. I have actually found the healing tools of people who really were sexually abused to have helped me the most.

What does it take to resolve issues with your mother? What specifically have you done to resolve issues with your mother?

Wilson

It took me not running away. The more I stayed away, the more the issues controlled me. Resolution came when I was able to tell Mom how these issues between us had affected me and let her know that I understood how she was affected, too.

Tim

Face what you have to do by yourself and what you have to do in dialogue with her.

Richard

Well I need to speak up, I can tell you that resolving issues with my mother has been the core hell of my life. When I was a little boy, my mother was very unhappy. My father was withdrawn and hostile, and she was isolated and lonely. Coming from a difficult childhood and having no awareness of how to deal with emotional issues, she found herself really struggling to keep it together. At a point when she was probably going through a form of mental/emotional breakdown, she used me to gratify her sexually. Even though I was probably about four, it was obvious to me that the story she was telling me to explain why she was having me do what I was doing made absolutely no sense, and that something deep and powerful which I didn't understand, and wasn't being let in on, was actually happening instead. I was both physically and emotionally repulsed by the situation, and responded in the only way I could think of, which was to resist passively. I sensed that this made her frustrated with me, and then I believe a wave of shame overcame her, and she pushed me away in a self-disgust which I took on as being about me. She then told me that I had to keep quiet about it or else she would cut my penis off.

Needless to say, I had a difficult childhood and adolescence. In eighth grade, I was so nervous at my new school that my shirt was usually soaked with sweat by 9:00 AM. I took a lot of drugs, particularly LSD, and found myself deeply split off from myself and depressed, and struggling mightily to maintain a facade of normalcy above it all. My first marriage ended when I discovered that my wife had lied to me about something she thought was unimportant but was actually potentially life-threatening for me. (It's a long story, and ultimately beside the point.) When I found out the truth, it was as though a chasm opened up in the ground and I was staring into the bowels of Hell. I had no idea at the time, because I had suppressed the memory of the incest to save myself from the risk of blurting out my secret, but I was reliving the moment when I discovered that my mother was a liar, covering up an evil whose depth I could only guess at, and forcing me to cut myself off from her emotionally forever. How could I know she wasn't planning to fatten me up and eat me? From then on, it would be a facade of connection, maintaining stability to survive but never really trusting ever again.

So, I immediately started unconsciously destroying the relationship with my wife, mainly through infidelity and fits of psychotic rage about God-knows-what little thing. And, naturally, she eventually left.

My second wife, to whom I have been married for quite some time, is not like mother. That is to say, she is grounded, and neither capable of not interested in playing emotional games. Nevertheless, I have belittled and verbally and emotionally beaten her up over the course of our marriage, as, I'm sad to say, I have my children (although I'm blessed at this point to be deeply reconciled with all three of them). At times of particular psychic stress, I would fly into fits of defensive life-or-death struggle with the shadows of my mother's blaming, lying, manipulating and withdrawing, lashing out at those who loved me with venom they couldn't remotely understand. It wasn't until five years ago, when my mother was critically ill and I found myself devoid of any sympathy for her, that I began to realize that something was missing from my otherwise exhaustive catalogue of childhood memories. And it has taken all of those five years of very hard work, marked by a painfully failed relationship with a female therapist and years of energetic contraction thereafter, to finally get to a place of real healing.

So what did it take to resolve my issues? Plunging into deep emotional process; retrieving the buried memory; seeing the parallels between my rage at my family members and the original rage I felt towards my mother; owning up to each of them (most recently and liberating my daughter) that I was abusing them because I was reliving my relationship with her; at last meeting one other man who had had a similar experience; AND, most of all, being really and truly loved by someone who has been able to see past the mass of my stuff to who I really am, and who has been willing to hold loving space for me to plunge to the very depths of my core with her and bring out the wounded, self-loathing shrieking child who got stuck there.

I also give thanks to the teachings of the Pathwork, which have guided me to understand all of this as a necessary wounding, to which I have spiritually consented, in order that I might come face to face with my own lower self and my own deviations from spiritual law, all of which pre-existed this incarnation. I don't dwell in victimhood, and I have compassion for my mother, who I am sure was in a Hell of her own when it happened and has been living in shame ever since. I wish I could have lived more of my life being able to be happy, but I know that spiritually I've done what I came here to do, and that's a real source of consolation. To the rest of my life!

What does it mean to be complete or resolve issues with your mother?

Wilson

For me it was losing the control she had over my mind and my relationships and my emotions. I don't think she ever changed, even to the end, but I changed and felt complete when she died. I could not wait for her to reconcile on her side, it may have never come. Completeness, to me, means honoring your Mother but then leaving and leaving the control with her.

Eric

I will toss in an answer for the question regarding the "what does it take to resolve issues with mom" question. This has been a great struggle for me that came to fruition last week. My mom has applied for disability. She had her hearing last week. All of the adventure leading to this point has been against my better judgment and advice, because, due to my work, I know the process and what she will experience.

Her attorney asked me to testify on her behalf. After my dad asked as well I agreed. I sat in the room while her life was pulled apart and her basic sense of identity was questioned. I also found myself so overcome with feelings of wasted anger and shame. I have spent many of the past 10-15 years hating who she had become. My mom's descent into physical and mental frailty in her 50's has been very difficult on the family. Her worsening mental health has been severe enough to require hospitalizations.

My shame is over my lack of ability to do anything about it. As I watched her in the hearing I realized how much of my own drive I projected on to her. In her early life, my mom was a single parent who raised two kids and worked as many jobs as needed so we would be ok. She is one of the strongest women I know.

Then, when I was in my late 20's and in grad school, she began to slide.

Our battles have been over her willful non-compliance with medication, appointments, and her lack of faith in, well, professionals like me.

The profound experience allowed me to simply say to her how proud I was and to testify to the court that she was not who I remember and that it was ok. I also told them why she needed help and why I was unable to be the one to give it.

Setting aside my own ego allowed me to finally be a son. Nothing more or less.

How do you treat your partner like your mother?

Wilson

Isolation and desertion in the tough times, especially the emotional ones. Wanting to control them, and finding that I couldn't, leaving in search of someone I could control. This is important to know so I will be more aware of it if it occurs again and choose a different action.

Laurence

An interesting question now that you ask it. In some ways, I am impatient with my partner, my wife. I expect a lot of her, sometimes ignoring the emotional obstacles that may make it hard for her to address some situations. I can be judgmental, too, which is funny because I think I learned this trait from my mother. At the same time, I can be pretty forgiving of my wife as I was my mother. I really think my mom had little idea about how to raise boys and she had three of them. I wish she could have been comfortable being more affectionate with us as I think then I would not have been so needy of affection in my subsequent adult relationships with women. I've always felt that my affectionate side actually came from my dad. He used to roughhouse with us as youngsters, but in a playful way reminding me of young bear cubs learning to play. I find that I am similar in approach in raising my 13 month old daughter.

Fredrick

Treating my partner as my mother is one screw up thing I can proudly say I have not done. I've been really lucky with my mother. She and I have always been very close, even now when I'm in late mid-life and she is old. We have a naughty sense of humor and a lot of fun together. Strangely, I've only once been seriously attracted to a woman who reminded me of my mother. That was a catastrophe for both of us! I seem to be more sexually bonded with the type of woman better represented by my sister. A Freudian would probably find me pretty vexing because of all that! My mother basically treated my father like someone who needed to be "handled." she was good at it, but I'm not sure it was good for their marriage even though they stayed together until he died.

What was your mother's image of your father and how much of that did you accept?

Wilson

This is a wonderful question, I have never thought of this. As I look back, I can honestly say that I bought NONE of it. In Mom's world we were all just satellites, anyway. My dad was my rock, he was the only one I loved and the only one I trusted. I made up my own mind about him even as a child. I can even remember at 10 years-old asking my dad to divorce my mother—I almost got a whipping for that one, and he told me never to say that again.

Tim

As for my mother image of my father, she sought to denigrate him; yet she has well had faults she tragically didn't feel the confidence to face. By taking her side, I did not get to know my father well.

What Insights did you personally gain from this chapter?

What do you want to commit to or re-commit to out of these insights?

Remember!
"Insight without committed action is only entertainment!"

Chapter 12
Shame and Our Emotional Wounds

How are our emotional wounds often our greatest gifts in life?

How do we forgive others and how do we accept the forgiveness of others?

How do you deal with shame as a man?

How does shame relate to guilt?

What is the cost of avoiding the emotional pain from our past?

What is your shame? What have you been ashamed of in your life? What can you do about it? What do you need to say or do to let it go?

What are you ashamed about yourself? What are parts of yourself that you don't want others to see or know about? What is it that disturbs you about another, that in reflection, you find lives inside of you too?

What do most men do with shame and emotional pain?

Did you ever consider that you can experience joy with grieving?

How does isolating ourselves in pain generally make everything worse, and what are alternatives?

What are constructive ways to deal with emotional pain, emotional wounds?

♦Martin's comments on this topic

♦Some of the gifts we get from our emotional wounds when we deal with them are courage and compassion. Illness and disease are what we tend to get when we avoid them.

♦In a men's workshop that I attended on spirituality conducted by Michael Meade, I remember two comments that had a big impact on me. One is that rituals often look strange, nonsensical, and useless to those who are not involved. This allowed me freedom from looking for the "right" rituals. And the other was that "ritual space" lets us face and move through our greatest emotional pain without feeling a sense of being alone. It forces us to face such questions as: How do I grieve? How do I deal with shame? For me I had just avoided it—or stuffed it—and, when I started to get in touch with it, it came up in buckets so much so that I had a hard time dealing with it. Men's work gives me a safe place to be when I am in pain, it gives me strength to move through it, and then support enough to let it go. It permits me to experience joy while moving through it. Looking for the "gifts" in emotional pain will often lead me to finding those gifts.

♦You will not uncover your wounds thinking about them in isolation. They will often keep controlling you like puppeteer's strings until you resolve them by interacting with your fellow men and the world in honest and new ways. When we hear the anguish of other men's wounds, it permits us to hear our own. The purpose is not to wallow in our wounds but move through them and beyond them, to eventually transform them into the gold that they are.

♦When you talk to people who have lived great lives they often reflect about how through dealing with their wounds they incidentally discovered some of life's best nuggets. I know this sounds like the finding of the "Philosopher's Stone" which transforms lead into gold. But spiritually it is the "Philosopher's Stone of Love" among those who share their suffering, acknowledge the pain, receive strength from the community of brothers, and then move to the next level of life. In other words, you come to see the gold that you extract from your wounds by looking for it and changing your own life. Since the content of your past cannot be changed, you can change your current understanding and interpretation of the event and the impact it has had upon you. This is part of the process of transforming your wounds into gold.

♦My particular wounds—feeling like a broken dyslexic who was "not good enough" and "not knowing who Martin is"—are actually my greatest gifts. They enable me to see things from a unique perspective. Because I did not know who I was and why I was here, I listened passionately to hear who other people were and what was their purpose. In the process I developed the ability to hear who they really are far beyond what they knew about themselves. My wounds gave me the vocation I love. My wounds and what they have done for me have made me a great coach. That does not change the fact that it still sucks to face the challenge of expressing myself in words and reading so slowly that I do best using "text to speech" software. What I am saying is this:

at some point I declared my wounds to be a gift that makes me who I am. When the old wounded feelings bubble up, I have my declaration to rely on.

♦Guilt and shame are interesting. Men are quite affected by shame. Guilt often refers to an act while shame refers to who you are as a person. When I think about wounds related to shame, one thing that comes to mind is my not being able to dance. The first time I really felt shame about this occurred after the humiliation of my ninth grade prom when my date left me because I was dancing like a geek. She said I danced funny and clearly was embarrassed to be with me. It had taken so much courage to ask her out and for me to get there. I was devastated. We seemed to get along well up to that time. In fact the evening ended waiting for my parents to pick me up on the school steps while my "date" was making out with a football player on the other end of the steps. This unresolved shame colored future actions. Since then I had often been made fun of, laughed at, or told how I dance like a girl. One time I went to a Halloween party as an alien covered up completely and I felt safe to dance. It really felt good to let go. At the end of the evening I won a $50.00 award for being the most unusual dancer and clearly "dancing to a rhythm other than of this world." I was re-humiliated and ashamed that I even tried to dance.

♦After I became a Success Coach, I made a list of all the things I thought I could not do, like drawing, playing music, and dancing, and I took them on. I found a dance therapist and told her I wanted her to coach me to dance like I was connected to the music. She said no one had ever asked that but she was willing to take on the challenge. After that I took traditional dance lessons and within a year I was able to really enjoy dancing. My wife Barbara, a former dance teacher and prom queen, thinks I'm doing great; our dancing together has healed her own wound from grammar and high school years when ironically only a few boys would dance with her because she was too good a dancer. Boy, did I move through a lot of fear getting to this point! But you can imagine how this opened up other areas of my life as well.

How does isolating ourselves in pain make everything worse and how do you convince a man that just because he did it all his life (like most of us) it is not part of him or any form of access to his power or gifts in life?

◆I want to share one of my postings from the on-line Men's Inquiry. "Today I am mad as hell at whatever got us men to choose isolation when we are in trouble. It is such crap. I realize I am not done talking about the "lone wolf" crap, and how cowardly it really is! It denies other men the blessing to contribute to a man, (and) it often drives a man into deeper depression. It does little to make a difference. I think we have lost more men to this than many great battles in war."

◆I remember the first time I had the courage to call another man and grieve on the phone. I was just dumped by a girlfriend and she emotionally gutted me. The man I called for support was my massage teacher, Scotty, who I apprenticed with. I remember that dialing the number was like fighting through great resistance. He answered and I said I was calling because I was in emotional pain but afraid to call him. Could he listen? He did! It changed my life. At first he said nothing just gave me his full attention. Then he said, "It's ok man." I remember where I was driving when I called him. The exact spot in the road. It was amazing how quickly I got over her after that moment. It was many years ago.

◆Have you let yourself grieve in the presence of other men? (men you have some trust with, that is.) Doing this at least once will truly change your life! It is the rare man who has dared to grieve in the midst of other men. Try it some time and see how it will change how you deal with life.

◆Let's not let another man die from isolation again!!!

The Men Address Selected Questions

How are our emotional wounds often our greatest gifts in life?

Allen

As we become aware of them, work through them, they wake us up to life. I know I am much more alive now than before recovery. But also as I become aware of the wounds, there is a richness and a depth to it. Lets me empathize with other people, for everyone has someone.

Bill

Once I had forgiven those who have hurt me, I felt liberated. Nobody is blameless, so it's silly for us to harbor ill will. I've found that each experience, however painful taught me something and I survived. Having suffered and being able to forgive makes one stronger and even less vulnerable. I don't wallow in my past emotional wounds because those perceived wounds are not who I am, they are just something that happened. If I do tell these stories then I'm making them my identity. I'm not the guy whose wife left him, I'm the guy who found there is much in this life to enjoy and every day is a bright new cup to drink from.

George

Only if I am away from the wounding situation, now the wound is there and needs to be healed.

Ross

My emotional wounds help me to see how I have become the man I am and why I sometimes feel the way I feel and do the things I do. This helps me to bring to consciousness the behaviors that no longer serve me and to work at changing them and to embrace the behaviors that do serve me.

Laurence

For me, they open us up to a better understanding of healing, forgiveness and grace. Learning to share my pain with others in a non-complaining way has been very useful. Feeling that we are not understood or that no one else has ever experienced the pain we are feeling is a trap. Sharing those feelings with others allows for the beginnings of healing. Learning that we are not alone, that others do honestly care about us if we open ourselves up to that caring, is an important lesson.

Wilson

In me, an opportunity for healing has often resulted from dealing with emotional wounds. These wounds shake me out of the complacency of routine life and force me to look deeply inside for strength and courage.

Dave

Forgiveness is a process, not an intellectual act, and I agree with much of what Jeanne Safer writes in *Forgiving & Not Forgiving: A New Approach to Resolving Intimate Betrayal*. Sometimes, for a variety of reasons, real forgiveness is not feasible, and accepting that fact is likelier to lead to peace of mind than feeling ashamed of being incapable of performing the impossible or pretending to have done something that remains undone.

Roy

Emotional wounds wake me up to what I am truly committed to and if I am not committed to anything they wake me up to that painful reality too!

Carl

Losing one of my 'second fathers' was such a tremendous blow that it taught me how deeply I cared, how much someone else actually (finally) meant to me. Similarly, when I had to apologize for not grieving with one of my friends when his father died, both of us cried together because of my oversight. It never happened with another; grief was sacred after that.

Horace

Not everyone agrees emotional wounds are often our greatest gifts in life. My observation is that most of us cling to our wounds with all the strength we possess and never consider letting them go. Even those who say they do are frequently challenged, and the idea itself is often not much more than an empty platitude.

If it is true for some, or to the extent it's true, the most important thing to know is that it doesn't come by accident. The Men's Weekend was never designed to be a cynosure—it is a step on the path, not the path itself. It takes work, hard work, constant work with oneself and others to stay on that path. More often that means clawing and scrapping and screaming than it does any picture of what it means to be liberated from the past. Most of us don't make it. We'd all like to think we do, but it's a lie—and you can tell who the liars are because they don't get it. They haven't shed their tears, they still believe in magic and miracles.

They want to save "us" before they save themselves. And ultimately, they are dangerous because power is their God. In my own case, I came from a family filled with shame. My mother was abused as a child, and almost molested by her father. My father was no less shamed based, though it was better hidden behind the façade of social prominence and religious orthodoxy. It wasn't enough that I inherited it—since it was all I knew—I added on to it for years—primarily by acting out sexually—not unlike the man who was recently a President of the United States.

In this, the relationships I developed through the Men's Division and primarily my team proved decisive. Particularly, it was the intimacy we developed, and the camaraderie. There is an inestimable value in having other men know this about myself. We're as sick as our secrets. That was what allowed me one day to say: "I don't have to do this any more." and to mean it. That didn't turn out to be the end of the story, but it was the beginning—a beginning for which I will be forever grateful.

Dan

My emotional wounds become gifts in my life when, and if, I finally pay attention to them and want to understand them. When I do that I learn enormous things about myself and then can make changes in my choices. From my observation and my experience, we often don't pay attention to our wounds; we just live with them and complain about the results.

How do we forgive others and how do we accept the forgiveness of others?

Carl

For years, I recalled an anti-Semitic slur made against me while in high school (by a fellow member of the football team). I forgave him and his remark. That was at least 20 years before he came to my place of business (he had shopped with us for a while) and asked for me to talk with him privately. I was puzzled about what he might say until he mentioned the 'football incident' when we were teenagers. He apologized repeatedly; both of us were tearful. Instantly, I respected him as a man of honor.

303

George

Our forgiveness is easier when the other(s) acknowledge and confirm the transgression. Our forgiveness is harder when the individuals in question have no clue. One way to transcend all of this is to lower expectations of others but to keep salient and running the smaller number of expectations part of our significant relations and connections with others. Lowering our expectations is another way of providing forgiveness in advance.

Ross

I forgive others by looking to see beyond their actions to try and find the reasons behind them. To be compassionate rather than judgmental. Perhaps I only need to forgive them if I judge them?

Dan

How do we forgive others and how do we accept the forgiveness of other? I haven't a clue. I guess an answer depends on what you mean by "forgive." If "forgive" means act like it never happened, I think forgiving is self-delusion. If "forgive" means moving on and not bearing grudges and exacting revenge, this is possible and necessary. The experience can never be forgotten; it will be part of my nature in direct relation to the size of the emotional impact it has on me in the first place. I need to understand how and when that experience triggers an emotional reaction in me, so I can step around its consequences.

Wilson

Forgiving others takes me some time. The idea of 'being wronged' and the injustice of that keeps true forgiveness out of my reach. The only way I can forgive others is to pray and release it to God; sometimes it takes several attempts before I can get full relief. I find it difficult to forgive the person face-to-face unless they ask for forgiveness. I make it easy to accept forgiveness from others by not running away from them or shutting myself out from them. I will 'stick with them' and let them know it is OK.

How do you deal with shame as a man?

George
Know it recognize it, do not permit one's self to endorse it, and assertively prevent others even from subtle and implicit attempts at shaming.

Ross
For me shame is feeling less than- that I am less than a man through my actions or my looks or beliefs etc. I deal with shame by avoiding negative judgments, by being compassionate with myself or by forgiving myself so that I no longer feel less than. This has not been easy for some of the things I have done and I am still working on this in some areas of my life.

Dan
Shame is about somebody else's expectations of me or their problems with me. I don't pay any attention to it unless that person really tries to push me around with their problems. Then I have to gather my strength and stand up to them as best I can to protect myself.

Wilson
I admit whatever is shaming me to someone else, someone that I trust. I pray to have it removed from me and I seek amends if there is another person involved.

Fredrick
I punish myself with endless work, trying to make up for it. It is exhausting and does not work too well.

Carl
How do I deal with shame as a man? Most humbly, I have apologized when I was a part of something shameful.

Arthur
My shame is to never be good enough, to never feel like I deserve anything good because of my inadequacies, and to not belong anywhere. I have used various ways of dealing with this and it depends on the situation. Sometimes telling that critical voice to

'F--k off, I don't need you anymore' is effective–a highly regarded spiritual practice! Other times just to notice it and see it for old stuff can be enough–so it depends where I catch it or how far it has run. If it has run quite a way and I am really feeling shamed then I can ask "What is the earliest memory of this?' to myself. If I feel there is something to be gained from exploring it, I will. Or I may just choose to feel the physicality of the feeling and lose the meaning so it fades as purely an uncomfortable sensation.

Allen

How do I deal with shame? Poorly. Seriously that is one of the core things I still deal with. For example my partner will ask if I still need to go to that support group each week. There are little comments from people I care about and I take them as shamming but I really don't know if they 'are'. I have to separate out what they say and remind me of who I am. My mother could shame with her sigh. How I deal with my shaming is bring it to my men's group and work through it until it is gone. I realize that a lot of shamming seems to come from my current partner. I could walk away from it but I realize that I will probably just have to work on this with another women. Personal work is like mastering an art. There is always room to improve and you can enjoy the process. Guilt involves other people and shame with myself.

How does shame relate to guilt?

Carl

If I had done something shameful knowingly, I would have felt guilty.

George

How does shame relate to guilt, for me? They are participating affiliates, with different though in excess equally malevolent bottom lines.

Allen

I think women have more guilt and men shame. Guilt has to do with what I did that is wrong, shame has to do with there is something wrong with who I am! This is important for us to listen to the fact that this is a core issue of men. I can make amends of what I did that came from guilt but dealing with shame I have to make amends to myself—where I have allowed others to convince that there is a core flaw in me.

Ross

I think guilt is about feeling bad about the consequences of my actions if they have had some negative effect on some people or me. It is closely tied to shame and I deal with it the same way.

Dan

Guilt—When does sorrow and regret for harm done become "guilt"? I don't know. I suspect that "guilt" is only an intense example of shame and is simply blackmail for something the other person thinks they're entitled to from us.

Wilson

To me, this is a cycle with shame generating more guilt and vice versa.

Wilson

Deny it and stuff it. Then it squirts out all over the place some other time or explodes

Arthur

The gift in my core wounds is the ability to know what is missing and deliver it as an act of service. Without this wounding I would have no idea about this work and would be 'someone else.' Guilt is 'I made a mistake.' Shame is 'I am a mistake.' Guilt for me is a way of realizing I have something to amend and this seems healthy. Shame is where this has gone further, to my being a lesser person for this indiscretion or mistake.

What is the cost of avoiding the emotional pain from our past?

Carl

What is the cost of avoiding the emotional pain from our past?

It reprocesses. Learning from it rather than avoiding it enhances awareness.

George

Facing the emotional pain is painful but as a Chinese proverb instructs, "a powerful medicine may indeed taste bitter." It I don't do it, it always hunts me down and catches up with me.

Ross

Sometimes the emotional pain offers a connection with the past and by avoiding that I may feel that I am letting it go and losing a connection with part of it that I want to remember and stay connected with.

Dan

Pain doesn't go away until it's healed. It can be out of sight and out of feeling, but as long as it's in me it affects the way I live, just as a physical pain affects the way I move and think. If the pain is denied and suppressed, I become unaware of how it is affecting my decisions and perspectives and incapable of adjusting them to remove the effects of the pain.

Wilson

If I understand this question, I never get past the pain if I don't acknowledge it and heal it. I stay stuck.

Roy

The wound just festers in my unconscious when I don't deal with it. What I see most men do and what I have done in my younger years is 'hunt' down the next attractive woman—which of course eventually turns the next relationship into the same pile of dung as the last one.

***What is your shame? What have you been ashamed
of in your life? What can you do about it? What do
you need to say or do to let it go?***

Dean

Talking about shame. I am ashamed I am a man. I was taught
that the feelings I now know as normal for males were wrong, bad,
and sinful. I was raised in a home with two parents; however
mother was the strong suit in the family. For some reason,
anything male was unacceptable. For years I wondered why my
father rejected me, and at this late time in my life, I see it was my
mother he was rejecting.

Oh to have better insight as a child, my life could have been so
different. I wanted recognition by a male. I was a middle child, of
three, older sister, younger brother—age difference being 4 years
younger than sister, 9 years older than brother. My father
worshipped my brother. He was everything I am not. I realized
after his birth, if I wanted any approval by family, I needed to
become a care taker for him. This at least allowed me into the
family circle, where brother was the center of attraction.

I vowed the first chance I had to leave, I would be gone, and
enlisted in the Navy as soon as I graduated from high school. This
was a culture shock. I had never heard swearing, and upon
entering boot camp, circa 1955, every other word was f--k, queer,
or piece of sh--. I had made it. The other recruits were everything
I ever wanted to be—a male, and no one was telling them to be any
other way. I was bothered by the physical appearance of them,
however. Being of English heritage, I am not a hairy person, we
are talking about chest, arms, legs, and elsewhere. Oh, how I
wanted to be like these guys. Fifty years later, I am not, but still
have the desire for this display of what I considered male. Talk
about misguided thinking. I encounter others who had the same
feelings as I. Wanting to be loved, approved, and a part of the clan
of men.

Lost my virginity at 20 with a cheap hooker, I think there were
5 of us, if you can believe, it was in Delaware. Really enjoyed it,
but still had this desire for physical male closeness. I married after
discharge, thinking a constant supply of available sex would cure
the desires in my mind. Forty-six years later, still have the desires,
both physical and mental. How different my life could have been.

I wish I could have been strong enough to say WHO I was, and take the consequence. Rather I chose to live a life of deceit, shame, guilt, all because I feared someone knowing WHO I really was. Not just my life has been affected, but my wife, who has NO idea, and also my daughter. In closing, my only child a daughter informed me 8 years ago she is a lesbian. Did I keep my secret well? I think not, for I feel in the bottom of my heart, I am responsible for her choice. Life goes on, and I live with my secret. My daughter is open to the world.

I have never shared this with anyone, not even my therapists of past. I hope this encourages other men to realize the value of emotional courage as it has me.

George
I am not willing to even share it here. I am barely willing to share it with myself. Clearly this is something I need to work on. I think a start would be making it less secret though in safe forums or interactions.

Barry
I believe that shame is one of most burdensome of all emotions, essentially acting like an anchor or ball & chain in one's life. In spiritual terms, such negative emotion prevents us from making conscious contact with God. I further believe that until a person honestly confronts and/or confesses his/her emotional pain, they will carry it with them through life. Healthy male relationships are a productive way to help cleanse such emotional wounds. I need to do more of it. To quote a friend, "Take my advice, I am not using it!"

Clark
What do I need to say or do to let go? I need to feel respected, to feel recognized as an individual, an individual that is unique, profound, and interesting all in my own right. I want acknowledgement that I can have and experience what I want. And I want for it to be acceptable for me to go the way I want. I want permission to be me. My father and brother both must see that my thoughts and vision are unique and stimulating and exciting for me. I want them to trust this thing called beauty that I desire. These men need to stop invalidating my existence, and I want to stop

suffering because of their lack of acceptance. I've needed to say these things to the men in my early years; I've need for them to hear this so I can develop into the creative and beautiful person that I am. I've felt enraged for many years because of their unwillingness to listen or allow. Through these years I have said: "I am angry at you, and I will not stop until you say that you're sorry." But it's impossible now, for you lay in grave. So, all that is left to contend with, is: the acknowledgment of what I needed then, and the self-love to seek my hearts desire now.

Barry

Through MKP, I learned how to reclaim all my feelings. And yes, grief and joy are very closely related. I always knew that at some level. The music that moved me was the saddest (Tchaikovsky Piano Trio, Dvorak Cello Concerto, Brahms Clarinet Quintet), but until I did the warrior weekend, that's about the only place I ever showed sadness.

And yes, the wound is where the strength comes from. In my case, never fitting in, not really trusting the love I got. From that, I formed my mission, to connect to everyone (co-create a connected world in balance).

When my now-wife and I had our third date, it was a wedding celebration for a New Warrior man and his new bride (MKP): her comment was she'd never seen so many straight men hugging before. It looked powerful and masculine to her. Took me 2 years before I felt comfortable doing that!

I now believe both my parents came from fear-based households, and lived "bound" by shame. As a result, I sometimes think I don't have ENOUGH healthy shame, because I'd sound off a lot and get lots of negative feedback, and keep doing it. And at some level, I have as much fear and shame as my parents.

Ross

I have in the past judged myself harshly and don't forgive myself quickly. As the media today in some cases focuses on men as perpetrators and or predators it can be easy for men to take on shame just for being a man.

Dan

How do I handle situations in which I am sorry for something I did to someone?—I tell the person I harmed what I did that I thought had harmed them, make what efforts I can to make them whole, and apologize to them. Sometimes I have to drive myself to this with a mental whip, but I've almost always been able to do this during the last 10-15 years. The best way of dealing with this, of course, is not to create the harm in the first place, and I'm getting better and better at that the more I know myself and express myself.

Wilson

My shame is my refusal to deal with my weight and my inability to sustain relationships. I believe they are tied together in that the weight keeps me from relationship. More shame comes in that I view both of these things as sin since they hinder me in my relationship with God. The solution is obvious—do it.

Carl

I am free of shame now. I just don't let it take hold of me. There is either something for me to clean up or let go of. That's it!

What are you ashamed about yourself? What parts of yourself don't you want others to see or know about? What is it that disturbs you about another that in reflection you find lives inside of you too?

Dave

This question is so tough I hesitate answering it. But, the answer is my sexuality. I'm 35 and am conflicted about my sexuality. It is just mixed up. It is somewhere in the middle. In the eyes of many, it is still taboo for a man to be anything but 100% heterosexual so that is my shame. Openly or overtly gay men disturb me because I see a reflection that is some of me. My shame also drives me to the "guilt by association" rule when I hear the voice say, "Get away, others will start talking." I know I shouldn't look to others and the outside world for validation or acceptance. It is one of my greatest faults…being too concerned about what others think or say.

What do most men do with shame and emotional pain?

George
Deny its presence and cover it with compulsive and/or addictive behavior. It's what I have done and it does not work very well!

Carl
I internalize it. I used to think I was a disposable friend to my friends and my wife. It took a long time for me to realize I am not disposable, God created me and I am a man of worth. It is too bad they did not see that in me. My wife finally told me, after almost a year of their encounters, that she had been seeing my male friends while I was out of town on business.

Dan
We're trained to "stuff our shame and emotional pain." The whole "men don't cry" brainwashing we get from the time we're babies—it's criminal. The only comforting thought is that often the ones who teach this lesson the loudest are the most hurt by the very men they taught. The price we men pay for sticking with this lesson is astronomical. What I don't understand is how men go on sticking with this lesson when they finally learn from their own experience that it is totally false.

Roy
Most men just ignore our shame and emotional pain and it either slowly destroys our health; we race to our latest addition to numb it through sex, alcohol, buying stuff etc; or of course we become part of the walking dead, emotionally numb.

Allen
Most men burry it in a place where the dogs always find it. There is not place to hide it well.

313

Did you ever consider that you can experience joy with grieving?

Ross

Yes I have experienced joy with grieving and I have done it. The joy I felt was the joy of allowing myself to grieve as a man over the ending of relationship. The joy of knowing that I was finally able to allow myself to cry, to be in touch with my grief and to know it was healing me to let it out and cry.

Wilson

Yes, I have experienced this in the release of addictions. I felt the joy of freedom from the addictions and the grief at losing a long-time faithful friend that worked for me for a long time. Also, one of hardest things in addiction recovery was losing all my friends, people who only had the addiction in common with me. I had to grieve the loss of the company along with the joy of freedom.

Dan

Yes, I have in fact experienced joy with grieving several times. I've also learned that emotions do not come one at a time. They come not in battalions but they do come in multiples, each with its own perspective on the experience.

Allen

Yes, and it is easy to forget. I am not sure that relates to crying with something that is happy, but I think it is the flip side of that. I think it is like grieving among men I feel safe to grieve with, I am in deep emotional pain but not alone.

How does isolating ourselves in pain generally make everything worse, and what are alternatives?

Dan

It makes it worse because we end up believing that only we can heal the pain, but we're in so much pain that we know we can't possibly heal anything ... and so no healing happens. For me the alternatives are two-fold: One, talk about it with someone, openly,

314

endlessly, emotionally. This someone has to be a person who will not dive in and enhance my sorrow or my feeling of helplessness, but who can hold me up until I learn how to swim in the feelings and help me find my way to my pain so I can understand what it is in me (not where it came from; what it means in my being). Two, to dig and dig until I understand what the pain means in my being. This is mostly about learning what the pain tells me about myself and how the pain will affect my perspectives and actions in the future. In some sense, I'm talking about incorporating the pain into my understanding of myself consciously.

Wilson

I become the hermit, internalized the pain and just let it spin around and around without release. The healthy alternative for me is to express this pain to another person that I know I can be vulnerable with and continued prayer for direction.

Fredrick

I agree that isolation adds to the pain and makes it morbid, but I also honor the basic privacy of the male nature compared to the female one. I resist what I view as a feminization of men as a result of the female biases of our psychological culture. I think we men tend to be better-equipped for dealing with difficult emotional things in ways other than shared words. I can make a lot of progress toward peace and equilibrium just left on my own in nature. So that is one way I deal with pain. I also get a lot of healing value just in the quiet company of a good male friend. We don't have to talk. Just sit together fishing or something often in nature.

What are constructive ways to deal with emotional pain, emotional wounds?

Steven

My biggest emotional wound was around sex and shame. I grew up as a Roman Catholic and was never told anything positive about me as a sexual being. Instead I learned that sex was dirty, and that I would go to hell for my bad thoughts. What resulted was a life of hiding and secrecy, where I didn't realize it was ok to be sexual and to celebrate that part of me. Those wounds showed up in my marriages and caused others and me much pain. The healing of those wounds has been powerful. I had to be willing to bring my shame into the light and share it with people I trusted. In return I learned to love all those parts of myself, and quit living for approval by others. Sex is nothing to be ashamed of. I think most of sexual perversion comes out of the shaming we do to young boys about their sex drive, driving it underground and into dark places.

Allen

To find a safe place to move through it, express it, forgive it. Sharing that with other people that can just hear it as the noise it is. That is having a place to vent or get it out!!!

Bob

I have to say, at 52, I still have difficulties to get rid of my guilt and accept as a part of myself what I am ashamed of. I must say though that I feel better and more in control when I acknowledge that shameful part of myself but without dwelling too much on it and letting it control my life.

What Insights did you personally gain from this chapter?

What do you want to commit to or re-commit to out of these insights?

Remember!
"Insight without committed action is only entertainment!"

Chapter 13
Our Anger, Our Fierceness and Dealing with Conflict

How do you define "anger" within yourself? How do you express it?

In the future what are specific ways you could deal better with anger and depression?

What are constructive ways of expressing your anger, rage, and fierceness?

What is the risk of "killing off our anger?" Do we have shame about it?

Where in your life do you allow yourself to just be aggressive or even assertive?

What is the value in honoring our fierceness? How do we know when we use it appropriately?

How can you use anger more effectively? Where is it appropriate to be angry? How do cultivate this energy in a positive direction?

How does "justifying anger" turn us into what we hate? How does 'reacting' with anger let anger run us?

How do we develop the way to be assertive without being aggressive?

What is anger and its relationship to sadness? How do you know to be angry?

How can we enjoy our differences? Maybe even enjoy a good argument? Do you consider that it is okay to agree to disagree?

Do you avoid conflict or realize that is a possible way for new learning, new creations and deeper relationships if you stay with it until its resolution?

Where in your life do you allow yourself to just be aggressive or even assertive?

How often are you too passive or non-responsive in your life and what does that cost you?

Do you understand it is never ok to rage against loved ones?

◆Martin's comments on this topic

◆Often what we hate in someone else is an unresolved issue within ourselves. Let me restate that. Often what I hate in someone else is something that I eventually find is an unresolved or unforgiven aspect of myself. In the New Warrior I-Group they use a great question to assist in revealing this information: "What I see in you that bothers me lives in me as . . . (fill in the blank)." When dealing with any unpleasant feelings toward someone it is useful to get clear what you are committed to in the relationship. You could be very angry with your child and feel that you "should not" feel like that. You feel what you feel, but what are you committed to and what actions will you take? Without the commitment of being a compassionate and loving father, all that remains is the feeling of anger toward your child. In The Men's Inquiry discussions we also revealed that speaking when you are 'in anger' seldom gets positive results.

◆I feel it is never appropriate to bring our anger to our partners or children. Get the energy out of the upset before addressing the issue with them. Often a harsh tone of voice attacking a loved one who has opened their heart to you is the same as hitting them with your fist. Now if your partner cannot stand any assertiveness toward getting something done in the world, that may point to an issue she needs to resolve. Often this kind of woman can only be with very passive men. For example, if you express concern about getting bad food at a restaurant and she is embarrassed and gets very upset by that, then that may be her problem. It is a subtle thing but some women kill off all the assertiveness in men then are disappointed that the men don't take any action. Men who have had this done to them describe it like this, "It's like she kicked me in the crotch then accused me of bad posture." Women would benefit from realizing in relationships that most men don't get subtle hints and do not do well with conflicting communication. Men need places to be assertive and aggressive or else it comes out "sideways" (a term from men's work). If you disagree, which I did 15 year ago, look at your own life and ask yourself are you really living up to your own potential as a man? I know I was not and I respect the man I see today in the mirror more than I did then. There is a great quote from John Eldredge in *Wild at Heart:* "How can you turn the other cheek if you have no cheek to turn?"

◆Some of the fears we have around conflict and aggression are due to the fact that we have not developed the ability to work through the issue or argument until it is resolved-which would allow a deeper relationship to evolve from that resolution. If you are walking around still mad about something, or if something easily re-triggers that anger, then YOU are unresolved with it. What I mean by working through a conflict is staying in the conversation long enough to get to a resolution or at least agreeing to disagree. If you cannot resolve it with the person, a good men's team is a great place to resolve it further. If I find myself in an argument that looks like I don't know if I can resolve it, I will sometimes go back to the question: "Where can we both be in agreement or what commitment are we aligned on?"

◆This is not meant to be a chapter of tips on how to deal with conflict. That will be a future book. This is for you to get insight from the responses of others, discussions with others using these questions, and the insights that you gain from exploring the questions in your own life.

◆Consider the value of have an argument to explore a new truth, not just proving you are right, and then being friends again. Many of us men have lost or never developed this ability. It is a wonderful ability if you are not attached to one position and committed to learning something new. You can even enjoy the value of being wrong since that will reveal a new learning. Some of my greatest insights both in my personal life and business life have occurred in the moments I was "wrong." If you don't have a mission to live out of then it is hard to let go of being right. Having to be "right" all the time would be a dreadfully boring existence. A way to start enhancing your ability to deal with conflict is finding safe places to practice taking on a conflict and staying with it until it is complete-meaning both parties are left with a sense of resolution and/or new understanding.

The Men Address Selected Questions

How do you define "anger" within yourself? How do you express it? How do you know you are angry?

Allen

I know I am angry when I am angry. Part is when I break apart into the four emotions, mad, glad, sad, and mad. It is a perceived insult. I love what the wise man said, "anger is a blanket over fear." When I am really honest with myself when I am angry and I look under the blanket, I am afraid of not getting what I want or of losing something. If someone slows on the highway in front, I am afraid I am not getting there fast enough. If someone violates me that is open and clear but if they violate someone I love it involves anger.

Kent

Oh anger, how well I know thee, from a sense of injustice to full-blown fury–a spontaneous impulse to powerful, possibly violent action. I have found that anger is an emotion that can all too easily bypass my brain and evoke a full body response. My immature use of anger was all too often a blind fury that destroyed all in its path, and rarely, in modern society, have I found that such an outburst is appropriate. Now, I recognize that a more mature application of anger is as a powerful fuel to confront injustice, to right wrongs, and to re-establish an order that works for the greater good. I think that anger can truly empower one to superhuman feats of greatness.

In my college days, my anger led to explosive outbursts and destructive behaviors. Slowly, I have learned to better control my anger and focus it on worthy projects. My repeated reflections on what caused the anger, and my review of possible appropriate responses have helped, but it has taken more time and effort than I expected to gain some control and avoid the initial "knee-jerk" response. I know that injustices still occur, and I still get angry, but I can better harness the power of the anger and use it as a fuel. I feel that learning to control and focus anger is part of becoming a well-socialized member of a civilized society. My conclusion is that it would be very good for individuals, their families, and society, if there were better ways to express, understand, and utilize the great power of anger.

Wilson

The definition of MY anger . . . that is a tough one. I know what makes me mad but defining it within me? It is something that keeps spinning around in my head and in my stomach, it keeps me awake, it is something that must be resolved - for my own sake. I can no longer just shrug it off with an "oh well."

The expression of my anger usually comes out in sarcasm. A quick mind and being handy with words make it easy to attack verbally at the core of a person that has angered me.

Roy

I remember how a wise man said that 'justifying anger' is the best way to stay asleep to one's life. That's reducing our awareness, but just blocking it does not help, and learning to harness the power and use it well is the best way.

Gary

Anger is the emotion I deal with the poorest. I rage over the foibles of people I've never met and the "insubordination" of inanimate objects that did nothing to harm me, but I still don't allow myself to connect to the "real" anger toward "real people" in my life. The way I go ballistic when I lose something, drop something or have a computer or other machine malfunction is pathological. My wife really hates me that way and I'm being a poor model to my son. Here I am a Quaker, a peaceful man, and when I hear about a child molester, or a politician I hate, or someone who did something ugly, my response is to want to see that person tortured, castrated, etc. (execution is WAAYY too easy on them!). And yet when I'm asked when I'm "really" angry, truth is, I have no clue!

Bill

Anger and even hatred rise out of fear, and fear from a perceived threat. I'm seldom angry, because I don't feel threatened.

321

If for some reason I do get angry I go out and work in the yard or take a walk or shoot basketball or go bowling. In those cases I'm usually OK in a short time.

To get angry over something can cause one to channel the anger for constructive good, if it is tempered with wisdom, joy and love. Anger for the most part is a response to a perception. One perception might be that something is not going to be OK, I'm losing control of the way I think something should be. But does everything have to be the way I think it should be? How bad would this be? Life would go on even if my expectations are not met. I can trade peace and contentment for the illusory idea that I'm losing control of a situation. Perception changed.

All this conflict is something beyond my control. The people have to see this for themselves. In a democracy, the people get the government they deserve. So you see my perception has changed. Only a foolish man tries to hold back the tides.

James
Some of the most powerful men's work I've seen is where the male leader had the participants yell at him. By setting a model where the leader is willing to completely let go of his ego, I can feel love and let go of anger, self- hatred, and experience love. When I know the leader can keep the container safe, and still allow rage to come out - that's very healing - since my father used to beat up me and my sister. As a leader, I encourage my participants to rage.

Dan
Anger warns me that something crucial to me, to myself, is being trampled on. It's taken me years to figure out how to deal with it, most of them spent repressing anger as I was taught to. Now, it seems I have a choice with anger - I can deal with the anger, or I can deal with the harm that triggered the anger. I used to deal - or try to deal - with the anger, but the effort usually failed to change anything. About all I accomplished was to reduce the raging feelings to some tolerable and safe level. For the last 15 years or so, I've found myself dealing with the harm that triggered the anger. This has been much more successful. The more I deal directly with the harm, the more the anger goes way, really goes away. Sometimes the harm has taken a lot of work to heal and the anger goes on (at an ever decreasing level) as a reminder to keep

working on the harm. Now, I see anger as the red cape waived at the bull. The bull's real problem is not the red cape but the matador who's out to kill him. The bull would be a lot better off spending his time and energy chasing the matador than chasing the red cape, which cannot possibly harm him.

Much of the anger message is really about protecting myself. I can't protect myself, of course, unless I know who myself is. So, dealing with anger for me was an unexpected by- product of finding myself. There's been another interesting by-product of finding myself. I've completely lost my fear of standing up and protecting myself quietly but forcefully. It's ceased to be a personality conflict; it's more a matter of deep principle, of the most fundamental kind of survival. I do it, often at a significant cost; simply because that's the way I live, like the color of my hair, or the nature of my skills.

Barry

It used to be that anger came up in me unexpectedly. It was so confounding to me because it would come out of nowhere. It would come out seemingly just to prove there is no real hope for friendship. It was violent in the way it cut people apart and get right at their soft spot. It was easy for me to justify when it happened. I would say they needed to hear the truth from someone.

It was for their good. And it was so eerie that it would almost always be true. But, it was done in such a way that it had an element of cruelty in it. When my victim and I were in a situation where we had to be together over time it would most always work out that we came to understand something about each other that we didn't know before. And, if we were able to stick it out we became quite close.

This method of interaction must have been inherited from my father without my knowing it. I saw it in him the cruelty and violence. It came on suddenly without apparent reason except in his mind. This even happened after he stopped drinking and coming home drunk but it was not as severe or physical as when he was drunk. When I was very young, around 4 or 5 he would tie my brother and me to the door knob so we wouldn't get into trouble and he could go out. When he caught me smoking at age 5 he stuck a cigar in my mouth and made me inhale till I was sick.

I think he even burned the bottom of my feet with his cigar. But, I also might be making this up. It was also a habit back in the 50's for not only my Dad but my teachers at school to grab me by one ear and take me somewhere like to their office or my room. I wonder if all that cracking I heard contributed to my eventual loss of hearing. Another favorite surprise was the Back of the Hand across the face. It happened lightning fast and left me seeing stars and ringing in the ear.

Anyway all this physical violence from my Dad coupled with what I heard in the way of hatred and his stories left some kind of marks on me- I just don't know what. The cruelty I personally witnessed in the public schools left other marks.

Of course, I've had strong anger in many other situations too numerous to mention. Anger is precious and dangerous to me and that's a reality that I embrace. I don't want to hurt someone needlessly. But, it might be that someone needs to be hurt in some way. It seems the only way to get through to some people due to the thickness of conditioning. Frustration brings anger. Anger brings action. May wisdom bring the appropriate action or the choice of no action? Thank You.

Arthur

I have projected my anger onto others for many years. Anger appeared inappropriately for me during this time because it was suppressed. I tried to get angry in deep inner work circles but would have to 'fake it until I made it' as they said. It never felt right or even close to the anger I could have with my wife who has her own issues with anger and therefore the perfect target for my projections. I actually felt ashamed because I could not access my anger or tears in these spaces.

What I realized was that my anger was with my mother so a bunch of hairy galoots were never going to get it out of me. My work with rites of passage opened me up especially to seeing the women facilitators working with the mothers in letting go of their boys and welcoming back young men. How much would my life be different to have had this?

I always thought my issues were with my father but it really was with my mother.

Fredrick

I haven't had a big problem with anger, I don't think. The last time I hit someone, I was probably nineteen years old. My wife and I squabble some, but it's mostly constructive in the long run. A colleague crossed me professionally in a big way, and I lost a fair amount of sleep over that one a few years ago. It was a war, and I think a righteous one since the stakes went beyond self-defense and into an ethical area that was important to me. I faced some hard lessons in terms of holding back vengeance when I was in a position to deal it out. I did hold to moderation, and I'm proud of that – although I am also proud of winning the war too.

Cliff

It seems to be a state of defense, defending my physical being translated into defending some inner position. The body tightens and a layer of armor goes up. The inner conflict of the physical manifestation vs. the mental judgments usually results in a silent paralysis. Then a cascade of resentments past and present and rationalizations to justify the right/wrong polarization takes place. I express it by holding this jumble of data and retreating into silent "stewing."

Daniel

I define anger as "reaching my limit." I have encountered something that I don't know how to address, or fix, or control, and I'm passed just being frustrated with it. How do you express it? I often internalize it. I will often tell myself that I am not able to handle whatever it is, and then give up because "I can't do it, or do it all."

Darryl

I've learned that my anger is really a family of related emotions. I see all sizes of anger in myself now: bugged, bothered, perturbed, annoyed, irritated, resentful, pissed off, mad, enraged, outraged, furious, and livid. I also see my being critical, judgmental, impatient and withdrawn as likely expressions of these angers. I know that I have a substitution pattern in which I'm at risk for showing anger when I am caught by surprise feeling scared or sad

325

Jack

I define anger as a feeling inside of me that involves a feeling of agitation and may prompt some kind of response or reaction to someone else.

I think that often I am one of those people who squelch a lot of anger but then it leaks out all over anyway, in irony, cynicism, and sometimes sarcasm. I can have a sharp wit.

Sometimes, though, I gear down and use the energy from anger to engage in some kind of constructive action to address the problem.

I think that what I just described above--taking constructive action to address a problem, is the best response to anger. It has nothing to do with violence or rage. It does mean being clear about what it is you are unhappy about. Sometimes, killing off anger means that this kind of useful action never happens. Interestingly, rage or over-aggressive responses to anger also have the same effect as doing nothing-and useful, moderate action, does not happen.

I see fierceness as a kind of determined protectiveness toward things that we care about. It implies a readiness to take action to be protective. Again, that action can be positive and useful, or a useless explosion of sound and fury. Constructive fierceness implies a willingness to do work to get something done, not just make a lot of noise about it. It also means being clearheaded enough to think, to be able to moderate your own actions, and to accommodate the legitimate concerns of other people.

Phillip

For me anger is about losing control. I don't like to show it, so I slow things down; I avoid and repress anger.

Wes

Anger is a feeling of frustration when what I want is not happening as fast as I want it to happen. How do I express anger? I let it churn in my belly and then I let go of the attachment I had to wanting something to happen before its time.

Marcus

I feel it often in my forehead as tension, sometimes in my jaw, sometimes in my belly. I experience it as intense energy. I've learned that when I channel this energy, I can accomplish a lot. I

326

notice that when I make myself wrong for feeling anger, I feel shame sometimes escalating to rage.

Frank

I define anger within myself as when I feel I start to lose control. I begin to get irrational and do and say things that I know aren't constructive.

Joel

The least common denominator here for me is ANGER:

Anger is an issue for me, because I block it, I internalize it. I was not allowed to be authentic to myself as I was growing up. The "boy" was not respected, honored or valued. I was diminished by my mother, and my father and was limited by her in my eyes. As I grew up, a lot of anger in me was never allowed to surface and resolve itself. I still do not have a handle on it, and simply 'avoid' conflict in the hopes that there will be no anger in my life. Unfortunately, this avoiding has a tendency to internalize the anger into self loathing and hostility onto others who are close to me.

Larry

Anger always has an object it is directed towards, either other people, myself or situations (maybe even the acorn that fell on my head.) I would define it as something incomplete in myself activated by outer events. Sometimes venting is useful, as a pressure release valve. Otherwise I hope I use it to explore what in me got triggered.

Jon

I was raised in a Catholic family and I was taught expressing anger was a sin. So, from a very young age, I learned to suppress anger.

Damon

Being a literal person, I'm giving a literal answer I am not one to suppress my anger, whatever or whoever brings me to anger gets immediate feedback of their effect on my emotions. The benefit is no game playing, no guessing. I have had people tell me that they always know where they stand with me and that is better that not knowing and trying to guess.

Rico

Anger is the inability to "be" with something. Anger is also not exactly a real feeling. Using an analogy, I like to think of emotions as smoke and feelings as fire. Big emotions are like to smoke from a fire. They in a sense are not the real thing, the fire is. Feelings tend to be a more subtle experience than emotions, which tend to be more big dramas. So the point is, to feel the feeling, as I feel it, it dissipates. If I just act it out, it compounds itself. Anger can be expressed through acting it out emotionally or physically.

Kobe

I define anger within myself as a strong and passionate position towards a particular idea or belief. Anger usually then presents itself when that idea or belief is challenged by someone; then I become angry towards that person. I usually express my anger violently (talking loudly or screaming about my belief) and sometimes passively (being with myself, alone and a little smug and righteous about my position).

Kyle

Anger has been changing in my life. Also, my seeing has been changing. Notice I don't say changed. That would take me out of the picture in the Now. I say changing because I am present in that continuum. In younger years I had anger and violence (physical and mental) come out of me at unexpected moments. I didn't understand. It seemed to want to subvert relationships from developing. My view of those times was always self-righteous because I thought I was getting at the root of something. I thought I was very insightful and giving the other person what they needed. In fact, it may have been true many times but there was one problem: It came out in such a way as to hurt them first. I justified this as my shocker so I could first get their attention. That part really worked. The part that didn't work was that it was not loving or kind in its delivery so it killed them and most of the time our relationship. I have deep regrets for hurting others in my life.

I hate government and insurance companies and large companies, all of whom insulate themselves from dispute or complaint or competition- all acting monopolistic and without social morality or responsibility. Their methods are despicable in their taking advantage of the non-fighter type of person and the rest of us too. I know organizations are made of people. But, I used to think not one person in ten was honorable. Now, I'm starting to see the hypocrisy in this. When I am really seeing myself I am the one who is not honorable.

My other anger, for authority is now mostly gone. But, only a few years ago when it was in high gear this was inconceivable. I recall one time driving in crowded conditions on a large street, a cop going in the other direction made a U-turn, maneuvered thru traffic to where I was and pulled me over. He approached my car with hand on his gun. I was enraged by his question: Where are you going? I said none of your business. It was a lengthy and painful process before I finally was allowed to drive on. But, I believed at that time I would be shot by this person who needed authority as much as I despised it.

When I later started placing myself in positions of authority, I began to understand more about the difficulties involved. I was intrigued and challenged to be first a coach and then a referee. That was only the beginning of my opening. There are so many dimensions to life.

My off-the-hip anger was just like my father's. I have no idea how it got into me because I hated that in him. But, after so many years in oblivion it is changing. I feel myself caring for others. I started to actually see in other people examples of kindness and honor. These examples have been having an affect on me. I do so much respect people with kindness and honor.

Randy
Anger for me is the unrefined bridge between realizing the fact that what is happening is contrary to my desire, and the frustration of not being grounded enough to get what I want—i.e.-I am stuck.

Todd
Anger is expressed by yelling. It is very difficult to control.

Willie
Anger is the disappointment that unmet expectations produce. Usually I let it out. It comes out in a quick rage that subsides in seconds. Frustration sometimes produces the same result.

Clark

I am a champion for what I call the petty and small feelings. It's all about me. Every few months I have a feeling of anger and frustration. It usually shows up as wanting to stab or shoot everyone. I call it the stabbity-stab and the shoo-tie-shoot feeling. I tell my team of men how I feel with the anger expressed. They check in and usually find that I am disappointed in not doing something I felt I should have—usually out of relationship with my customers or the men—usually not telling the truth about something I promised to do. After I tell the truth about it I feel better and in power. I am on a men's team so that men can tell me the truth with all the ugly attached to it. It stings, but I change faster if its not sugar coated or ignored.

Bill

I feel anger as a powerful emotional response to the perception of being the object of an injustice. I usually don't have any opportunity to express it, because whether my perceptions are accurate or not, few people around me seem to hold themselves accountable to behave justly or even have the slightest interest or understanding in the concept of justice. Therefore, it becomes difficult or impossible to hold anyone responsible for their actions and resolve the anger in a traditional way.

Jake

Anger rises up out of deep roots. I feel the flow seemingly initiated by an outside event but in truth it comes from something unresolved within my own psyche. I felt frustration as a child and young man resulting from my un-athletic stature and growing up in a household dominated by women. These issues denied me comfort in my earlier years and later became triggers.

I learned later the anger offers the opportunity to see these and other of my unresolved issues mirrored in others. Fortunately, I was not forced to bury this emotion as it flared up in childhood. Ironically, however, I was manipulated to feel guilt about expressing it. As a teen I used anger to fuel aggression when threatened and although I lost more of these occasional fights than I won, the emotion provided the adrenalin to stand up for myself. This owning of my personal values is the gold in anger. The rust is the trap I fell into when I misdirected the anger and lashed out at an innocent bystander, usually someone I loved.

My strategy to deal with the detrimental effects of anger has been to allow the emotion to surface in me, then catch my reaction and hold it for examination. I look for unfinished aspects of my growth in what I see to diffuse aggression. Although this does not always work, I challenge myself to take this path of growth rather than strike out or swallow the emotion.

If I know I am in the presence of a real threat, either physical or mental, I use the power sparked by my anger to defend and stand up for my beliefs. I channel the energy into verbal expressions and have not had an escalation into physical confrontation for years. I rarely try to consciously trigger others into explosive exchanges thereby avoiding unnecessary conflict. However, as stated above, I can be fierce in defending myself and others with words.

Chad

My world has the best security system money can buy: Fear and Anger. Fear is my emotional and physical energy equivalent to statements like "It's going to hurt!" or "He's going to eat me!" Anger is my emotional and physical energy equivalent to statements like, "NO!" or "Stay back!" or "Stop that!" The Fear subsystems are the tripwires and motion detectors and solenoids and snuffers in my psyche, in my body. They are there to alert me of the possibility of harm. They set off alarms.

So whenever some real or imagined threat breaches some real or imagined boundary in my world and trips an alarm, I feel something along the spectrum from mild concern to apprehension to full-blown terror depending on the perceived threat. Fear is always about the future. It's always anticipatory. What could happen in the next second or the next year?

The anger component is my protective response. Anger protects me from what fear alerts me to. It's the active response component of my security system: arsenal, guards, attack dogs, MACE, whatever.

Joseph

The truth is I don't get angry with anyone except sadly my wife and kids sometime.

331

In the future what are specific ways you could deal better with anger and depression?

Wilson

I have learned to wait until I have cooled off to address any anger issues. Prayer is vital and solutions come to me, usually overnight, as a result. As far as depression goes (anger turned inward), I no longer allow myself to wallow in that pit for too long. I seek someone out to visit or partake in an activity—generally, being around another person pulls me out.

Laurence

I find that opening myself up to the love of my family and close friends is most helpful. Holding and playing with my year old daughter does remarkable things for me. It helps me gain perspective and be thankful for the blessings that I have.

Daniel

Through trust and sharing; I have recently found that if I am willing to be vulnerable (with the right people). I don't have to be all and do all. There truly is strength in weakness, and relationships are formed that actually have depth and are not based just on looks or accomplishments. I'll admit that it is not an easy thing for me to trust, but as someone once said "If you continue to do what you've always done, you'll always get what you've always gotten."

Darryl

When I begin to think clearly about my anger and I determine that it is not a substitution for scared or sad, then I start looking for its meaning, which is that somehow I am experiencing a violation, either real or imagined. When I act in a constructive way that redresses the violation, then I feel complete and my anger, rational or not, disappears.

I almost killed myself with my rage in the days before I learned how it worked in me.

Tyrone

First, I use the 24 hour rule; don't react in any way until I've thoroughly thought through the issue for 24 hours.

Wes

In the future, I plan to begin to express what it is that I want, to find out if other people are interested to help make it happen, but still being unattached to the outcome.

Chad

I once had my whole mental world wired with high-voltage electric fence that would hurt you if you touched it. My fear and anger looked like one and the same. Then I replaced that with a boundary that would set off ear-splitting sirens, turn on blinding lights, and bring snarling dogs to the other side of the fence--all to scare you but not necessarily hurt you. Now some of my inner world is available to visitors. Like a city park. And like a park, it's got some rules and hours of operation and all that, but you're welcome to hang out. Other parts of my inner world are wired with firm but polite "private area" signs and invisible fence. If you ignore the signs and trespass, it sets off a silent alarm in my head. So I can identify the intruder, decide how dangerous the threat is, and take some course of action from simply ignoring you until you go away to actively repelling you. I've still got a few very private areas bristling with high-voltage, razor wire, killer dogs and shotguns, so to speak. But it's a small area. It's very well posted, very well defended, and very far from the public areas. If someone tries to breach that most private area of my life, to push their way in uninvited to my heart and soul—or my home—I assume they intend to do me or my loved ones serious harm and they deserve what they get.

Cliff

If I can't readily talk my anger out with either its instigator or a benevolent third party I could still get the energy out by some vigorous physical movement and vocalization. That seems to be important to get energy out/flowing....it doesn't have to make sense or follow any mainstream theory. Energy at least moving diffuses and is easier to manage than energy that I hold in and allow some external trigger to prick...... like removing the top of a pressure cooker while it's still on the flame. That's okay if you like that much excitement in your life but I'm getting too old for it.

Andrew

I've been reflecting on what's been going on with me these past few days and wish to share a few observations and commitments about anger.

My chronic, generalized anger inevitably results in my telling myself stories about the feeling. This requires me to be "angry at ____, because ____." In whatever story I weave, I necessarily make myself the victim, in that so-and-so has now "done something to me." It's very disempowering.

Moreover, the rage coursing through my body gives me an artificial sense of power. (I suspect, in fact, that I'm addicted to the cocktail of brain chemicals produced by the anger.) A truer sense of power would stem from a quiet confidence, in which there existed many possible responses. Such a quiet confidence, in addition to being less exhausting for me, would be much more innately attractive to others than my bubbling rage. This is important, since much of my anger springs from or is exacerbated by my sense of isolation.

Soooo, I've been thinking of some daily practices I can begin to implement. As I mentioned, I'm often my own worst enemy, and the change here needs to be an "inside job." I've decided for now to do two things:

1) Actively practice gratitude multiple times each day. I will attempt to remember this practice whenever I catch myself slipping into a funk, and am intentionally developing a habit of doing it whenever I hear a car horn, alarm, siren or telephone ringing.

2) In the words of John Maxwell, putting a "10" on everyone's head: expecting the best of them. This one is a real challenge for me. I was working with it today and noticing just how much I like seeing others be wrong and inept. So, for now, this means paying attention to my harsh judgments of others and reminding myself that I'm not getting richer, happier or healthier by virtue of this judgment—that wallowing in the judgment does me a disservice. By letting it go, I'm also breathing in gratitude that I'm growing healthier and more loveable by virtue of this practice.

I have asked my men's team to remind me of my commitment to these two practices. I've been playing with them today and intend to make them habits. I am asking my men's team to provide me any feedback or suggestions, they have. After all, even if I think their idea is lousy, I get to practice #2 above.

Phillip
Let it happen. Learn how to display it constructively.

Kobe
I think that by understanding, and actually 'looking at' the position I'm holding is a start. I could then possibly see the other persons' position better. With this knowledge, and some empathy with myself and the other person, I could possibly shift either my position or theirs towards one another a little closer. I could see that being 'positional' and 'righteous' about a particular idea or belief totally collapses any understanding of anything outside of my own world. As the position subsides, so does the anger.

Kyle
There is no future. This illusion makes me only think I have control. I don't. I can only observe what is (now), and digest that. If I try to judge it, or correct or change it, than my trying prevents my seeing what really is.

Marcus
I breathe into the places in my body, I give myself permission to feel it, and I often do something physical to move the energy. I manage my anger better when I'm exercising regularly.

Frank
Just stay in control. I can reason and debate with the best of them, I have no reason to let my emotions get out of control. Focusing anger in a constructive way versus a destructive way is something I need to do.

Rico
Instead of acting it out, I have found that by developing a "witnessing presence" I can begin to make some headway on dealing with it. Through witnessing the feeling of anger it begins to dissipate. When I act it out, it tends to feed on itself and perpetuate itself and run me over and over. I have found that only the witnessing presence has the power to burn through historic anger. Witnessing over time slowly empties the pall of historic anger until there is much more room in the psyche.

Willie

I want to find a way to slow it down. I want to find a way to express it that is both safe for myself and those around me. I don't know what those are.

Randy

To immediately offer myself self-respect and trust. And, to wake up to the fact that it is ok for me to feel and have this emotion, for this emotion is a guiding light—no self-condemnation.

Damon

If I am unprovoked, there is no rage to deal with. Treat me with respect and I will treat you with respect.

Bill

Give up traditional resolution. Seek to achieve inner peace with the new social reality that few hold themselves accountable to behave justly. Since this is a self-distorting approach, I loathe it. But as a last resort, it may be all that is left to me.

Larry

Wait to calm down, write or journal out what I am experiencing and use a tool I teach called 'Feel, Want, Willing." First state what I am feeling. This works well if you can do this to the person(s) involved. Then when they have heard that, tell them what I want, and what I am willing to do to have it. Example- I am angry you did not call me on time. I want you to be timely and considerate in the future. I am willing to do the same for you.

What are constructive ways of expressing your anger, rage, and fierceness?

Wilson

I have found that I have to wait a while but I do not avoid or deny my anger. I will go the person and tell them, 'You know, this really made me mad and it upset me". Sometimes, it is news to them and sometimes it is an opening for either resolution or a deeper relationship - I have experienced both solutions. Fierceness is another issue . . . I have found that my fierceness is threatening, especially to women (large size, booming voice). My being passionate is usually misinterpreted as being either fierce or 'too aggressive'. I feel I am viewed as a threat unless I am flat and emotionless. This troubles me and creates problems for me.

Bob

At 51, I am still a teen when it comes to dealing with anger and frustration. Learning to cope with them proves to be a very painful process by which I have to get rid of my pride. And frankly, I feel naked and vulnerable without that pride. I know that there are ways to harness our male anger and that frustrations come from of perception of things. I know those things but can't feel them.

Blake

This is a tough one. I had a supposedly confidential experience with a male friend (close, but not that close - not one of those friends from my adolescent years, and yes someone I know through my wife's circle) wherein I deliberately expressed my rage, not at him but in front of him. This was not an out-of-control rage, but I did reveal how deeply I felt about what I was saying. The response I received was highly judgmental, and soon thereafter I learned my confidence (that I expressed anger, not necessarily what I was saying) had not been kept. I naturally felt not only betrayed but ashamed. The experience was in the context of working on my personal growth. The lesson I took from this was that efforts to help one grow are often feeding a pathology of the "helper" having to do with control, ego and who know what else. You need to make sure you are in a safe place to explore your anger.

Bill

To hold someone accountable for the injustice they cause is a constructive way indeed but not necessarily effective. So the question becomes, "What do we do when a constructive approach becomes ineffective?" Reluctantly I must admit, as I think all honest people must admit, when constructive approaches become ineffective, all we are left with is destructive ones. Since that is unacceptable, the world should be working together to correct it's ill social environment. I feel sadness that it does not seem to be doing so.

Daniel

To find places or activities where I can channel my anger, rage, and fierceness—things that are productive or beneficial to the community, to friends, or to myself.

Cliff

Being assertive is a more balanced expression of these emotions. It allows and tempers the extremes.

Wes

Looking into myself for answers, questioning the feelings and why they are there, and being open to listen to the possible answers as to why my body/mind feels the way it does.

Fred

Martin, thanks also to you for your kind words and YOUR courage to ask us. I wish more men would have compassion for what it takes for YOU to ask us for responses to questions that will HELP our lives and then answer them so you don't have to ask twice!! Your kind words are also an inspiration to all of us as well.

More along the same lines:

More constructive ways of expressing our anger would be simply to talk about it and hope for people to understand. We also need to learn how to do it properly and not in a way that would scare people away.

I allow myself to be aggressive when I need to get something done. I value doing a good job over all else and I need to be aggressive at times to do so. I am not sure about any value in honoring our fierceness.

Being angry in a constructive sense is being angry for the right reasons. If somebody persecutes somebody you know, then use it for that. Using anger for all the right reasons helps, especially when somebody tries to get you to do something that you know is wrong.

Reacting to our anger constantly is when it owns us and we do not own it. It is like letting it control us rather than we controlling it. Justifying anger can turn us into what we hate if we do not use it for a justifiable purpose.

We become assertive by not being aggressive when we try to say that our answers are our be all and end all and that we do not want to discuss it anymore.

Anger in relation to sadness is when we scare people away with our anger by not using it constructively. We may have regret for using it for that purpose. I know to be angry when we are constantly persecuted for no reason at all. However, it can make our anger engulf us and then we explode.

We can enjoy differences by being around others in order to have a balance. It is okay to agree to disagree but even that has its limits.

Sometimes conflict cannot be avoided especially when we have a difference of opinion with others. We are all different and our environments make us different—hence the differences that we have.

Rico
Focus and dedication to being present.

What is the risk of "killing off our anger?" Do we have shame about it?

Wilson
I think men could very well lose their anger. Appropriate anger is OK in my book, but we have been feminized to the point that the expression of ANY anger is viewed as negative. As young boys, we are punished for it, as men the women in our life punish us by passively attacking us. There is shame in having anger but there should not be. We did not put that shame there.

We loose our ability to protect what is important, go for what we truly want, and lack the commitment to stand up for what we believe putting this burden on the women in our lives.

Phillip
Anger doesn't go away - it becomes rage. Rage destroys men and relationships from the inside out. I feel less than a man when I fail to stand up for myself, and I lose my sharp edge. Who admires a dull man? Therein lays shame in disguise.

Daniel

I believe that "directed" anger and fierceness are strengths, and to kill them off or to allow them be suppressed gives over to our fears. Do we have shame about it? Yes! Responding to our anger and fierceness takes courage—a boldness if you will, and I, for the majority of my life was convinced that responding with strength and boldness was wrong. I was taught that to be bold was prideful, and that too was wrong.

Darryl

In my judgment I have been given the ability to feel anger for a purpose, just as sadness and scare are signals that have purpose and meaning for me if I am willing to read them. For someone to try to take away the reality of my emotional life would be the deepest kind of personal violation, like trying to take away my sight, or my hearing, or my sense of touch. I need my aliveness and awareness to be whole. So, yes, attempting to "kill off" my (or any man's) anger and fierceness because they remind folks of violence and injustices that men have committed is a strategy that will never work. It is okay to be fierce and angry about injustice. I feel enraged about fools like Karl Rove manufacturing a war and sending thousands of young men and women to their deaths in order to make George Bush electable. I feel furious that my 16 year old daughter is bombarded by demeaning, objectifying images of so-called sexy women role-models. I feel angry about continuing modern racism all around me. I feel really angry that the women I love and those I don't even know don't feel safe to walk, jog or just be outdoors at night.

It's not whether we men are fierce or angry. It's what we are fierce or angry about—in the service of what? And whom?

Chad

If I kill off anger, I lose my ability to: 1) defend myself and my loved ones 2) defend my values (protest injustice) 3) feel any other strong emotion—if I block anger, the log jam blocks the flow of everything else in the river, too.

Anger is the energy that gives me the ability to defend myself, others, and my values with my words, my actions, my facial expressions and body language. Anger is what gives all that power, credibility, consistency, effectiveness.

Roy

There is no killing it off. There is just suppressing it so it comes out either with an explosion against someone that does not deserve it or just damaging my own body by containing it. It is just energy. You can direct it in constructive ways or un-constructive ways.

Kobe

Killing of your anger for the sake of not being angry, in my opinion, is to ignore your beliefs and ideas. Anger should be embraced, because anger points directly towards our beliefs and ideas. Anger always points to something significant about ourselves, so it should never be shamed.

Cliff

Killing off—that's a fool's game. Anger is a normal response. It just gets misplaced or we don't have models or modeling on how to appropriately deal with it. And yes, there is shame around anything that some authority figure that we accept as true (our country, our parents, etc.) tells us, like "Don't do that!"

Willie

I know if I don't express my emotions they will come back to bite me.

Randy

The risk is that I would become something inhumane; a piece of synthetic with no ability to feel, relate, and connect. It is used in the most primitive-form to protect, and in the mid-form to guide, and in the higher form to inspire....I will never stop feeling this beautiful passion.

Marcus

I cherish my anger and rage as a powerful masculine part of me; it reminds me that I'm alive! I judge that our feminized society has marginalized men's anger and labeled men who get angry as dangerous, this makes me angry!

Rico

Anger can be used to accomplish things but it is an act, not real. If used as fuel over the long haul, it is a misguided motivation. It tends to backfire on itself in the long run. In my experience, things accomplished through anger mean little to the soul's genuine growth or the true strength of a human being. Feeling anger as opposed to acting it out, doesn't kill it off, it burns it off, while burning we grow stronger. There is no shame in that.

Frank

Sometimes killing off anger prevents things from getting done. If something is making me angry, I need to address it. Sometimes it takes raising my voice to get people to notice that I am serious. I don't think there is any shame in it, as long as the anger remains controlled.

Kyle

It doesn't seem likely I will 'kill off' my anger. And mentally I don't believe it is nature's way. This is not a control issue to me. This is about my body. When I'm angry, I am anger. I didn't say I have anger. I said I am angry. So, who is it that would be in control? I know we have some social mechanisms that may kick in but it seems theoretical to bring them in when my real lessons are stored in my bones.

Jon

I think it's safe to say that as an adult, I don't know how to express my anger. I am well aware that there are many things in this world that are worth getting angry about. I no longer believe that it is a sin to express anger; however, I never really learned how to do it.

What can happen to me is that I become afraid of that inner feeling of anger—the anger threatens to take over the situation, and I am afraid to let it do that. I don't know if I'm afraid I'll physically hurt someone, or if I'm afraid I will look stupid, or what ... but for whatever reason, I experience a certain amount of paralysis when I try to express anger.

A place I do allow myself to express anger or fierceness is playing racquetball. Also in performing, I like to act in theater, and to do improvisational theater. Doing that gives me a great opportunity to act out the emotions that I am pretty much unable to express in my 'real' life.

Damon

An early death from a host of physical ailments brought on by the flood of adrenalin flowing through your veins with no outlet.
Do we have shame about it? I am not ashamed of a pure human defense programmed in my genes.

Bill

The risk is that I will become an automaton, bereft of authenticity. I have done a tremendous amount of work to resolve false shame; and so I know that even though I have done my best and failed in successfully expressing anger, I am not defective. However, shame also involves confidence, or our capacity to live effectively in a given environment. I have made myself the man I choose to be, a character consistent with my values. However, the social environment I find myself in is not one that rewards such men, so confidence is impacted and perhaps some small shame arises from being stuck in an anti social environment.

Wes

Killing off anger is an illusion. It will still be there, growing into rage, waiting to be expressed. Killing off fierceness is also an illusion. It will still be there, waiting to be used. Exercising fierceness is a fine way to work through the tough issues and to increase my energy output. It's not the only way or always the most effective, but it's a wonderful tool to be able to have at the ready. Do I have shame around it? Each individual deals in a different way. I have had some shame involving showing anger, but I have pride with it on occasion, too.

Larry

Fierceness and anger are not the same, although some people grow up seeing that model and equate them. The risk of 'killing off our anger' is that we have a world full of men too passive to get anything done. Women know these men for they feel tired around them.

What is the value in honoring our fierceness? How do we know when we use it inappropriately?

Wilson

There is value in our fierceness because it is truly part of who we are. When we deny it, we deny ourselves - we become less that what we started with. Inappropriate use of fierceness is when people are hurt; my most common sin is using my fierceness to control others through intimidation.

Daniel

I don't feel that I've learned this yet. It is appropriate in survival and protection of family and loved ones

Kyle

I do honor (this means 'accept' in my book) my attributes, fierceness being one of them. If I don't honor my attributes what is that saying? It's saying I don't believe I'm sufficient. But I am sufficient because nature is perfect in its balance and harmony. And I am nature. I know I may not be able to fathom it nor understand the whole picture, but it delights me to consider my miniscule contribution to the whole.

Wes

Fierceness is a wonderful healthy attitude of self-acceptance. Honoring fierceness (as well as passive behavior, if that is what is what the body chooses) is one way to generate health by allowing the flow of emotion to circulate and be free. How do we know when we use it appropriately? In the moment, we just know.

Rico

Fierceness is an innate quality of the soul. It comes naturally when we are fully present.

Cliff

It can connect me more to what I perceive as my bedrock, that part that is truly me and not made up by observing outside sources.

How can you use anger more effectively? Where is it appropriate to be angry? How do you cultivate this energy in a positive direction?

Eddy

I have found that showing anger is usually non-productive—and the key word here is "usually," for there are times when showing anger is useful, even necessary. In most cases, remaining calm and collected is the most effective way to deal with a person or a situation. People become very defensive if you show your anger. However, there are times when you must display anger. For instance, if you've tried every other strategy without success, and it's important that you get your point across, showing anger may be the best way to get the other person or party to listen. Even then, however, yelling at the other person or party isn't productive—one can show anger without going berserk.

Wilson

Effective anger for me is the anger that forces me to seek resolution to an issue. Like I said, I have to wait a while but I must resolve the situation or at least express myself on it. Calm expression of anger, for me, is effective.

Appropriate anger: "You, give me MY money!" "Stop hurting him"

To me, acknowledgement of anger generally makes it turn into a problem solving situation. Calm, verbal expression of anger is important to me.

Steven

I've always related to this quote:

"I never work better than when I'm inspired by anger: I can write, pray, and preach well. My whole temperament is quickened, my understanding sharpened, and all mundane vexations and temptations depart."

– Martin Luther, German religious reformer

My own experience with anger has been profound. I grew up with a father who beat the crap out of me and my brothers and sisters. I know now that he didn't know better, but I was angry as I came into manhood. Since I didn't know any healthy ways of dealing with my anger, it came out in rage, and I often scared the

345

people I loved. After doing some therapy and other personal work, I learned how to process my anger, and found ways to release it. It was amazing. All of sudden I had this power to let go of something in a healthy way, so I did, every time something came up that made me angry. Then I had another profound awareness, which takes me back to the quote by Martin Luther. I was in the middle of a divorce and a split with a business partner and in both cases was being taken advantage of. I was pissed. And my therapist told me something that rocked my world. When I expressed a desire to do some work to let go of the anger, he encouraged me not too. He said that the anger might be a valuable ally in my negotiations and in my quest to take care of myself during this situation. He was right, and it's become a valuable ally ever since. But it took all the initial awareness about healthy processing and all that to open me to the idea that this emotion which I was terrified of my whole life, could be so critical to loving myself.

Kyle
Perhaps punching someone would be of use sometimes. Sometimes talk just isn't enough. Wouldn't you like to get Bush in the ring? Are we being brainwashed that physical contact is a no? I'd like to see some old fashioned fist fighting instead of arbitration. And how about honor of dueling and the age of chivalry. Wouldn't it make you be more authentic if you knew you could die if someone challenged you? That would help me overcome my fear of fighting and release something horrible yet primitive in me that sometimes wants to get out.

Cliff
To address injustice and to protect the weak and the innocents.

Werner
To defend my family and my own life. With awareness it may be used in controlled ways to get someone attention when other means have not worked.

Daniel
By remaining focused and deliberate in our actions.

Kyle

Any place, no limits at all. How to be angry? I don't know I'd rather be genuine and not rehearse.

Wes

Cultivating anger energy into a positive direction can be done a variety of ways. Depending on the source of the anger and the various arenas of expression, the body by intention finds the appropriate way. Sometimes, in retrospect, there might be regret about a display of anger, but in the moment, all expression is the appropriate expression. Even a 'mistaken' expression, is key to being aware of the need to deal proactively with the stress.

How does "justifying anger" turn us into what we hate? How does 'reacting' with anger let anger run us?

Wilson

I have found that even if I believe I am justified in my anger, it does me no good to hold on to it. Anger does cloud resolution and generally it will build impassable walls.

Allen

I just does, and it is hard to explain. If I am so determined to not be someone, I unconsciously focus on that person and slowly become them. It reminded of the 'dark side' in Star wars and how they turned Anakin to become Darth Vader, by giving into his hate. There is some type of physiological twist.

Kyle

This reminds me of my so-deceptive mind and why I don't trust it. I realize that when I had the most anger in my life I thought I was the on a white horse and did no wrong. I was angered by authority, yet I wanted to control. I was angered by deception, yet I was not honorable. I was angered by insensitive, unthinking people- yet I did not know kindness. Hell yes, I was angry at myself wasn't I? I sometimes see this even now my reaction to someone who is doing or saying something that I myself have a problem with—alas when someone tries to give me advice when I

347

am not asking for it. I think they are audacious and resent that they think they know what's good for me, that they think they have 'arrived' and pretend they have no problems, that they are bragging how good they are. But, this is what I catch myself doing—giving advice as though I know, bragging how good I am, etc. Do you see?

So there is all this opportunity out there to learn about myself from watching my reactions to others (instead of getting mad at them). This takes a lot of energy to be so attentive.

Chad

The more I know my fears—recognize them, understand them, work through them, accept them and deal with my shame at being afraid—the less I am run by them. There are not as many alarms and not as loud. So I get angry less often and less unconsciously or automatically. Or I can pretend I'm not afraid and not angry and walk around directly or indirectly, aggressively or passively, whacking the hell out of anyone who trips a wire in my world.

Wes

In general I 'hate' being in situations of hate. So if hate is the source of the anger, then justifying that anger will surround me in a sphere of hate by welcoming it into my life. This still might be the appropriate expression in any particular moment. So I'm okay with the world as it is, and sometimes that means that I "need" to be hating. When is reacting with anger letting anger run us? This is just a point of view. Are we running the anger or is the anger running us? Both views can be seen to be true if you believe it.

Daniel

Reacting with anger demonstrates a "limited repertoire" of responses to a given situation. I get angry when I've exhausted all the possibilities, I don't know what to do next, and walking away doesn't seem to be a viable option.

How do we develop the way to be assertive without being aggressive?

Von

I personally like the notion of assertiveness versus aggressiveness. Assertive behavior is simply defining one's personal boundaries (often defined by values, principles and time) and guarding those boundaries with conviction. One of my important lessons learned in maturity, is that I am not obligated to do what others expect me to do. My personal mission, values and goals determine where such boundaries are. Of course, without such personal definition, one experiences the kind of pain and shame. Further, I have learned that I am NOT obligated to explain myself. A simple, courteous, no, or a quiet exit from a room will often suffice, rather than making an emotional outburst.

Dan

Fierceness and assertiveness vs. aggression and control. For me, fierceness and assertiveness are based on me and protection of my self. Aggression and control are focused on my doing something to you. Once I try to do something to you, there's going to be conflict and resistance. There's no way I can win. Even if I have over-powering force in the end, I will pay a large cost and probably won't end up with any real protection for me and myself anyway.

Anger in men has an odd role to play. For reasons that maybe the sociologists can explain, men have always been allowed to express anger when every other emotion is prohibited to them. I'm convinced that men have all the emotions we have words for just like women and children, that, since anger is allowable, all of their emotional feelings get funneled into anger, that, because men express all of their emotions via anger, they believe that's the only emotion they have, and that, if men would find, name, and express each of their emotions, anger would be considerably less in the world and men could process their anger effectively.

Wilson

Through practice. Men's groups are excellent places to practice resolutions and express emotions that may be misinterpreted outside of the group. I learned skills in these groups that I successfully took with me to the outside world.

Chad
The best book I have ever read on this subject is Malcom Smith's, "When I Say No I Feel Guilty." It's the original assertiveness training manual based on the program he developed for the Peace Corp back in the 60s. Such a brilliant, brilliant book, and I think it's out of print.

Kyle
By watching ourselves and noticing what's going on right now. Not trying to do anything about it, just noticing what is. That is what gives up the facts and the body will know what to do.

Wes
Again, this is unique to each situation. But I would say that intending and then acting on the intention to change my thoughts and beliefs about being assertive without being aggressive. I like to use affirmations sometimes. I might say or write down a statement indicating I want to be assertive, and then repeat it in my mind to see if I can say it so that it rings true in the core of my being.

Tom
Becoming more assertive is not one of my goals at present. I am an American who has been living in Japan for many years, and this experience has helped me to develop more objective views of my country than I once had. During my visits to the U.S., I am able to see good and bad points that I had never noticed while I was still living here. Unfortunately, one of things I have observed is an ever-increasing degree of assertiveness in all walks of life here. Indeed, I reckon that we are now in danger of becoming a nation of pushy, self-centered loud mouths. I think this sad development has occurred as a result of we American men and women (and especially women perhaps, in recent years) being taught over and over again the importance—nay, the necessity—of being ASSERTIVE. "Speak up!" "Make yourself noticed!" "Insist upon your rights!" "Push ahead!" "Don't take 'no' for an answer!" These mantras have been drilled into us since early childhood. But

we are rarely taught the benefits of being good listeners, or of being cooperative, or of being quietly competent and steadfast.

I think assertiveness is probably one of many character traits found in successful business men and women, but its value is currently overemphasized in America.

Daniel
For me it's by trying new things, putting myself in unfamiliar situations, and gaining new experiences.

What is anger and its relationship to sadness? How do you know to be angry?

Wilson
For me, concealed anger breeds depression. I cannot live with either.

I am not certain that I consciously know when to be angry - anger is an emotion that rises up in me when I am faced with personal injustice, judgmental remarks, being ridiculed when I am giving it my best.

Arthur
Under my repressed anger is sadness. This I knew theoretically but had not found it in me until I returned from a rites of passage camp.

The first instance was when we had just finished the training camp and as we left the land, oldest man to youngest, the women trainee facilitators stood periodically along the dirt track and we sung the honoring of grandmother and grandfather song Puresominee/Puremominee, and this affected me so much that I wept the whole journey home. The women were the catalyst! These tears felt like such a relief – a weight was lifting.

On a subsequent camp I had been touched by such beauty that I had never known to be possible when one of the camp cooks spoke a Rumi poem 'Looking for your face' and it just moved me. When I returned home I felt a real urge in some way to relay to my wife this beauty but whatever I said was just not hitting the mark. Over a period of 2 or 3 days I still felt this urge to share the experience, but it seemed the message was just not getting through.

351

Finally one evening she said she actually did not want to even be in the same room as me. I went to the spare room and lay there and felt the tears welling yet there was something blocking them. I had a sudden realization that I had been here before, that as a child I lay there no longer able to cry because what was the point – NO ONE WAS COMING, NO ONE CARED. I knew that place deeply etched in my psyche and here I was again totally recreating the experience with the dutiful assistance of my wife!

Thankfully she appeared soon afterwards, not too benevolent but 'over' all this and she said to me 'come back to bed.' So the story has a shift, someone did come and what a gift in many ways. I returned to our bed and wept uncontrollably in her arms firstly for me, the little boy who felt so helpless and could affect nothing with his tears, and then my tears went out to all children and I was saddened for the shame and hurt that seemed insurmountable. My wife understood me and this situation a bit better. So did I. It was beautiful.

I memorized that poem that had affected me so, and was reciting it to my mentor over the phone and he said 'You know this is about you.' Here's the poem;

LOOKING FOR YOUR FACE – by Rumi
From the beginning of my life
I have been looking for your face
but today I have seen it

Today I have seen
the charm, the beauty,
the unfathomable grace
of the face
that I was looking for

Today I have found you
and those who laughed
and scorned me yesterday
are sorry that they were not looking
as I did

I am bewildered by the magnificence
of your beauty

and wish to see you
with a hundred eyes

My heart has burned with passion
and has searched forever
for this wondrous beauty
that I now behold

I am ashamed
to call this love human
and afraid of God
to call it divine

Your fragrant breath
like the morning breeze
has come to the stillness of the garden
You have breathed new life into me
I have become your sunshine
and also your shadow

My soul is screaming in ecstasy
Every fiber of my being
is in love with you

Your effulgence
has lit a fire in my heart
for me
the earth and sky

My arrow of love
has arrived at the target
I am in the house of mercy
and my heart
is a place of prayer

Kyle

Sadness seems like the passive side of anger—when there is
nothing to be done or nothing wants to be done or nothing is
sufficient to be done. I realize there is great sadness wherever I
look. Maybe this is what drives us to hide things from ourselves,

wanting to keep continually occupied and noisy. In this way it seems easier to deal with the superficial, made-up stuff, beliefs in various things, gods, behaviors, future. I wonder if we are doomed to be miserable or if there is any possibility of understanding sadness.

Phillip

I am reminded of a quote from an episode of *The Sopranos*: "Depression is anger turned inward." I have been depressed at times in my life when I didn't know I should be angry. I have to be more conscious of my needs and feelings to avoid depression and properly vent my anger. I also need meaningful relationships with other men.

Chad

Sadness is my feeling of loss and pain at the harm that fear tries to warn me about and anger tries to protect against. The sadness is always the same—I'm sad that someone has discounted, neglected, abandoned, disrespected, abused or otherwise harmed me or someone else or something of value—whether a forest or an idea or a spirit or a child. But I can't feel the sadness until I identify the fear that triggered the anger, and express or acknowledge them first.

Probably 90% of the time I can eventually find the sadness under my anger. I think the other 10% of the time, it's there but I can't get to it, because—and this is funny—my fear kicks back in and says, "No! It's going to hurt too much to feel that sadness." So I keep working on it.

Daniel

I would define them both as "over the top" emotional responses. By that I mean that you can only prepare yourself for what you can anticipate. At some point the circumstances will go beyond all that you have prepared for, and you will experience an emotion like anger or sadness. How do you know to be angry? Sometimes it's just a "knee-jerk reaction," but at other times when I've prepared, or had a similar experience, I have a bank of information to access for alternative responses.

How can we enjoy our differences? Maybe even enjoy a good argument? Do you think it is okay to agree to disagree?

Kyle

It is essential to disagree with everything. That way I can examine it fresh for myself. If I can only be innocent and without agenda than I can say anything to anyone without giving offence. But, that is the rub– without agenda!

Cliff

I am still learning that debate can teach me something and is not just "Oh my god a tiger is coming!"

Werner

I have the chance to grow, learn something new, become wiser, even learn how I am wrong, and it gives me a way to be closer to someone who I may stay further apart if I did not accept our differences.

Daniel

We can enjoy our differences by first appreciating and not fearing our differences. Maybe even enjoy a good argument? I don't know yet what it is to have a "good argument." As I mentioned earlier, conflict and I were like oil and water. I have, though, reached the level where I am willing to go through the pain (my perception) of an argument if I value the individual, or the potential outcome seems worth it. Do you consider that it is okay to agree to disagree? It is, absolutely, okay to agree to disagree. We are all different with varied experiences and backgrounds. Our differences are what makes life exciting.

Do you avoid conflict or realize that is a possible way for new learning, new creations and deeper relationship if you stay with it ?

Kyle

Conflict has been painful at times. It has also produced and cemented my most valuable relationships. At times it's difficult

355

and at times it's fun to take conflict as a part of my life, not something to be avoided. Like problems in general, my life is full of them everyday and moment. Logically, mentally to fight them is to waste energy and be in stress. Problems (and conflict) are not negative. I make my living and my friendships from them. Evolution. My cells reproduce from them. My body becomes stronger from them. I increase my intellect from them. What's the problem?

Cliff

By going through this series of questions I am seeing a more accepting attitude toward anger, maybe even making friends with it so that it doesn't run me or at least feel like that.

Chad

One of the blessings and curses of having a nervous system brain is that my protective systems can kick in automatically in about a hundredth of a second. I go from the alert—fear—to a protective response—anger—quicker than I can consciously think. My animal brain runs through whole fear and anger cycle in a split-second. I might not even actually feel the feelings or know why I just bristled at somebody. If I want to learn, I have to re-enact and re-create and slow down that machinery to figure out why I react to things, the way I do. I have to reverse-engineer the complex security system and trace the wiring back to hidden memories of old threats and harms until I say, "Oh, that's why I wanted to punch that guy in the face."

Daniel

In the past I would run from conflict, and though I am still not comfortable with many types of conflict, especially when it's personal, I do my best to "work through it."

How do we kill other men off with our silence?

Cooley

I believe the most significant way we kill one another off is by avoiding one another (stony silence). It makes me uncomfortable to see another man up close and personal, because I might have to

356

share myself. He may ask how I feel. Even worse, he may provoke my fear and judge me less than a man. I am not practiced at sharing, and I might give too much if I open up. It is my armor that protects and isolates me from other men. Notice how we tend to go away when we are ignored? You could have retreated at any point in this project, but you haven't. I appreciate your persistence, and I admire your courage. I am proud to be part of what you are trying to create.

Bill

I don't know if my contribution can be very helpful in this context, because I am very isolated and disillusioned with the concept of community. Because of the financial and emotional roller-coaster that started when my ex wife decided she didn't want to be married anymore and because of my disabled teenage son, I have had to reach out to community for help a number of times, not because I wanted to or thought it would do any good, but because I was desperate and had no where else to turn.

I am now isolated and hopeless toward the concept of community because I was basically ignored what feels like a hundred times by men who claimed to be more emotionally aware and connected than average, in more than one community, no matter how desperate our situation was, including being on the street with kids.

Frankly, my judgment is that the concept of mutual support in community is merely a mind game played by affluent men to comfort themselves about their own complacency. Men are on their own, without hope of support, and that is the fundamental reason men harden themselves emotionally. Nothing occurs in a vacuum. Men are emotionally hard because they find themselves in a hard environment because of the way we are treated in the world; and the way men are treated in the world is as hard today as it ever was, if not worse.

My spiritual practice enables me to have a measure of inner peace despite this experience, but my relationship with community will probably be negatively impacted for the rest of my life. Sorry but that's what my experience has shown me.

There were very few bright shining exceptions of men who really show up emotionally and otherwise, with love and sincerity and understanding and respect for my family when we were in

357

need and reached out for support, and these few exceptional men have enabled me to hold onto the belief that the universe is a fundamentally friendly place in spite of many troubling experiences. I owe those few men a lot. So I am not killed off, but my relationship to community is.

Where in your life do you allow yourself to just be aggressive or even assertive?

Willie
In my specific area of expertise, where I know I'm right beyond a shadow of a doubt.

Rico
Wherever necessary.

Daniel
The area of my life that gives me the most satisfaction—my work with neglected, mistreated, or abandoned animals. Working for and even fighting for their benefit and their rights—a place where I am willing to ignore my own fears and inadequacies for the benefit of others.

Kyle
I don't want to be contrived, just to be who I am.

Wes
In situations where my body's energy has decided that it is the best expression. In the past, I haven't needed to use it that much as my goal was to be OK with the world as it is. But now I'm learning that my goal is to be OK with the world as it is with me wanting to be assertive (aggressive doesn't feel right to me) in it.

Phillip
I am rarely aggressive, but I allow myself to be assertive in the workplace. (I don't have an interest in sports, which I imagine satisfies this need for some men.) My professional relationships are emotionally disconnected, so I don't have to worry about hurting anyone's feelings. I go for what I want and make it

happen, because I have been initiated in this arena. I have been more passive in my personal relationships, because it is difficult for me to assert my needs. I have not been properly initiated in this area.

How often are you too passive or non-responsive in your life and what does that cost you?

Darryl

This is embarrassing. I wish I were better. There is pressure from all my male programming to pretend there are not areas where I am passive—non-responsive. But the truth is I want to avoid conflict. I don't see the point of always telling the truth in my primary relationship if it is simply going to lead to another useless argument, so I choose to become passive and non-responsive about my partners' violations, broken agreements, and failed commitments. Then the frustration and hopelessness grows in me. I don't respect myself. And I carry around a sense of impending relationship doom. It's just a matter of when...

Woody Allen said to the psychiatrist, in effect, "I don't want you to cure my brother from thinking he is a chicken.......because we need the eggs."

Daniel

I have lived the majority of my life in passive or non-responsive mode. Things would happen to me, around me, with me, or without me. My attitude was "I am not in control, and what happens to me is always someone else's decision." That attitude has cost me love, has cost me success, and has allowed me to see myself living "at the bottom," surviving on the scraps the world is willing to throw my way.

Phillip

Passivity has been a way of life for me. It is a controlled and risk-free mode of interacting with others. They allegedly can't hurt me if I don't respond to their stimuli; there is no pain if I ignore it/them. This way of life costs me my happiness by repressing my emotions and creativity.

Larry

It costs aliveness and intensity. I am too passive sometimes, although sometimes I am not sure if I made the best choice or not.

Kobe

I'm often too passive about many things; most of which are associated with other people. I tend to give the other person "space" to be angry, sad, annoyed, happy, and therefore don't interact much with them. I justify this under the guise of "giving respect" to the person. I mean, who am I to say they shouldn't be angry, sad or whatever. Writing these answers, I could see that interaction is perhaps exactly what that person requires at the moment to get to "their" ideas or beliefs. The outcome of this is: it costs me countless opportunities to contribute to other people, which is what I say I'm all about.

Willie

I'm often too passive, and it costs me my spine. I don't always know when to take a stand. Is this case important enough to rock the boat or not? I don't know where that balance is.

Rico

I have only been too passive or non responsive when I have not been willing to be fully present in the moment and in my life. When one is fully present, all ways of being are available.

Cliff

I am probably too often passive by nature (as an introvert) and that costs me in self esteem, self definition, and more open engagement with others.

David

I try not to be passive or non-responsive, but there are times both in personal issues and in business that I have chosen that course. In many years of military service we used to call decision making like this as "picking your battles" or "knowing when to bet your bars". The latter referred to betting your Lieutenant bar or Captains bars on decisions when perhaps taking a more passive approach would be more appropriate.

The cost of being passive is high - where you may continue on a path with your personal or business relationship, I have found that continued passiveness over a period of time has cost me losing out on the most important relationship I have - the one with myself.

Kyle

I am seldom passive. I am probably opposite. Although while we are in the judging vain of too much... or not enough... I'll confess that something's re-hash a situation and wish I would have said or done something differently. But, I am seldom in doubt in my everyday acts. I seldom over think something. I guess I trust my bones to come up with what is needed at the time. This is not blowing my horn–I can't help it. This is just the way I'm built. Those who are passive have qualities I aspire to like gentleness, kindness, patience and much more that I need.

On the other hand I'm putting myself in workshops and in front of audiences to help me learn how to "get out of my own way" when I'm nervous or tight, like doing a spontaneous performance. I find this stimulating and frightening but full of lessons and challenges and opportunities to overcome my fears. To live fully, to not be dead or partially dead until it is time to die–why not?

Damon

If you cannot express your feelings, your needs, you get what you deserve – nothing. This is not a license to be disrespectful but to state your needs and your rights to have your needs met.

Frank

I am almost always too passive. I have a hard time saying no. I often commit to things that I shouldn't commit too and it almost always raises my stress levels.

Bill

Almost daily–authenticity.

Wes

I think that I am as passive and non-responsive as I should be. Some people think I'm way too much so, but I think that when I am not responsive the energy of the moment warrants that I am that way. The cost is not an issue to me. The important thing for me is not to judge the passive behavior as bad or good. It is or was the way I was, which is what I was at my core.

What Insights did you personally gain from this chapter?

What do you want to commit to or re-commit to out of these insights?

Remember!
"Insight without committed action is only entertainment!"

Chapter 14
Finding our Tears and Learning to Grieve

Our deepest tears are how we abandon ourselves.—*Rumi*

How did you find your tears? How do men cry or grieve?

What are ways of resolving losses in our life?

What have you found to be the best way to handle anger and depression?

Do you turn to men, women, or isolate yourself from more emotional pain during a crisis?

What does it mean to experience your negative feelings so that they pass through you vs. stuffing them or avoiding them?

What is the cost to our lives of not crying or grieving? And when does crying or grieving not work?

What works in transforming emotional pain?

Can you remember the very first time you ever cried about anything?

If you stopped crying or grieving, can you remember when, what happened and what decision you made about the event that happened?

How do we model for younger men finding safe ways or places to cry or grieve?

Some types of tears are safer for men to express than others, what are they?

How do you get to the tears below the anger?

How have you found to grieve and not feel alone?

◆Martin's comments on this topic

◆As a child I did not receive any "pressure" from anyone to cry but figured out quickly that it was not cool to do as a boy at school because those that did were picked-on and made fun of. At some point during my high school years I decided that not only was crying not okay but that emotions were the core of problems. In fact while other boys were trying to figure out how to get girls, I had decided that I would never reach spiritual enlightenment if I

363

did not rid my self of all emotions. Of course I was just as interested in girls but at that time spiritual enlightenment seemed less complicated to take on than dealing with girls. This made for an interesting adolescence. Of course the experiment did not work, but it did teach me the cost of cutting off my emotions and later I learned how much fear I had generated trying to live entirely in my head.

♦In one of the Raleigh Men's Center workshops on, "How Do Men Cry"? I started tearing up as I described my experience of being at a funeral of a friend's father the day before. I was moved by my friend's description of his father's life—including the good as well as some of the difficult times. While he was talking, tears came to his eyes, but instead of stopping and giving himself time to regain his composure, he just kept talking. The tears came and went for him as he spoke about his father in front of the group, some deep and others mixed with laughter, but he kept talking.

♦In the men's workshop I unconsciously changed the topic slightly as I spoke about this to keep my tears from flowing. A man from the group asked, "What was that?!" "Go back to that." What are those tears about now?" At first I said I thought it was because of the courage my friend showed, then I sat with my own feelings a moment and it came to me. The tears were about the many years that I had spent suppressing my own emotions. These were tears of lost years. I also mentioned how at the beginning of the funeral, when I first walked in, I felt very emotional and did not want to show it. I remembered what another man said in a discussion about developing the ability to cry inside. Instead of trying to block the tears, I imagined that I was crying inside and the process kind of worked. I felt less like I was blocking my emotions. It's a technique that I use today to feel the emotions of sadness, grief, or just being deeply moved by life fully on the inside but not always letting it show on the outside.

♦This is why men's groups are so important. I thanked the participant for the artful way he had kept me present to my feelings. He replied, "I learned to do this from you." I was deeply touched.

♦This experience let me think about another question: How do we support or model for younger men finding safe ways to cry or grieve? There are clearly safe places to have tears. Suppressing feelings is not a solution but a way to create disease or even misplaced rage and violence. Finding safe places to express our feelings is very important.

♦One of the shocks I had while getting more in-touch with my feelings, before I got involved with men's groups, was how negatively the women I dated responded to my tears. One woman said, "You're the type of man I always wanted and now I am angry and scared." Another one encouraged me to open up then said, "That's enough!" I think we underestimate how many women are still influenced by the idea that their partner should be strong and that being strong does not include tears. I think we have an obligation as maturing men to honor women's fear of our tears, but that does not mean we should deny our feelings.

♦When men suppress their feelings they are not suppressing just good feelings. They are suppressing sadness, grief and shame. Many of us have spent more than 30 years or more of our lives suppressing sadness, grief, and shame, leaving us with a lot of emotional baggage to move through when we start exploring these feelings. My experience is that this pain is of a different quality than a woman's pain (not more, not less, just different), and it seems to me that it is asking too much from our wives/partners to be on the same wavelength. That's the beauty of having a men's group or men's team. Here we can develop supportive relationships with male friends where we can safely express ourselves! It is such an exhilarating feeling to be able to release these feelings in a safe and supportive environment.

♦I have experienced men supporting me compassionately through tears, and it is unlike anything I have experienced with a woman supporting me. A man supports another man moving through feelings with "compassionate attention." This gives a man a safe space to fully experience his feelings, undiluted by touch, and allows him to move to a new depth in his capacity to experience emotion. We need to have compassion for our wives' or partners' fears of our most painful experiences, even if they do not recognize these fears. With the girlfriend who said she felt angry and scared on seeing my tears, I asked her what she thought was the reason for her reaction. She said she was still affected by the stereotype of men not crying. I asked how I was or appeared after I had cried. She acknowledged that I was more confident and stronger.

♦Consider "honoring" women's fears of our tears, for when a man has the courage to address grief that has often been suppressed for years, it can be scary to be around. This is the value of men supporting men though this grief. The unconscious training that strong men don't cry affects us all. A solution, as I've said so many times now in this book, is to develop safe men's groups or places for our emotions. This is one of the best places to "bring our grieving." It will take time for you to develop a team of men that you have this safety with, but the payoffs are truly worth the journey. Going through this journey interestingly enough allows a man to be more available to hear the emotions of the women in their lives.

♦These are just ideas and suggestions. Let me restate that I am only interested and committed to what makes people, lives, and relationships work. How have YOU learned to move through this pain in your life? How have you healed these wounds? What's behind anger? For me it is often sadness and tears.

♦A men's group can become a safe place to express your feelings. A place to experience your feelings and not feel alone. I would invite you to ask, "What are other places where men have found safe avenues to cry or grieve"? For me, in the car driving is one. I cannot just let my tears come when I am very sad. I usually need something to stimulate them and to be in a safe place. Often the car with the news on has this effect. Sometimes being at the movies creates that safe place in the dark theater. In the real world there are safe places to cry and there are not. That's what we can teach our sons when we make the path ourselves. If we don't model how men deal with emotions constructively our sons will pick it up from their peers, TV, or worse, the movies.

The Men Address Selected Questions

How did you find your tears?

Bob

This question is closely linked to the one about anger. If only I could cry! Honestly I think I cry more often than most men do, that is maybe twice a year. How do I deal with emotional pain? I suck it up. I tell myself that life is not perfect and that nobody, including God, has ever promised me I would be happy. That being said, I have a propensity to engage in self-destructive behaviors when I am wounded with the result that I add guilt to pain. If I could just find a way to cry and not feel so alone I think my life would be much better off.

Bruce

I find my tears in quiet moments going deep into myself. I find a deep hurt or an inspired joy. When I center on the feelings of sadness or joy, embracing that specific feeling, feeling it to its fullest, tears develop from deep within my body. I feel my soul cry for the hurt or the joy. This only happens when I am in a very safe place. Generally I am alone. Occasionally I have been with trusting individuals, and in some situations have felt a connection with many of them allowing the emotions to fully express themselves in their presence. After the tears have seemingly drained my body of all fluids I feel peace after the hurt and elation after the joy. The tears act like a huge eraser sweeping away the chalk from a chalkboard seemingly written years ago.

Allen

It is very important. For me it can be experiencing something very happy. It's about realizing the importance of finding safe places to cry and letting it out—or I can feel real good about doing something and tearing up. Of course I have to rein that in at work in business places. I will take some risk with some people at work—but not many.

Arnold

I remember going through my adolescent years feeling emotionally frozen, a little overwhelmed by events in my family—the death of my father, and then my mother's very difficult remarriage five years later. I started to see a counselor while I was at the university, and still living at home. I realized that I still had lots of tears to shed, but couldn't seem to let them go. So, one evening when the family was out, I started to drink lots of tea—those tears have to come from liquid somewhere. And I started to cut up onions. This was a very mechanical strategy worked. I thought about some of my losses and painful aspects of the situation I had grown up in, and the tears came. I think that I had bottled the sadness up because there was no place to take it to. The counselor, however, was able to listen to me and hear me without taking anything personally and nothing went further than him. As an adult, I do not think that I have cried a lot, but in times of pain, I have had no problem with crying hard when that is what I had to do. I think that it's necessary. And of course, I can get affected at movies or when reading material that moves me.

I think that crying, and tears, are healthy and normal at times. At times it is important to hold back tears, perhaps to show strength. Tears can also be used to manipulate, and it is important to hold back tears that may overly influence someone else.

One of my concerns as I hear people talk about crying and tears are that some men now talk about "breaking down" and speak about tears in the language we use for serious pathology like a "nervous breakdown". I think that it is important to not talk about tears or the underlying feelings, like sadness or loss, as pathological. I think that when we do that, we can turn the sadness into inappropriate anger or use drugs or alcohol to wash those feelings away. When we get rid of these feelings without dealing with them, we fail to take necessary action to address problems. I think that can be one of the useful things about anger, though—it can give us energy to get things done that need to be done.

Another concern that I have is about how people talk about "closure" related to grief and sadness that is related to loss. As I hear people talk about this, I get the impression that there is an idea afloat in our culture that once you have grieved fully and properly about something, you will never ever be troubled by

368

feelings about that again. I think that this idea is dangerous. I think that the fact is that some losses will reverberate throughout our lives and will have new implications as we go through each succeeding life stage. I have sometimes wondered about how much I still think about my father, who died nearly fifty years ago. I cannot say that I am troubled very much by feelings about him, but sometimes I do feel sadness or anger in relation to his early death. I have come to accept that this is normal for me. This kind of loss does have implications all through your life, and you cannot cut yourself off from the reality of that—as you reach each new marker in your life, these kinds of losses influence what is possible and what is not, and what kinds of choices you are willing to consider. In some ways I think that this makes all of my decision making richer. I am less likely to accept glib solutions to complex problems. In some ways, the early loss of my father gave me a kind of premature wisdom. This was in no way a full compensation for this kind of loss, but it was not bad to have that, either.

James

When I finally gave up 'looking good' I discovered crying as one of my greatest joys. I had a man share with me that he felt like he was being reborn from crying. To be able to cry requires balance of attention - knowing we are safe in the present makes it safe to let go of the past.

Dan

For me, there are all kinds of tears—tears of anger and frustration, tears of loss, tears of awe, tears of joy, tears of beauty and stunning creativity. At bottom, though, I think they are all overwhelming emotion about something that touches me, myself, at its most fundamental level. As far as I am concerned, every tear is important and precious and needs to be shed and listened to. When I've been able to listen to a tear, I've learned important things about who I am, and how I really operate, and what's really important to me.

Suppress the tears, and you lose all that information and you end with all that emotional energy roaring around with no place to go. For men, as I explained somewhere above, it usually gets released as angry violence. The extreme, of course, is that the emotion never comes out, and the doctors can tell us what that does to men's health.

As boys we're taught that tears are a sign of weakness, of failure ... mothers and fathers delight in impressing the lesson right and left. That lesson strikes me as an abomination because it deprives the boy of an invaluable route to learning who he is and, therefore, being who he is. Then, I spent the next forty plus years trying to cope with tears as if they were lions to be tamed instead of unicorns to be followed.

I remember, as clearly as I see this computer screen, the first time I cried to the depth of my being. I was in my early forties, divorced, with my three visiting kids (10-13) upstairs in bed. I sat downstairs reading a biography of Clementine Churchill, Winston's wife. All of a sudden, for no reason that I ever could identify, I was engulfed by wracking sobs. I sat there at midnight sobbing my soul out, terrified that I'd wake the kids and have to show them a sobbing father. It was probably 45 minutes before I felt confidently under control. I was physically more exhausted than I ever had been before or since. Twenty years later, I still have no clue of what triggered the tears or where they came from, although I have some guesses. In the days afterwards, I felt cleansed, emptied, refreshed, as if I'd cleaned out a badly clogged pipe. Somehow I also felt free to act and think more independently, out of the box, about myself.

Since then, I've cried a lot but almost always for joy, or in awe, or in sheer pleasure of some moment of beauty or creativity. I feel so close to who I am in those moments. Well, I also sometimes feel embarrassed or shy over the tears flowing down my face. The more I know and respect myself, however, the less I care who sees these tears; they're just another way for me to enjoy my self. The angry and frustrated tears are harder to deal with; they usually mean digging into my self to find the message they carry and then to protect my self. These often carry hurt with them, but I've found that the message they carry is never frightening and hurtful and that healing happens fairly easily when I stand up for my self and draw a boundary protecting myself. I can't claim that I easily forgive the person or institution that has stepped on my self or that I readily give them much room to move in the future. But, for me, that's not anger, its pride in my self.

Ronald

Despite an affectionate nature with those close to me I am solitary with my emotions. Joy and laughter are part of my public face, sadness and depression never are . . . ever. There are two contributing factors I think and as I explore them I am aware of the difference between analysis and rationalization. The first is I am relatively even keeled. The pendulum of my personality does not have a wide swing. I am interpreted generously as being stoic and uncharitably as unfeeling. Neither characterization is accurate.

The "still waters run deep" adage is, in fact, appropriate to me. But the depths refer not to my moods but rather to my thoughtfulness. It takes time for me to come to grips with my emotions and I have learned not to express them until that time is done. The expression then is usually private.

About six weeks before my father died we played a round of golf. The golf course had always been our neutral ground. All through the difficult years of father/son relationships we could always share a mutual interest and some time away from the complications of life. He was a pretty good player and had passed on some of his skill to me. As often happens, the son had grown to surpass the father. On this particular fall day I had not played much and did not play my best. My Dad had an excellent game and we arrived at the eighteenth tee all-square. His drive and approach were good and mine was slightly better. As we got to the green he lay a dozen feet from the hole and my ball was about ten feet away. His putt was good but mine came up inches short. He reached into the hole and retrieved the two balls first tossing me mine and then his with its distinctive blue dot marking and laughingly said, "Here, keep this one, it rolls straighter." I thoroughly enjoyed both the game and my defeat and tucked the ball into my bag. It was the last time we were to play. Two days later he was diagnosed with cancer and all too soon he was gone.

Through the winter of my loss I never cried. Once, a few days after he passed away I went down to my den and took out the family albums thinking this would bring on my tears. Instead I found myself inwardly celebrating the wonderful life we had shared together. There was a joy in the pain I was feeling. It was the realization that I had had something special in my life. I did not feel sad at that moment, just thankful.

The months passed and once again came the inevitable Spring with its tasks and chores, one of which was the cleaning of my golf bag. Alone in the garage I removed the clubs and other paraphernalia that accumulates over a season and lastly the pouch with the balls and tees. There in my hand was a slightly muddied ball with blue dots. I could say that for the next hour I shed a tear or even that I wept. That would not be accurate. I bawled like a baby. My mind and body were spasmodically wracked with an uncontrollable venting of emotion. The walls of the garage were assaulted with my sobs and curses as I railed against the unfairness of it all. It was too soon. I was not ready to lose him. It was not rational; it had no meaning to anyone but me.

The time of grieving had passed for all the others who were dear in my Dad's life, but it was my moment. It was time for me to move on as well. I miss him still twenty years later. Of all the men in my life, he was the man.

Wilson

Mine have come by honest examination of myself in places of safety. These safe places are few and far between and most of them are shepherded by women. I wish I had men that I felt safe enough to share these with.

Gary

For me, it's been more tantrums, not crying, except for Brahms, Dvorak, etc. chamber music, until the New Warrior Training Adventure. Now I can cry, and know it won't last forever. I even did a process with my men's group over my father's death where I deeply grieved with the men just giving me attention. It is impossible to express how freeing that was, how what is suppose to take years almost happened in a moment. I know its masculine and it is the nurturing quality of masculine.

Fredrick

Tears come very slowly to me, if at all. I can cry listening to Van Morrison, and I cried when my beloved cat died. Otherwise, I almost never cry. I used to give myself grief over that, assuming that there was something wrong with me. But after a while, I gave myself a break about that. I don't know if it's true that "men don't cry the way women do." I used to laugh at that idea. Now I am not so sure. Rather than generalizing about men, I'll stick to speaking of my own nature – I have come to believe that my natural way of experiencing grief is more private, and to accept that about myself. There are things wrong with me and things I need to work on, but I am also very wary of our vulnerability to internalizing judgments that have nothing to do with reality.

Steven

I love crying. But there were many years during my early adulthood when I didn't cry at all. I think it was about 11 years that I hardly cried at all, except for one time that my brother and I talked on the phone after a long disagreement. But otherwise I was clogged up. I grew up like a lot of men my age, being told as a kid to "stop crying or I'll give you something to cry about". So I stopped crying. I had to do a lot of work to give myself permission to let the tears come, and once I did, boy did they come. I can now cry at the drop of a hat. I'll cry during a breakfast with a friend, at movies, with just about anybody. Sometimes the cry is quick, and sometimes it's deep and long. When my mom died I thought I'd never stop crying. But I did, though I still grieve when I need to. Crying in the presence (and with the support) of other men is one of the most powerful experiences for me. It seems to erase some of the shaming I got from my father early on about crying. The ironic thing is, my Dad has gone through a transformation of his own, due to a lot of things, including Mom's death. And now he cries all the time, too. That heals me as well.

Roy

When I first started opening Pandora's box of my feeling I was with the worst therapist of my life. He just encouraging it, and it came like a river of tears that seemed it would never stop. It was not until men's work later on that I realized that a man needs to find or create safe places to find his tears. And I found that work or in the presence of his wife is not necessarily the safest place to move through his deepest wounds.

What are ways of resolving losses in your life?

Wilson

For me, the most important thing was acknowledgement of the loss and the pain of that loss- only this opened the door to healing for me. You have to start naming that undistinguished mass of feelings, listen and give a name to each one.

Allen

Again, getting it out. Sharing it with someone helps me to accept it and also helps me to realize that I have so much else. When I am by myself I focus on that is all there is.

Roy

To keep alive the good aspects or memories of the person and feel the loss fully.

What have you found to be the best way to handle anger and depression?

Bruce

I suffered off and on from depression for about 20 years of my life. I am now 37. Getting out of that stagnant state was the most challenging endeavor of my life. A lot of it was due to deeply entrenched anger. This anger was centered on my loss of self or/and spirit. Initially this anger was directed at my parents for denying myself to live in an emotionally safe environment, therefore I fell into recluse. Later, I developed anger at myself for allowing my parents to have that control over me and for not allowing myself to express and live as my truer nature.

Once I recognized the anger (a multitude of times) and the feelings associated with the depression I was able to get a better handle on them. This process of assessing and labeling the emotions happened a multitude of times over many years. The greatest relief was in journaling my feelings and activities. Exposing the anger and feelings over and over allowed me to assess there relevance to the current situation. Over time I found that the old tapes were only impacting my current situation in

374

negative ways and became less relevant. It was then I sought to adopt new feelings more applicable to the current situation. So in conclusion, defining the emotions of anger and depression, what is causing them and not allowing them to take control is my way of handling these emotions.

Laurence

It means you take a healthy approach to your emotional life. I attempt to honestly examine my feelings, both positive and negative, so that I can discover our true underlying motivations and sometimes it works! Understanding this, I can move forward with my life and get closer to an understanding of others and of whatever spiritual force guides us all. Buried emotions never stay buried, for me the come up in in-appropriate ways. They will surface again and the longer they stay buried the greater the impact of their ultimate resurfacing.

Wilson

What have I found to be the best way to handle anger and depression? By not ignoring either of them. By acknowledging them, bringing them into the light of day, talking about them, reading about how others handled these issues, and taking action to insure I had tools to defend myself. My tools were: speaking with someone, taking activity initiatives, prayer.

Roy

Sometimes by hanging out with male friends and just connecting on some other issue, by laughing about stupid things we did together years ago, by bringing it to my men's group and really getting in touch with the anger followed by the sadness.

Do you turn to men, women, or isolate yourself from emotional pain during a crisis?

Wilson

My tendency is to isolate but I have forced myself past that stage. Now, I turn to a female professional friend who I have known for many years that I trust. There are few men I really trust to lean on in times of emotional pain. The rawness of it makes most of them run since the relationships are not as developed as I need them to be.

Allen
I used to isolate, then my second choice was with women. Now it is with my brothers of my men's group.

Bruce
I either isolate myself or turn to a woman I can confide in, this can put stress on my partner. I turn to woman because they will generally provide the nurturance and the non-judgmental stance that I am seeking. However, there is one male friend who can provide the safe arena needed to share my emotions. I really had never thought of cultivating male friends close enough that I could turn to them. I wish I had that.

What does it mean to experience your negative feelings so that they pass through you vs. stuffing them or avoiding them?

Laurence
It means you take a healthy approach to your emotional life. I attempt to honestly examine my feelings, both positive and negative, so that I can discover our true underlying motivations and sometimes it works! Understanding this, I can move forward with my life and get closer to an understanding of others and of whatever spiritual force guides us all. Buried emotions never stay buried, for me they come up in inappropriate ways. They will surface again and the longer they stay buried the greater the impact of their ultimate resurfacing.

Bruce
In the past six months I have been able to allow my negative feelings to pass through me rather than stuffing them. In the past I engaged and negatively embraced them. Now I am more likely to recognize them, assess their value in the moment and let them go. It is a beautiful feeling to know that I can have more control over my thoughts and feelings. This is not to say that I don't recognize

and feel the negative feelings, I do, and I find their sting isn't so strong when I don't allow them to linger for lengths of time.

Wilson
By letting them pass through and allowing myself to experience these feelings I do not give them any power over me. If I ignore them they run me and ultimately ruin me.

How do men cry or grieve?

Wilson
Privately. Stoically. Or not at all. If they have developed real male friends they may just spend time with them, mention the problem, the other man just listens and hangs out with them. Some of us develop close enough male friends that they can move through real deep pain. I have been with some veterans really grieving and it shakes the earth. It is an extraordinary gift to be part of and the men look 10 years younger but exhausted afterwards.

Gary
For me, it's been more tantrums, not crying, except for Brahms, Dvorak, etc. chamber music, until the New Warrior Training Adventure. Now I can cry, and know it won't last forever. I even did a "tombstone process" (a Shadow Work TM piece) with my father's body before they cremated it. I know it's masculine.

One "New Warrior" theory is that calling the training that was a clever way to get men to reclaim their "warrior" when the truth is, in middle age, the warrior is in decline, while the lover (and grief) is in ascendancy; whereas their female partners of the same age are going through the opposite!

Roy
I think many men hid out in opinions, intellectual babble, or worse to avoid being authentic, being exposed, being real, being connected. I know since I used to be like that. It's like the kid hiding behind a small object with most of his body exposed thinking that he can not be seen. We will do anything as men to avoid dealing with difficult emotions, of course women seem to over indulge in them to avoid moving through them.

Bill

I want to share a quote that I think expresses my views on this topic the best. "Your joy is your sorrow unmasked. The deeper sorrow carves into your being the more joy you can contain. Joy and sorrow are inseparable. When you are weeping.......you are weeping for that which has been your delight."

Kahlil Gibran – "The Prophet"

For me and most men it has taken us a long time to figure this out.

What is the cost to our lives of not crying or grieving? And when does crying or grieving not work?

Bruce

To me, the cost for not crying when needed, only delays the processing and letting go of the emotional garbage. Like garbage not property taken care of it only accumulates and begins to stink, making it more of a challenge to recognize the depth and ability to clear it out. Crying doesn't work for me if I'm not in the right emotional state and I feel the place isn't safe.

Wilson

I have seen physical hearts damaged by the retention of grief. We pay the price, one way or the other. Crying and grieving does not work for me if I stop myself, or am stopped by someone, before I complete the process. The grief keeps spinning around and around and manifests in another area of my life. I knew a man in my men's group who was dying of hardening of the arties. The doctors gave him no hope so he started doing things to 'live' knowing he would die soon. He joined our men's group and said that he was determined to 'break through this emotional stuff". Boy did he. Within a year he almost seemed like a different men. He becomes more confident, he lead groups of men dealing with grief, he found a life partner who he has married. He figured he was going to die anyway so he stopped going to the doctor. His new wife insisted he get a checkup which he had not had within a year and a half. The doctor could not believe it, the problem was gone, I mean really gone. If I had not known him personally I would not believe it.

What works in transforming emotional pain?

Bruce

More recently I like to recognize the base feeling associated with the emotional pain: sad, mad, angry or shame. Once I recognize the feeling and feel it, not allowing too much time to pass, I seek to find the goodness in the pain and transform it by allowing a positive feeling to replace the negative feeling. Depending on the situation and my mindset this can be a real challenge or fairly easy. The beauty is often just recognizing the impact the negative emotion is having on me and knowing I don't need to allow it to bring me down.

Brad

Overall, what I my experience of myself and other men teaches me is that we often have a false suffering. This false suffering is called apathy (from Greek apatheia=not to suffer), and arises because we refuse to identify with the victim and identify with the persecutor instead.

Apathy is accommodation to the pain and the victimizing system or situation. It means we really go to sleep, and hope to protect ourselves against pain by being 'above and beyond' it—that is, immortal divinities. It is only the gods who do not suffer. Finding our tears, for me, means recovering my pain. This involves recovering our true memories of myself, both individually and as a group/community. Recovering our memories means bringing back our feelings and tolerating them. To remember (re-member=to join again) is more specifically an 'un-forgetting' (to 'unforget' is the Greek word for 'truth'-aletheia), because we have (outside awareness) chosen to forget our suffering,—to forget the victim within myself and the community. Instead of positively not forgetting and remembering, we chose to make myths, which as the derivation of this word shows, is a 'covering-up' of a truth that the persecutor, the immortal god with me, does not want to know. Because the god cannot remain immortal or even a god in the sight of suffering that arises from his dominating actions. This is the reason why gods and tyrants force their victims to be silent and invisible.

But to recover our feelings means we have to step out of our identification with the persecutor, because it is the persecutor that sees the suffering one as shameful and 'beneath' him. So along with memory of the victim goes the choice of solidarity with the victim. To remain with the victim, with the pain, breaks the power of the dominating persecutor in us. It is in the dominator's defeat at the hands of the victim that means liberation for the individual and community. Only suffering (freely chosen), heals suffering. And the only way I know for me to choose freely my suffering, is for me to "tell" it to another who himself is capable of tolerating the feelings I project into him. As I see this man not collapsing under the burden of my feelings, and who then hands his unclasped self back to me, I am then enabled to (at least begin) to live with my own feelings.

Roy

When I learned that I could cry with God and not feel alone. When I discovered that God could hold me like a lover and let me weep. In those moments when I experience my tears are almost embraced in joy. Let me be real this not a clear thing, I cannot even guarantee that I did not make it up. But I just took on that it was possible and at times it feels real. I remember that comment that a real ritual space lets us move through painful emotions and not be alone. That is the experience of joy I mean. When I remember this, my tears heal me.

Wilson

Going through it. Another man being there with you during the transformation that has been through the same process and successfully come out the other side. It is like a woman can understand the pain of childbirth easier than a man. A man that has done work on himself can help another man pass through deep emotional pain as well. If you have not experienced I know it would be hard to believe. I have.

Can you remember the very first time you ever cried about anything? What decision did you make after that and does that decision still apply in your life?

Barry

Yes. I was a small child then. Someone told me to stop and I really did. I don't even remember who it was. But I never cried again to later in life.

Wilson

No, I really can't remember the first time I ever cried. I do remember that crying for me (as a youth) was associated with anger - and both were undesirables.

I didn't allow myself to cry when my father died, it took me decades to grieve the loss. It took me even longer to be able to cry freely - I certainly have no problem now.

Roy

It is a distant memory about loosing a balloon and crying. The other memory is watching the other boys when they cried and how people reacted and thinking, "it's not good to cry".

If you stopped crying or grieving, can you remember when, what happened and what decision you made about the event that happened?

Blake

I cried once in front of my wife - on the eve of our marriage, she demanded I confront my mother over an issue on which my wife later learned she had been wrong. Before (or just after - my memory may be fading) the confrontation, I sobbed. In retrospect, I believe that may have been a turning point in our marriage in terms of my wife's respect for me. Crying and capitulating to her unreasonable demands. It had been many years since I had cried. Other than getting choked up at movies, weddings and funerals, I have not cried since.

Barry

The little child in me figured that no one would help me stop my tears so I stopped them myself. Years later, I realized that I was living my adult life as if crying was not acceptable without knowing why. When I finally figured out the source of that programmed resistance, I was open to expressing sadness and grief in a beneficial way.

Roy

I bought fully into 'boys don't cry' and I am not sure it is good to teach boys to cry in any place but more to find and have safe places to find their tears. I don't think the world will change that much by the time the boy grows up. I can not remember the specific time but I just know to show 'negative feelings' in any way was 'not good'. Over time these feeling just became a blur from my neck down, an undistinguished blob that I did not understand. When put on the spot to have feeling, I came up with answers that got the questions to stop for if they were the wrong answer I would get criticized more. Bad therapy encouraged me to move from no feelings to feeling on my sleeves, which was not much better. My first wife acted as if she was embarrassed by it and the worthless therapist acted as if was wonderful. It's not ok for men today to show our feelings in any place!! It took a lot of work in men's groups to be ok with the feelings I have, but not always 'sharing them with everyone', just having them. Also finding a therapist who understood men's work helped—and just because they are a male therapist does not mean they are any good at this!

Wilson

When I did stop crying at a youthful age, it was because I considered it a weakness and was ashamed—which caused it to back up for years and years and years. When women ask us to 'share our feelings' do they know what a massive backlog we may have. We haven't spent 20 year, stuffing good feelings but bad ones.

How do we model for younger men finding safe ways or places to cry or grieve?

Bruce

I think it is absolutely necessary that they be surrounded by trusting and non judgmental men and women so that they feel comfortable in expressing their tears or grief. Certainly men within this circle can model it by expressing their tears and grief. To me, it is absolutely imperative that the person expressing the tears and grief not be scorned, shamed, judged or felt that their expression is not needed or welcomed.

As a mature adult, I find myself tearing up more often than I did as a younger man. I suppose that such behavior is a result of being more open and compassionate to the pain that others experience. However, I have learned that being more compassionate does not mean that I am weaker. In fact, I can now experience such emotions more openly and then reach out to the person(s) experiencing that pain in a more productive manner.

Wilson

I am not certain on this one. I have done it by allowing myself to be emotional in front of them and show them that they grief was not permanent - I did make it to the other side and released the grief. Finding a place? If it's not the church or an honest Men's Group, I am not certain there is a safe place in our society.

Roy

I share stories with younger men of times when I moved through grief at times when I think they may be feeling grief. Of course if I had not done enough work on this issue myself I would have nothing to give them.

Some types of tears are safer for men to express than others, what are they?

Wilson

Tears of victory, joy, and celebration are ok. Tears shed at 'giant' emotional losses - parents, mates, etc are ok—as long as it is just a little bit. Tears about fear are not ok. Tears about loosing things are not ok. But we men truly fall in love with things for better or worse!

Roy
I have found that really deep grieving is NOT okay in most places. A little bit of tearing up is okay if it's quickly wiped away and ignored—and then it has to be about some major loss. Like the old war movies where you see a soldier go through total hell and he breaks down for a minute or two until his buddy says "come on, snap out of it." No wonder we're so emotionally stuck!

What Insights did you personally gain from this chapter?

What do you want to commit to or re-commit to out of these insights?

Remember!
"Insight without committed action is only entertainment!"

Chapter 15
Keeping the Fire Alive

What would be possible if you had a group of men in your life like your closest brothers? Men who supported you in staying aligned with your mission; men you could trust, who gave you strength to be the best father, husband, and leader in your life. Maybe you have a team like this in your life. If you do, consider yourself blessed. So many men do not.

It is my intention that this book will open both men and women to the value of men resolving issues from their past that unconsciously run them. Because without our past resolved, our vision of the future is distorted. This is the core mission of men's work—to help create a strong foundation that makes life a game worth playing.

Some further thoughts on men's work: it is about celebrating masculinity, about teaching integrity and accountability, giving us more access to our laughter and tears, as well as enhancing our lives; it's also about reclaiming the gift of our personhood, sonhood, fatherhood, brotherhood, and the fellowship of other men; it's about addressing the joy and beauty of being a man in a way that does not dishonor women or other men. Men's work is about men supporting other men by being fully self-expressed in their own lives in such a way that honors others' lives; it's about learning about the area where we experience most emotions, between our neck and our waist; it's about distinguishing and being able to express the full spectrum of emotions; it's about learning how to have healthy, close relationships with other men; it's about how to move through painful emotions instead of avoiding or suppressing them; and it's about learning what's beautiful about being a man, a husband, and a father.

The mature man has access to both compassion and strength, knows the roles he plays in his world, and is fully engaged with life with fire and passion. A man dominating and controlling his environment has no access to his true fire or passion for he has to set up structures in his environment to compensate for this absence.

If you have read up to this point without taking some new actions in your life, then I doubt if you have gained much value. If you have read and paid attention to the insights that arose, taking new actions, then you have let me contribute to you. You have contributed to my living my mission, and I thank you.

So what are you going to do today to connect to your own passion and fire? Find your edge that keeps you fully engaged with life. Take on life like building a blazing campfire that burns bright with beauty, service and passionate energy, warming the hearts of family and friends who gather around the fire with you.

"This is the true joy in life, being used for a purpose recognized by yourself as a mighty one; being thoroughly worn out before you are thrown on the scrap heap; being a force of Nature instead of a feverish selfish little clod of ailments and grievances complaining that the world will not devote itself to making you happy."

-George Bernard Shaw
Man and Superman, Epistle Dedicatory

Appendix
About Creating a Men's Team or Group

By now you probably realize the importance of being part of a men's team or men's group. Regardless of age, It is a chief ingredient in the metamorphosis of boy to man.

Here are a few suggestions on creating such a group or a Men's Inquiry meeting. Use them as guidelines, paying attention to what works in your own community.

Step into the role

The most important thing to do is to see yourself as a part of the group, a member of the team, with a specific and important role.

Contact men who have already participated in a men's group, access their wisdom and experiences, and let them contribute to you.

Read books on men's issues or on how to start a men's group, such as *A Circle of Men: The Original Manual for Men's Support Groups* by Bill Kauth. The Internet is a good resource for information, book listings, and other web links. The Triangle Men's Inquiry Meeting web page: www.TheMensInquiry.com is a good place to start.

Get clear on the vision

Write down what you see is possible for the men to learn from the group and how their own lives would be enhanced if they had a team of men *really* supporting them on the journey of life. Make sure to include yourself in this picture.

Another useful question to ask yourself: "What do I specifically want or need out of a men's group?" Write down why you are qualified to start this group and a list of men that you know who could benefit from being in such a group.

A scientist, with two young children, contacted me about starting a men's group, but he was apprehensive about creating the group because he felt underqualified. He said, "Look, I am not a psychologist, I have no qualifications to start such a group." I told him that I thought he was extremely qualified! He was a concerned father, husband, and obviously interested in connecting with other men. "This is not a therapy group." I told him. "We are coming together to support each other because that's what healthy men do. Also, the best way to get other men to take a risk and open up is to model it yourself."

Each time before I begin the Men's Inquiry discussion, I ask myself this question: "How can I really give myself away, and what can I share about myself that will encourage other men to speak honestly?" How can I demonstrate emotional courage to inspire the men to do the same? There is no way to fake this. This is about taking a risk and making changes. It does not have to be big, something small is often better. Something like, "I just was not as straight with my brother about what I want related to (fill in the blank) today and feel a bit bothered by that."

Select the questions
For example, one universal topic we have covered is:

"How does resolving Issues with your father give you more freedom?" This naturally leads to other questions, such as, "How do you resolve issues with your father when he is not available or doesn't seem to care?" Then, for example, a man may share something personal, such as, how he wrote a letter once saying exactly what he needed to say to his father to resolve the issues, although he didn't actually send the letter

The Men's Inquiry structure

See Chapter 2 for a timed outline of the Inquiry format.

Opening the meeting
An example of what the facilitators may say at the start of the meeting:
"Welcome to The Men's Inquiry, we start on time and end on time. We have a brief time for introductions and updates. Then we will explore the question of the day till about 9:15 PM, and then take time to review insights and actions we want to take. Men are

asked to honor the confidentiality of each man here. That means what is said here stays here. You are welcome to share your own personal insights and I encourage you to use this for new actions in your own life. Men are asked to do their best to speak from their own experience, speaking in the first person as though just sharing your own life is a contribution to the other men. Please only give advice if it is specifically asked for and, if you want advice, ask for it. Remember that listening and giving your attention to the other men is as great a contribution as sharing your own experiences.

Ground rules
These can be printed and handed out, or read aloud at the start of the meeting.

1) Start on time / end on time.
2) Ask that confidentiality be honored. That means what is said here stays here. You may share you own insights but not the words of another person here.
3) Do your best to speak from your own experience, in the first person vs. someone else's idea. For example "I feel X about this" vs. "Men tend to or we tend to."
4) Advice is welcome only when someone asks for it. Realize that your attention and sharing your own experience is the greatest contribution and makes this inquiry provide the most value.
5) You may raise a hand if you relate to what is being said as a simple validation.

Being present
In the first half-hour the facilitator asks the men to introduce themselves, share a significant event and "anything you need to say to be fully present here tonight." He might also say: "You can pass. We will go counter clockwise. Who would like to start?"

The facilitator keeps the talk flowing and makes sure men stay on introductions and don't go on too long. If it is a larger group (over 8) you need to be especially vigilant so that individuals don't ramble and take too much time.

Introducing the question

After introductions and updates, "throw" the question out. "The question tonight is:..." Ask who would like to start. Then be quiet. If no one speaks, just sit in the silence listening and looking softly around the room until someone breaks the silence. This is a very important point.

Keeping the conversation flowing

The facilitator does not 'correct' any man but leads both by example and questions. Unlike facilitators in other settings, he is also a participant!

If several men are dominating the conversation, you can intervene and ask some of the more quiet men if they have a comment. Don't push it. If a man truly runs on, you may have to stop him, but it is best not to do so very often. You can say something like "John, I see you are very passionate about this, but I am going to stop you to get some other men's input on that."

Let the conversation flow from one question to the next. Make notes of ideas and listen for emerging sub-questions that come up to discuss. Let it flow. The key is the connection it creates, not that you stay on the exact topic. If the question seems complete very early, introduce a new question. If it happens near the end, then just wrap it up a little early.

Between 15 and 25 minutes before the end, wrap it up no matter where they are. You may say, "We could continue this for a long time, but I am committed to starting and ending on time. We will each talk one last time so that everyone has a chance to share whatever insights they've gained from this discussion and what they are willing to commit or re-commit to out of this insight. To quote the founder, 'Insight without action is just entertainment.' So, who would like to begin?"

Closing on time

Then end on time, even if the men are not done. This is about setting up a structure that creates something men can rely on and about honoring our word in relationship to time.

A closing comment may be: "Thank you all for having the courage to come here and contribute. If you have any suggestions or new questions, let us/me hear about them. I look forward to seeing you next month!"

Encouraging interaction

At some point be sure to mention that "we encourage men to also meet outside the group, so consider trading phone numbers and email addresses and meeting for coffee outside the meeting. You may meet with someone from the group because you would like to continue a conversation with him about one of the questions. You may want to meet with him about a similar hobby, work or issue. You may even want to meet with someone if you notice you don't seem to be getting along well and want to discover what that's about."

Also remind them to be attentive to issues they have brought up in the group that they may not want to bring up outside. Let the man take the initiative of bringing up a sensitive topic about himself. You can do this by sharing your own issues on the topic when you meet outside and see if he follows. If not, drop that topic and just hang out with him.

Listening for new topics

Listen for any issues that come out of the current meeting that would be good questions for the next meeting. I find making notes during the meeting to keep track of topics that come up is a big help. I often will let the men know in the beginning that I take notes only to keep track of the meeting, my own insights, and if I hear something that may make a good question for a future meeting.

You can have multiple questions for one meeting. If so, you may choose to type them out and hand out copies

What are possible challenges that someone should watch out for when considering a men's group?

I think one of the greatest challenges in any group is over-emphasizing that something outside of us is the sole cause of a problem that can make us into helpless victims The problem with this is that there is no self-responsibility. You become a victim who has to take aggressive action against the victimizer, and then you get stuck in a win/lose situation.

Another challenge is not having enough accountability and focus in the group. This lets the drift of life take over and the group floats to a level of superficiality and mediocrity, and then dissolves. This is why a certain degree of accountability and a theme or focus is necessary. Also, if the group has no connection to a greater purpose, it can be at risk of eventually becoming a self-absorbed group and will usually just dissolve.

It is an amazing experience when men get together and explore important questions openly and honestly...Inquiry has a clear purpose, goal, and end point. This is intrinsically appealing to men because it is focused.

Imagine how you could create time for something that costs only a few hours a month in time...an investment that would pay you back in untold ways that would profoundly improve the quality and depth of your relationships...that would enlighten you and your loved ones. Yes, getting involved with a men's group does take time, commitment, and courage to reap the real benefits. However, this is true for anything worth having in life.

If you want to start a Men's Inquiry group, get in touch with me and explore the resources on www.themensinquiry.com. You can purchase the recordings of The Men's Inquiry to hear a group in session. You may also want to join the on-line Men's Inquiry* at: http://health.groupsyahoo.com/group/TriangleMensInquiryMeeting/

Please note that the on-line Men's Inquiry is a starting point; the real work is accomplished one-on-one relating to other men and within in-person groups. .

For more information about additional resources, products, and presentations visit our websites at:

www.TheMensInquiry.com
and
www.TheWomensInquiry.com

Martin Brossman, founder of The Men's Inquiry, is available for interviews and presentations both on issues related to this book and Success Coaching and Training.

Contact information:

Martin Brossman
4441 Six Forks Rd. Suite 106-251
Raleigh NC 27609 - USA

(919) 847-4757
Martin@CoachingSupport.com
www.CoachingSupport.com

Thank you for buying and reading this book!
If you have gained value from it, consider purchasing a copy for a friend.

A portion of the proceeds from the sale of this book will go to support The Men's Inquiry, The Women's Inquiry, and the Triangle Men's Center (www.trianglemenscenter.org).

About The Author's Involvement in Men's Work

Martin Brossman's path with Men's Work started in 1994 when he read the book *Iron John* by Robert Bly. Two years later he attended the *Sterling Men's Weekend*. That experience inspired him to create The Triangle Men's Inquiry, holding the first meeting on October 18, 1996. He has faithfully continued the meetings monthly to date, free of charge.

On November 10, 2000, he created the on-line *Men's Inquiry* which has connected hundreds of men around the globe in online discussions. He has participated in many other on-line men's discussion groups as well as helping with their conceptual design. He leads the online *Men's Inquiry* group and facilitates the Raleigh in-person Inquiry meetings. In 2003 he created the women's version of this work with online and in-person meetings called the *Women's Inquiry–TheWomensInquiry.com*.

Martin has been a supporter of the Raleigh Men's Center and has been involved in their annual retreat every year since it started. He was actively involved in the first Wake County Public forum on men's issues with over 400 participants in 2001. That year he convinced a local magazine to dedicate one full issue to Men's Work, guaranteeing it would be their most successful issue to date–and it was! He has been on radio talk shows about men's issues, including *Waking Up with Carolyn Craft* on Sirius Satellite Radio (Lime.com) and assisted Warren Farrell, author of 6 books on men's issues, in Farrell's workshop on relationships. Martin has published numerous articles on men's issues that have been published in web and print publications. In Spring 2002 he gave his first live poetry reading on men's issues at St. Andrews Presbyterian College.

The New Warrior Men's Training has been especially important to Martin, along with the ongoing value of the related support group (I-Group). With great honor in 2007 he received the Ron Hering Mission of Service award from the ManKind Project.

Martin has offered mentoring and support to men around the world wanting to get involved in Men's Work or start their own men's groups. Currently a spokesman for the value of men's work, Martin gives presentations on various men's issues to groups of men and women.